# EATING CHINESE: CULTURE ON THE MENU IN SMALL TOWN CANADA

'Chicken fried rice, sweet and sour pork, and an order of onion rings, please.'

Chinese restaurants in small town Canada are at once everywhere – you would be hard pressed to find a town without a Chinese restaurant – and yet they are conspicuously absent in critical discussions of Chinese diasporic culture or even in popular writing about Chinese food. In *Eating Chinese*, Lily Cho examines Chinese restaurants as spaces that define, for those both inside and outside the community, what it means to be Chinese and what it means to be Chinese Canadian.

Despite restrictions on immigration and explicitly racist legislation at national and provincial levels, Chinese immigrants have long dominated the restaurant industry in small town Canada. Culturally isolated, Chinese communities in Canada were often strongly connected to their non-Chinese neighbours through the food that they prepared and served. Cho looks at this surprisingly ubiquitous feature of the small town through menus, literature, art, and music. An innovative approach to the study of diaspora, *Eating Chinese* brings to light the cultural spaces crafted by restaurateurs, diners, cooks, servers, and artists.

(Cultural Spaces)

LILY CHO is an associate professor of English at the University of Western Ontario.

Interior of Club Café, Chinese restaurant, Innisfail, Alberta, 1927.
Joanne Hui illustration based on image courtesy of Glenbow Archives.

LILY CHO

# Eating Chinese
Culture on the Menu
in Small Town Canada

UNIVERSITY OF TORONTO PRESS
Toronto Buffalo London

© University of Toronto Press Incorporated 2010
Toronto Buffalo London
www.utppublishing.com
Printed in Canada

ISBN 978-1-4426-4105-1 (cloth)
ISBN 978-1-4426-1040-8 (paper)

Printed on acid-free, 100% post-consumer recycled paper with
vegetable-based inks.

**Library and Archives Canada Cataloguing in Publication**

Cho, Lily, 1975–
   Eating Chinese : culture on the menu in small town Canada / Lily Cho.

Includes bibliographical references and index.
ISBN 978-1-4426-4105-1 (bound)     ISBN 978-1-4426-1040-8 (pbk.)

   1. Chinese restaurants – Canada – History.   2. Chinese – Canada –
Social conditions.   3. Chinese Canadians – Social conditions.   I. Title.

FC106.C5C58 2010      305.895'1071      C2010-905445-8

University of Toronto Press acknowledges the financial assistance to its
publishing program of the Canada Council for the Arts and the Ontario
Arts Council.

This book has been published with the help of a grant from the Canadian
Federation for the Humanities and Social Sciences, through the Aid to
Scholarly Publications Programme, using funds provided by the Social
Sciences and Humanities Research Council of Canada.

University of Toronto Press acknowledges the financial support for its
publishing activities of the Government of Canada through the Book
Publishing Industry Development Program (BPIDP).

# Contents

# Illustrations

# Acknowledgments

I could not have written this book without the generosity and support of many people. I am indebted:

To Stephen Slemon. To Karyn Ball, Donald Goellnicht, Vijay Mishra, and Heather Zwicker, who read all of it the first time around.

To the Social Sciences and Humanities Research Council of Canada, the Aid to Scholarly Publications Program, and the J.B. Smallman Fund at the University of Western Ontario.

To Brad Bannon, Allison Hargreaves, Kiel Hume, Cristina Ionica, and Alia Somani for research assistance that went well above and beyond.

To Richard Cavell, Diana Brydon, David Chariandy, Sneja Gunew, Smaro Kamboureli, Roy Miki, and Eleanor Ty, who told me I was writing a book when I forgot.

To Siobhan McMenemy and Ryan Van Huijstee, who believed it was a book. To the anonymous readers of the manuscript whose thoughtfulness and thoroughness made this book better.

To Apollo Amoko, Ian Balfour, Melina Baum Singer, Jesse Brown, Jenny Burman, Eric Cazdyn, Katharine Charlton, Alison Conway, Margaret DeRosia, Jeff Derksen, Katherine Ensslen, Todd Ferguson, Aaron Hankewich, Emily Hill, Camilla Ingr, Joanne Hui, Alice Jim, Greg King, Martin Kreiswirth, Kinsley Kreiswirth, Larissa Lai, David Lloyd, Sue Malley, Richard McCabe, Sophie McCall, Mary Helen McMurran, Corey Mintz, Marni Mishna, Alex Panther, Thy Phu, Joe Rosich, Matthew Rowlinson, Mia Sheldon, Joshua Schuster, Ken Singer, Kim Solga, Cheryl Suzack, Karen Tam, Rei Terada, Bryce Traister, Sasha Torres, Pauline Wakeham, Dorothy Wang, and Keri Zwicker, whose friendship and guidance have seen me through the hard parts.

To Zachary Green for all the pies, and so much more, which got me through the home stretch.

To Fred Wah for the Diamond Grill menu and for writing poetry that got to things I knew but did not know how to say.

To my family.

To my parents, who dreamed of something other than what they knew at the Shangri-La Restaurant in Whitehorse, Yukon Territory. It no longer exists, but that is not what matters. Their courage and love make everything possible. This book is for them.

EATING CHINESE: CULTURE ON THE MENU
IN SMALL TOWN CANADA

# Introduction

The sidewalk ends at the N.D. Café. Clumps of prairie grass sprout up along the edge of the sidewalk separating it from the unpaved road in front. A single street lamp towers above the café a short distance past the end of the sidewalk. Obviously, nobody walks here anymore, but people might drive by on their way to somewhere else. The café itself is a one-storey building with a small addition (kitchen? living quarters?) jutting out of one side. The front windows have all been broken and are now draped with plastic. Someone must still care about the building. The modest false front is still bright white, with the letters 'N, D. Café' painted clearly in black. The paint on the side of the building, sanded down by the wind, peels away in great strips. It stands alone, solitary on a street that seems more solitary still. I wonder what else would have stood beside it. I wonder whether the people who ran the café were ever as lonely as the building seems to be now. The grey-blue prairie sky, the colour of a threatening summer thunderstorm, looms enormous in the background.

The photograph has no date. It came to me in the post from an anonymous radio listener after the local public radio station broadcasted a short interview they had conducted with me about a project that, at the time, I could only vaguely describe.[1] I knew it would have something to do with restaurants like the N.D. Café even though, at the time, I did not know that the N.D. Café existed. I knew it had something to do with the people who would have lived and worked at the restaurant, even though, at the time, I did not know their names. I knew it had to do with wanting to make sense of the presence of the N.D. Café, and other restaurants like it, on the main streets of towns such as New Dayton, Alberta.

In 1917, Hoy Fat Leong came to New Dayton, Alberta, Canada, with his son Charlie Chew Leong.[2] They owned and operated the first restaurant in New Dayton, buying the land from Jim Reid, a local landowner, on installments. The New Dayton Café had two tables and a countertop. In 1923 the restaurant was destroyed by fire. Charlie rebuilt the café, and the new restaurant had four tables, stools, a glass counter, and modern gas lamps (a big improvement on the old kerosene ones). There was a soda fountain and you could order from a small but varied menu that included canned veal and spaghetti, tamales and chili con carne. There was no Chinese food on the menu at all, although Charlie Chew had printed his name right on the front of the menu under the title 'proprietor.' You would dial '4' to reach the restaurant through the local switchboard.

The N.D. Café was documented in the late twentieth century. In 1995 Calgary's Folio Gallery published a series of black and white photographs by George Webber titled *Requiem: The Vanishing Face of the Canadian Prairie*. Two photographs of the N.D. Café are a part of the series. In one, 'Abandoned Café,' a fluorescent tube hangs over the empty restaurant interior (figure 1). The glass counter has been ripped out and the drawers and cupboards are empty. The old cash register has been taken out and there is a hole in the wall where it once sat. The linoleum is coming up from the floorboards. You can see where the glass counter stood by the colour of the linoleum. In the second photograph, 'Mr and Mrs Chew,' Charlie and his wife stand in front of a glass counter filled with goods before the closing of the café (figure 2). The photograph was taken in 1988. The Chews are old. In both photographs, there is the sense, as the subtitle to *Requiem* suggests, of things in the process of vanishing, on the verge of disappearance. The New Dayton Café, a Chinese restaurant that no longer exists in a town that no longer exists, seems to exemplify an object of disappearance on the Canadian small-town landscape. Like the prairie grain elevator, it seems as though its time has passed, that the restaurants which remain are little more than anachronistic reminders of another time, another history.

But has it really disappeared? After all, you can still drive into almost any small town in Canada and expect to find a Chinese restaurant. Chinese people still seem to work in them. While the N.D. Café has closed its doors, another Chinese restaurant in the New Dayton area (now amalgamated and officially a part of greater Lethbridge, Alberta) has taken its place. A requiem is meant for that which has passed, that which has died. The idea of a requiem is contradictory and perhaps premature given that, for all intents and purposes, neither the prairie nor the Chinese restaurants that dot the landscape of its small towns can be considered to have passed on. But what interests me even more is the *persuasiveness*

1   'Abandoned Café.' George Webber. ND Café, New Dayton, Alberta, 1993.

of the narrative, of the news of the prairie's death and passing. Not only does the idea of a requiem for the prairie *seem* to make sense, but the situating of the N.D. Café and Charlie Chew at the heart of the requiem also *seems* natural. Still, what is normal about announcing the death of something that has not died? And how has the migration of Hoy Fat Leong and Charlie Chew Leong to a small, dusty town where there were no other Chinese people, where the possibilities for loneliness and isolation must have been as big as the prairie sky, become such a naturalized feature of small town Canadian life? Too old to be recuperated within the new narratives of multiculturalism and too new to be a proper object

2   'Mr and Mrs Chew.' George Webber. New Dayton, Alberta, 1988.

of wistful histories (although it is certainly getting there) the small town Chinese restaurant is an awkward reminder of the ways in which modernity sometimes stammers, prematurely announcing the death of that which is not yet dead. The persuasiveness of the narrative of the requiem signals the readiness with which we declare the passing of that which is too old for the present and not quite old enough for 'real' history. It is what Meaghan Morris recalls in a different context, as that which comes too soon, too late.[3]

Within the contradictions of being too soon, too late, the small town Chinese restaurant poses a problem for a modernity that wants to move on without it. It is strangely visible and yet invisible – a sign of the passing of time and the death of prairie life, and yet still one of the last places where one can find a proper beef dip sandwich. It is at once everywhere (it is hard to find a town without one) and yet almost nowhere in contemporary discussions of Chinese immigration, diasporas, Canadian multiculturalism, transnational migration patterns, and global movements of people and capital. One of the central concerns of this book is this paradox of visibility. Spaces such as the N.D. Café and people such as Charlie Chew seem to have no place in contemporary Chineseness except perhaps as a feature of that which has passed on and is now past. There is a sense that no one goes to small towns anymore, that what really matters are the increasingly multicultural mega-cities of the first world. And yet, it is precisely at the moment when something is declared to be outdated that the investment in the dating of things, their situatedness in history, reveals itself.

This book seeks to redress the premature requiems for these restaurants that are not yet dead or gone. Indeed, I want to suggest that these restaurants illuminate both the difficulty of sustaining the presentness of the past in Chinese diaspora and the need to do so. The small town Chinese restaurants of this book are those where the menu is divided between Chinese and 'Canadian' food offerings; where the Chinese food items are not differentiated by regional categories such as Szechuan or Hunan, but by genres such as 'egg foo yong,' 'chow mein,' and 'chop suey'; and where there is a preponderance of Naughahyde. They are not found in cities. They are not in Chinatown. These are sometimes the only restaurants in town. There are similar restaurants in other countries, but I have limited the scope of my project to those in Canada in order to create a coherent archive for discussion. Even though there are tantalizing parallels to be drawn with small town Chinese restaurants in Australia and the United States, for example, I recognize the particular differences attendant upon the immigration histories of Chinese communities in those countries. While focusing on small town Chinese restaurants in Canada may seem like a limiting critical move, my hope is that it is an enabling limit that allows for a sense of the larger issues of diasporic identity and community through an engagement with a very specific manifestation of Chinese diasporic culture.

The N.D. Café, and the restaurants that came before, after, and around it, enable a consideration of the possibilities of a perpetually forgotten and yet persistently present story of diasporic arrival. The undated photograph from the un-named photographer opens up for us a crack in the story of the Chinese migration in Canada. It is a dialectical image that, as Eduardo Cadava notes with regard to the use of photography in Benjamin's writing, 'interrupts history and opens up another possibility of history, one that spaces time and temporalizes space' (61). This project falls headlong into this interruption. I want to look for the ways in which the N.D. Café has not so much disappeared, but has been submerged, and to look at what it means to recover it, and other spaces like it, as crucial sites of diasporic arrival.

Chinese settlement in small towns across Canada has a long history and this settlement has profoundly affected the restaurant industry in Canada. As Edgar Wickberg notes in his history of Chinese immigration, one of the primary types of early Chinese communities could be found 'in those places where a large number of Chinese worked for non-Chinese companies. The largest enterprise was, of course, railway construction, but there were similar communities at the coal mines in and near Wellington, at the sawmills in Burrard Inlet, near the fish canneries in New Westminster and Skeena, and on farms at Harrison, Clinton, Cache Creek, and 150 Mile House' (24–5). Thus drawn by the work that was available, Chinese immigrants went to small towns across the country. During the latter part of the nineteenth century, in conjunction with the building of the railway, Chinese immigration extended eastward beyond British Columbia. Wickberg observes that 'the railroad greatly affected the distribution of Chinese communities on the mainland of British Columbia' (24). Not only did Chinese communities develop outside of urban centers such as Vancouver and Victoria, but the census figures also show that a significant number of Chinese immigrants worked in and arguably transformed the restaurant industry in the places where they landed. According to the 1931 Canadian census, Chinese people made up less than one per cent of the Canadian population, and yet one out of every five restaurant, café, or tavern keepers was of Chinese origin. More than one out of every three male cooks was Chinese (Reiter 30). As Wickberg's work on the Canadian census shows, 40 per cent of Chinese people in Alberta in 1921 worked in the restaurant industry (310). That number rose to 60 per cent in 1931. The numbers are even higher in Saskatchewan, where 50 per cent of Chinese immigrants worked in restaurants in 1921 and an astonishing high of 70 per cent in 1931 (ibid.).

These dramatic numbers point not to the Chinese population in the Chinatowns of Vancouver, Calgary, or Toronto, but in small towns across the country. While statistics can only be a part of the story, these numbers do suggest that looking at Chinese restaurants in terms of diaspora culture means looking at the small town restaurants that are connected to the legacy of early migration and that continue to serve up 'Chinese and Canadian food' on the main streets of towns such as Ponoka, Swift Current, and Nelson today.

Closely following the development of the railway across the country, the rise of restaurants on the main streets of small western Canadian towns is also the story of a Chinese diasporic community in development. As Donald Wetherell and Irene Kmet note in their work on the evolution of small towns in Alberta, the placement of railway routes was one of the most important factors in the establishment of a town (13). In addition to the east–west route operated by the Canadian Pacific Railway, several other lines, including the C&ER, the Grand Trunk Pacific Railway, and the Canadian Northern Railway, operated in Alberta alone in the late nineteenth and early twentieth century. Along all these lines towns developed, main streets were established, and businesses emerged. 'The few business people of non-European origin were usually Chinese. Initially operating small general stores and laundries, they soon began operating cafes' (117). Wetherell and Kmet observe that, in addition to 'serving food to the many commercial travelers, to farmers and their families in town for the day, and to local people without cooking facilities,' small town cafés also 'served as informal meeting places, providing an important social opportunity for townspeople and hinterland visitors' (227). From the beginning, these cafés illuminate the curious role of Chineseness in the development of small town life.

My call for a turn to the non-urban is not simply about a locational or purely geographic shift, but is also a conceptual one. In *The Country and the City*, Raymond Williams writes that 'the country and the city are changing historical realities, both in themselves and in their interrelations' (289). I take from Williams's consideration of the city and the country the understanding that these are conceptual categories where the historical is produced by a set of specific narratives. In a similar vein, the non-metropolitan space of my inquiry is a conceptual category as much as it is a material site. The premature requiem for small town Chinese restaurants that have not yet disappeared also indicates a discomfort with the non-modern as a feature of the present. Indeed, those who arrive to work in the kitchens of Chinese restaurants do seem very far removed from the modern multinational entrepreneur with his handful of passports and the latest-model mobile phone. The small town Chinese restaurant illuminates a collusion between the idea of the non-urban and that of the non-modern in the increasingly triumphalist accounts of Asian arrival. In this latter vision, Chinese in diaspora are, as the title of Lynn Pan's book proposes, 'sons of the yellow empire.' They are no longer 'coolies' and laundry workers, but rule, according to the title of Aihwa Ong and Donald Nonini's study, 'ungrounded empires' and networks of transnational capital. And yet, the collapsing of contemporary Chinese dishwashers and short-order cooks with the non-modern belies a historicist investment. I read in the relegating of the non-urban to the non-modern a divorcing of the modern from the historically constitutive; that is, the desire to keep the past in the past is also the desire to keep the past from intruding into the present. In reclaiming the small town Chinese restaurant as vital to contemporary Chinese diasporic discourse, I suggest that these restaurants function as a locus for examining diasporic culture. In particular, they lie at the juncture between old and new diasporas.

The delineation of old and new diasporas refers to what Vijay Mishra and Gayatri Spivak delineate as the old diasporas of slavery and indenture and the new diasporas of transnational migration. Spivak asks, in 'Diasporas Old and New,' 'What were the old diasporas, before the world was thoroughly consolidated as transnational? They were the results of religious oppression and war, of slavery and indenturing, trade and conquest' (245).

While this distinction between old and new diasporas has not been significantly taken up in subsequent critical discussions of diaspora and postcoloniality, I want to return to it because these categories open up a way of understanding the heterogeneity of diasporic communities while still attending to the continuities of specific historical experiences of displacement. As Mishra notes,

> I keep the distinction of the 'old' and the 'new' not because the binary has to be defended or that the binary is incontestable; it is made because Indian intellectuals of the diaspora (Appadurai, Radhakrishnan and Bhabha, among many others) presume that the lives of the Indian NRIs (the 'new' diaspora of 'non-resident Indians') constitute the self-evidently legitimate archive with which to explore the histories of diasporic subjectivities. They also tended to presume that the 'new' presents itself as the dominant (and indeed the more exciting) site for purposes of diasporic comment. (*Literature* 3)

This distinction between old and new diasporas remains one of the clearest ways of attending to the unevenness within diasporic communities with long and diverse histories of migration. Mishra notes that highlighting the particularilities between old and new Indian diasporas in his essay is more than 'a purely heuristic desire for a neat taxonomy' ('Diasporic' 442). He draws 'attention to the complex procedures by which diasporas negotiate their perceived moment of trauma and how, in the artistic domain, the trauma works itself out' (ibid.). Mishra's identification of the old Indian diaspora with the traumas of indenture passage points to ways in which the experience of the passage shapes diasporic communities. Implicit within the distinction between old and new diasporas lies the problem of involuntary and voluntary displacement. Extending Spivak's and Mishra's project, I suggest that the 'old' diasporas of indenture and slavery are not fully distinct from the 'new' ones of jet-fuelled transnational mobility. Rather, these diasporas are contemporaneous and can draw attention to the ways in which the past is constitutive of the present.

Certainly, there are crucial differences between the Chinese communities born of railway workers of the late nineteenth and early twentieth centuries, and those of the wealthy transnational capitalists from Hong Kong who migrated in the late twentieth century out of anxiety over the return of Hong Kong to China. And indeed, the multiple-passport-carrying businessman from Hong Kong might be the first to insist upon the difference between himself and the impoverished Chinese who crossed the Pacific a century earlier out of desperation and for lack of any better options. Separated as they are by time, history, and class, it seems fanciful at best and just plain mistaken at worst to claim them both under the rubric of 'Chinese diaspora.' Nevertheless, there is something that connects them. It is more than just the fact of China as a space of origin, or race and ethnicity, or even the experience of displacement, be it voluntary, involuntary, or something in between. It seems to me that one of the most powerful possibilities of diaspora studies lies in its exploration and illumination of what it is that connects these two disparate figures. They are not temporally or historically static. There were wealthy merchant-class Chinese migrants long before there were passports. Poor Chinese still migrate out of desperation and for lack of better options. When they arrive, as Jennifer 8. Lee reveals of Chinese migrants in the United States, many still end up working in Chinese restaurants in small towns. As she notes of the migrants who were on the ill-fated *Golden Venture*, which crashed into New York's Rockaway Beach in 1993, over '90 percent of the *Golden Venture* survivors were involved in the Chinese-restaurant business' despite having been scattered into the heartland of America (110). 'The *Golden Venture* was in essence,' she writes, 'a delivery of Chinese restaurant workers to the United States that had gone haywire' (110). Marked by an inexhaustible demand for cheap labour that does not require language skills, the North American Chinese restaurant continues to be a landing place for Chinese migrants with few or no options. The old diasporas do not exist only in the past and the new diasporas have been in place for a long time. The distinction between old and new diasporas does not necessarily describe a series of historical stages in the development of a particular diasporic community. Rather, this distinction can be more usefully deployed to articulate the ways in which the old diaspora is constitutive of, and coeval with, the new.

In their seeming anachronism, small town Chinese restaurants illuminate the coevality of the old and new Chinese diaspora. At once old in their connection to Chinese camp cooks who worked on railways, farms, and in lumber camps in the late-nineteenth and early-twentieth century, they are also new as consistently and persistently visible Chinese businesses with connections to a merchant class of migrant who has money to invest. In his documentary series *Chinese Restaurants*, Cheuk Kwan's telling of the story of 'Noisy' Jim Kook's restaurant illustrates the ways in which the small town restaurant is both old and new. Jim Kook has run the New Outlook Café in Outlook, Saskatchewan, for forty years. Using the birth certificate of a Chinese migrant who had passed away, Kook came as a paper son. Although all of his five children worked in the restaurant, none of them takes on the business. Instead, Kook sells the restaurant to a new immigrant couple, Ken and Ruby Chan. Wetherell and Kmet note that even though 'cafes were among the first businesses established in a town, many saw a rapid turn-over of owners. For most, it was a marginal business' (228). These restaurants are businesses to be passed on, not within families but across communities. In its retention of the shape and form of a place constructed by a paper son of the old diaspora, the New Outlook Café is old. And yet, as a space for new migrants such as the Chans who come as investors, it is also a part of the new diaspora.

Chinese restaurants mark not only the connection between old and new diasporas, they are also spaces of interaction between Chinese and non-Chinese communities. Long after the railway was completed and the lumber camps disbanded, Chinese restaurants continued to be one of the few consistently available spaces of cultural interaction between Chinese immigrants and their 'host' communities. Across spaces of cultural contact, the West has often had the orientalizing power of translating the East. As Shu-Mei Shih suggests, '[it] is not that there is an ontological lack or wealth of translatability between Chineseness and Westernness, but that the conferral of that translatability and opacity is itself a historically determined and *affective* act conducted in the field of unequal power relations' (115). Navigating and, as I will show in chapter 2, successfully re-scripting power relations in order to define 'Chinese food' for non-Chinese consumers, Chinese restaurants operate as a curious juncture of interaction and relation between Chineseness and Westernness. Because I want to understand how these interactions and relations contributed to the shaping of Chineseness in diaspora, my understanding of the restaurant is grounded in thinking of it as a culturally productive space rather than as a cultural object. I understand the Chinese restaurant not as a reflection of Chineseness or small town Canadian culture, but rather as a cultural site that is productive of Chineseness, Canadianness, small town Canadian culture, and diasporic culture more broadly.

From Brillat-Savarin's oft-quoted aphorism 'Tell me what you eat, and I will tell you what you are' to Roland Barthes's discussion of steak frites and French national identity,[4] it has become something of a given that there is an intimate connection between what we eat and who we are, between food and identity. Much of the academic work in this area has emerged in the field of anthropology and sociology through discussions of food culture and food ways. While this work has helped shape my thinking, these analyses tend to focus on the meanings that can be read into the production and consumption of food rather than that which comes out of the *interactions* around food in the restaurant. Although it is tempting to read a semiotics of the menu through the kind of work that Mary Douglas and Margaret Visser have accomplished in their readings of menus and the rituals of dining, this type of reading risks assuming a sameness in the experience of eating Chinese.[5]

And yet, even a cursory look at Chinese restaurants reveals the remarkable range and diversity of the experience of what it means to 'eat Chinese.' In attending to this diversity while also taking up small town Chinese restaurants as a coherent, culturally legible space, my approach to the Chinese restaurant as a cultural site owes much to Meaghan Morris's work on shopping centres. In 'Things to Do with Shopping Centers,' Morris demands a critically differentiated understanding of shopping centres. For Morris, shopping centres may be '*minimally* readable' as being the same everywhere, but looking at the differences between them 'involves predicating a more complex and localized *affective* relation to shopping spaces, and to their links with other sites of domestic and familial labour, than does the scenario of the cruising grammarian reading similarity from place to place' (393). I take from Morris's work the commitment to the specific histories of cultural sites and an emphasis on the productivity of the interactions between people and places. In this sense I examine the restaurant as an actively localized space. I explore the multiple interactions situated within and around the space of the restaurant in order to arrive at a sense of the ways in which these interactions produce the culture of the restaurant.

Tracking the transformations and interactions that render the small town Chinese restaurant as a cultural space poses a problem: that of readability, minimal or otherwise. How does one read a restaurant? It is as much a problem of methodology as it is of the 'text' itself. What makes up a restaurant? Of course, a restaurant is more than the food that it serves – it has an architecture; it is a gathering space; it is the kitchen and the dining area and the swinging doors which connect the two; it is the menu and the space of the counter. As Rebecca Spang's history of the rise of the eighteenth- and nineteenth-century French restaurant makes clear, the restaurant became a restaurant through a specific economic and political history.[6] The things that make up the restaurant, which distinguish it from other public eating spaces, emerge out of this history. Moreover, the things which distinguish the small town Chinese restaurant from other restaurants also emerge out of a specific history which is related not only to the rise of the European restaurant as a cultural institution, but also to the history of migrant Chinese labour in Canada and the interactions between Chinese and non-Chinese communities. How can the interactions that produce the space of the restaurant be rendered visible and readable? What are the protocols for such a reading? What does it mean to not only read a space, but also to read for its transformation through the interactions between diners and cooks, communities and families, histories of migrancy and memories of diasporic arrival?

This book reads the small town Chinese restaurant by taking up a range of diverse texts: folk tales and rumours, menus, Canadian folk songs, art installations, and literature. I have chosen each text because of the way it illuminates a different facet of the restaurant as a cultural space. These representations are in no way comprehensive. They are, however, symptomatic of the kinds of interactions and affective relations that constitute the cultural productivity of the space of the small town

Chinese restaurant. Each of the texts I consider reveals something different about the persuasiveness of the premature requiem for the restaurant that has not yet passed.

One of the commitments of this book is to look at diasporas as communities that have been forged out of the dynamism and contingencies of relations – between diasporic subjects and across diasporic and non-diasporic communities – rather than as ontological facts. That is, I am less interested in thinking of *the* Chinese diaspora than I am in examining the processes through which Chinese diaspora communities emerge. This book understands diasporas as communities that form out of relations between and across the diasporic and non-diasporic, and thus not on the basis of imaginary connections to an imaginary homeland (as Salman Rushdie suggests);[7] nor on the basis of a collective historical wound that must be constantly nursed as 'ethnic abjection.' (as Rey Chow suggests);[8] nor even along the problematic lines of racial or religious identification (as Avtar Brah, Stéphane Dufoix, and Khachig Tololyan suggest).[9] All of these positions are valuable in that they describe particular conditions of diasporic subjectivity. However, it seems to me that much of diaspora theory has worried a great deal about the descriptive elements of the diasporic, about being able to name and distinguish the diasporic from the ethnic, the racially segregated, the traumatized and dislocated. This anxiety over who might count as diasporic suggests not only the capaciousness of the category of diaspora, but also the ontologization of diasporic agency in current discussions. These anxieties signal what Jasmin Habib notes as the problems 'inherent in defining or describing a "diaspora" as a thing rather than as a process or a relationship' (16). Rather than worrying over who might be counted as diasporic and who should have their claims to diasporic membership revoked, I am committed to showing how diasporic communities emerge out of the relationships within and across diasporas.

In this commitment to comprehending the mechanisms of community in diaspora while at the same time questioning the bases of these mechanisms, diaspora theory shares some of the goals of feminism. As Morris notes, 'Whatever their differences, most feminisms have been marked, at least in their creative political phase, by an experimental approach to the present, a desire to shape the future, and an enterprising attitude to representing the past. In other words, feminism is sceptical but *constructive*' (xiv–xv). Diaspora studies can be skeptical of many things: of what it is that brings diasporas together as diaspora; of how to understand the histories of diasporas; of postcolonialism; of race; of nationalism and nation-states. But it is also constructive in its commitment to the possibility of community despite dispersal and dislocation.

The double movement of diaspora theory's skepticism and constructiveness has helped me to grasp the ways in which the Chinese restaurant, as a problematic site of cultural identification, is nonetheless a location of Chinese diaspora culture. David Scott points to the diasporic sense of connection across time and space, with reference to Kamau Braithwaite, and acknowledges it as 'an obscure miracle of connection,' as that which is neither for nor against essentialism, but which understands diasporic community as constituted within an 'evocation of a community of those for whom slavery is the name of a trial and a tribulation, and Africa the name of identity\difference' (127). In the spirit of Scott, this book explores ways of understanding the Chinese diaspora, through restaurants such as the N.D. Café, as communities for whom indenture and migrant labouring is the name of a trial that is not just a feature of the past, and China not simply a homeland spurned or lost. After all, the inevitable double question that the racially marked diasporic subject must bear over and over again – Where are you from? No, no, where are you *really* from? – indicates that entities such as 'China' have to mean something more than just geo-political spaces or coherent zones of cultural difference. That incredulous double question – incredulous because it disbelieves any answer other than the one it already knows – also signals the necessity of recognizing the history of involuntary dislocations within a present that seeks to retain that history as merely a feature of the past.

While diasporic theoretical approaches make possible my thinking in this book, part of what has been most useful for me in thinking through this project is to understand the places where the Chinese restaurant does *not* fit, where it becomes a problem for diaspora theories. Where older diaspora theories focused on the paradigmatic Jewish example, and more recent theories have tended to examine either the South Asian diaspora of indentured labour and NRI's or the cosmopolitan intellectual traditions in postcolonial criticism, there has been less focus on the serial formations of East Asian diasporas. The Chinese restaurant functions as an illuminating locus of the old and the new diaspora. Its proprietors' persistent identification and problematization of Chineseness far from anything else that might be recognized as Chinese suggests that diasporic formations can also be incredibly lonely and isolating even if they are bound by notions of community. If we take seriously Rey Chow's warning against submitting to the lures of race and blood as bases for belonging (WD 118), how do we read for the ties that bind diaspora communities? This book is an extended conversation with and through diasporic theory that is grounded in the small town Chinese restaurant.

In chapter 1, I distinguish diasporic agency from postcolonial conceptions of agency through an exploration of two moments in the history of Chinese cooks serving food to non-Chinese consumers. The first is one of subaltern history and culinary resistance. It occurs in Hong Kong, January 1857, only months before the Sepoy Rebellion in India. From the colonial archive, we can read a story of poison, deception, and, ultimately, panic fuelled by rumour that cannot be contained. I juxtapose this narrative with that of a different moment of culinary resistance, one that does not even have a place in the colonial archive, but circulates as a folk story, a tale told over *mah jong* tables of the *lo wah kiu*, old villagers in the new country. It is a story about the sour sweetness of agency in diaspora embedded on the contemporary restaurant menu. Put against each other, these two narratives suggest the importance of the relationship between the postcolonial and the diasporic, and some of the problems of reading for agency in the precariousness of migrancy.

Chapter 2 attends to this problem of diasporic agency further through a reading of Chinese restaurant menus. From the 1923 menu of the N.D. Café, which offered no Chinese food at all, to the contemporary menus of restaurants that contain the now familiar offerings of chop suey, chow mein, and fried rice, these menus are texts that both define and critique the concepts of Chineseness and Canadianness. This chapter argues that understanding diasporic arrival to include non-metropolitan settlement enables a conception of Chinese diasporic agency that is not only spatial, but also temporal. That is, as I will show through a reading of restaurant menus across different periods, the restaurants contain within them an assertion of a different temporality. Within this reading of temporal resistance, this chapter also makes a connection between an alternative temporality and the work of memory.

Chapters 3 and 4 engage with the problem of diasporic spatiality enmeshed with the conceptions of alternative temporality in chapter 2. Chapter 3 examines the representation of the Chinese restaurant in two folk songs, Sylvia Tyson's 'The Night the Chinese Restaurant Burned Down' and Joni Mitchell's 'Chinese Café/Unchained Melody.' Although both songs refer to the restaurant as a disappearing or disappeared object, the chapter argues that this use of the restaurant as a site of loss signals a larger problem of nostalgia as *structural* to the public sphere. Chapter 4 continues the discussion of the problem of space through a discussion of a series of art installations called the *Gold Mountain Restau-*

*rants* by Karen Tam. This chapter explores the incipient situatedness of diasporas and ways of reading their emplacement in places of 'arrival.' It argues that the Chinese restaurant functions as a diasporic counterpublic sphere where diasporic culture is not only shaped by the relationships maintained with the spaces of origin (such as China, imaginary or otherwise), but also by the spaces of arrival.

Chapter 5 takes up what David Scott calls 'a demand of black diaspora criticism' (127). I understand this demand as one that revolves around the problem of transmission, of attempting to grasp what it is that makes diasporic communities diasporic. What are the ties that bind? In the context of the black diaspora, Scott takes this demand to mean 'that it neither wants the cultural nationalist dream of a full and homogenous "blackness" nor the postmodern hope of an arbitrary, empty, and "unscripted" one' (127). If it is not race, or nation, or even just the experience of displacement, what constitutes diasporic community? This chapter explores these questions through the poetry of Fred Wah and argues that a first step away from the bind of the oppositions of cultural nationalism, on the one hand, and deconstructed Chineseness, on the other, lies in stepping outside of the ensnarements of historicism. I suggest that the debate on the problem of Chineseness between cultural nationalists and deconstructionists remains within a historicist frame of reference and that this debate mirrors the split debate in literary criticism on Wah between form and content. Embracing the difficulties of Wah's text, I read for the ways in which *Diamond Grill* and *Waiting for Saskatchewan* put forward the notion of a transgenerational memory.

One of the goals of this final chapter, and of this book overall, is that of situating the longing, sadness, hunger, and homesickness of what it means to be in diaspora. I do not mean to valorize the melancholic, or to indulge in narratives of victimization and wounding. But I also do not want to write off diasporic melancholia as only naive, misguided, and therefore dangerous. Those in diaspora often know better than anyone else that there is no home to which they can return. And yet this knowledge does not make that homesickness any less legitimate. If the logic of the wound is that it must be cured in order for the wounded subject to move forward, then the basis of that logic must be questioned. Perhaps we need to embrace the coevality of sadness and pleasure in diaspora, the bittersweetness of being within communities of dislocation.

It is this bittersweetness that colours my sense of what it means to eat Chinese. One of my first memories of eating anything at all, and my first inkling of what it might mean to eat Chinese, came on a thick milky-white ceramic plate edged with dark green stripes piled high with freshly made onion rings. It's the kind of plate you still see in some Chinese restaurants, old diners, or amidst piles of second-hand dishes at thrift stores. They are sturdy and seem to last forever. The onion rings did not last long. They were hot and golden, crisp outside and still steamy in the middle. The back of my thighs stuck to the Naughahyde of the booth. My legs dangled far above the linoleum floor. I remember these onion rings with a combination of deep pleasure and sadness hovering at the edges. I used to think onion rings were Chinese food because we were Chinese people and we cooked and ate Chinese food. Those onion rings that I ate on summer afternoons in a nondescript Chinese restaurant in a nondescript town in the middle of what felt like nowhere are a problem in that, for me, they are both terribly Chinese and not Chinese at all.

Later, eating onion rings made by the same hands, hands that were even more deeply lined, more scarred, and sad, all I could think was, Why did you come here? At one point in *Diamond Grill*, Fred Wah asks, 'Why Trail of all places?' (87). Why some place where we knew no one? When we had no job, no friends, not even a place to live? Because of a rumour. 'Because there was a rumour in Calgary that you could get a job in Trail' (*Diamond Grill* 87). Because there was a rumour of gold. Because there was a rumour of possibility. Because there was a rumour that it had to be better there than it was here.

Let us begin then with rumour and eating Chinese food.

*Chapter One*

# Sweet and Sour: Historical Presence and Diasporic Agency

Sweet and sour pork is one thing in English. In Cantonese it tells a very different story. This chapter is a meditation on the significance of that difference. Thinking about the story of the naming of sweet and sour pork in Cantonese I came to questions about the relationship between postcolonial and diaspora studies, and the question of agency. These questions brought me to another story of food and naming that is set in nineteenth-century Hong Kong. Through two stories of food and rumour, this chapter is concerned with the problem of reading for agency not just in the slenderness of historical narrative, but also in the precariousness of migrancy.

I will begin in Hong Kong and close somewhere in small town Canada. It is also a trajectory that moves from the postcolonial to the diasporic. I am aware that this chapter seems to move from the specificity of Hong Kong and postcoloniality into the vagueness of an un-named small town somewhere in the vastness of the Canadian landscape and the quality of dispersion that characterizes diaspora. It is not that the space of diaspora is necessarily so vague, but rather, as I will show, that it is marked by a precariousness that flourishes in dispersion.

Let me turn then to the first meal: Hong Kong, 1857.

At the time, many Hong Kong Europeans bought fresh bread daily from the E Sing Bakery belonging to a Chinese man, Cheong Ah Lum. On 15 January 1857, large numbers of that European community became violently ill. The colonial police were called in; the investigation was immediate; and it was soon discovered that the cause of the January 15th illness was this: arsenic in the morning loaves. Fortunately, for the colonialists, the arsenic had been added to the loaves in such large quantities that most of the poisoned Europeans vomited at once and thus ejected most of the poison from their systems. Although Ah Lum, the owner of the bakery, had left that same morning to Macau with his family, they soon tracked him down. At the trial, he claimed to have known nothing of the incident and that his own family had also been violently ill that day. The real crisis began when Ah Lum was acquitted at the trial. Fifty-two of his workers were jailed and ten were tried. It was eventually decided that the Chinese government in Canton probably incited the poisoning, but no proof was ever found. Mass arrests followed the poisoning and thousands of Chinese were deported. Ultimately, 26,000 Chinese people left Hong Kong that year.[1]

In the Ah Lum affair, as it came to be known, we are confronted with a colonial dynamic where anti-colonial political agency is, at best, dispersed. There is a massive overdetermination. It brings the colonial government to the vexing problem of an obvious occasion of criminality where there is no clear single agent. Fifty-two workers were arrested. Ten were tried. But Ah Lum himself, the man whose name became synonymous with the entire incident, was acquitted. And there were no answers. Despite the attempts of the colonial government to bring justice to the colony, the discourse of rumour and panic amplified the incident; very quickly, the poisoning moved beyond Ah Lum, beyond the fifty-two incarcerated workers, beyond ten convicted felons: it amounted to mass arrests and mass deportations. The Ah Lum affair touched the skittish nerve of the British community.

In the introduction to *Elementary Aspects of Peasant Insurgency in Colonial India*, Ranajit Guha offers a way of reading for peasant insurgency despite the paucity of non-elite, non-colonial primary historical materials. Examining colonial documents, Guha suggests that the colonial archive betrays itself. In the uncertainty, the gaps of that archive, there is the possibility of reading for a peasant rebel consciousness.

> For counter-insurgency, which derives directly from insurgency and is determined by the latter in all that is essential to its form and articulation, can hardly afford a discourse that is not fully and compulsively involved with the rebel and his activities. It is of course true that the reports, despatches, minutes, judgments, laws, letters, etc. in which policemen, soldiers, bureaucrats, landlords, usurers and others hostile to insurgency register their sentiments, amount to a representation of their will. But these documents do not get their content from that will alone, for the latter is predicated on another will – that of the insurgent. (Guha 15)

In the spirit of Guha's project, we can read in the colonial archive of the letters, dispatches, and laws for the history of anti-British Chinese insurgency.

Sir John Bowring, then governor of Hong Kong, communicated the news of the poisoning to Her Majesty's Government in Britain in a letter that is itself a performance of a futile attempt to contain the fear and panic that gripped the colony. Writing on the morning of the poisoning, Bowring details the increase of various security measures and begs twice 'to impress [upon] Her Majesty's Government the urgent necessity of sending at once, from India if possible, a Force of not less than 5000 men' (Hong Kong Public Records Office, CO, 129-62, at 95). The letter begins with references to a series of previous despatches of previous ordinances concerning the security of the colony. Bowring refers only ambiguously to the poisoning: 'I now forward copies of four Government modifications, issued in connection with that Ordinance and *the existing condition of things*' (PRO, CO, 129-62, at 93, my emphasis). Bowring's letter attempts to maintain the formality of official correspondence. It outlines the official response to the crisis in the form of the actions they have taken: the appointment of a new assistant to the superintendent of police; the increase of the police force itself by one hundred men, fifty English and fifty Indian; the hiring of a merchant steamer to patrol the waters in the bays and creeks surrounding Hong Kong until English gun boats arrive. Bowring only gestures to the poisoning. His letter suppresses the news of the poisoning until it explodes at the end of the letter into a full-out admission of panic. It is not until close to the end of the letter that Bowring describes the events that lead to these new security measures:

> Incendiarism was the only subject of our apprehension till this morning when a diabolical attempt was made to poison the foreign community by putting arsenic in the bread supplied by the Esing [*sic*] Bakery and largely used in the town. The principal, one Alum [*sic*] is said to have absconded to Macao, and I have this instant written to the Governor of that Settlement desiring assistance in his apprehension. (Ibid. 94)

After detailing the news of the poisoning itself, Bowring closes the letter with his second entreaty for military reinforcement and declares that 'these may be necessary for the defence of the Colony, and certainly are for the assertion of our Treaty Rights, the security of our Trade, and the very maintenance of our position in China' (ibid. 95). It is finally only in the postscript that Bowring permits himself the admission of a moment of personal panic. Scrawled at the end of the letter, Bowring adds: 'PS I beg to apologize if anything should have been forgotten at this last moment – I am shaken by the effects of poison, *every member* of my family being at this moment suffering from this new attempt upon our lives' (ibid. 94). Only after five pages of official reporting does Bowring finally arrive at an explanation for the actions he has taken. His emotional anxiety only resurfaces all the more powerfully in the postscript – the attempt to script the poisoning after the fact of its occurrence.

In 'The Prose of Counter-Insurgency,' Guha notes that there is a quality of raw, instantaneousness that accompanies primary historical documents written first-hand by those who had the most to fear from anti-colonial resistance. It is a quality that is suppressed, contained, and controlled in secondary and tertiary historical treatments. In the case of Bowring's first letter reporting the poisoning, Bowring's own attempt to suppress the rawness of his fear makes the tenor of his panic all the more vociferous.

In the panic of Hong Kong, January 1857, I cannot help but hear the echo of Meerut, May 1857 – the beginning of the so-called Indian Mutiny or Sepoy Rebellion. Word had reached the British that chapatis were being passed, from hand to hand, in the villages surrounded by the British military cantonments. Homi Bhabha's essay 'By Bread Alone' suggests that we might read the agency of the chapati not in the ambiguity of the content of the message embedded in the chapati, but rather in the productivity of rumour, the contagion of panic. Moreover, the chapati frustrates the colonial desire for a single agent of history. Bhabha's conclusion is in part that the power of the chapati narrative lies precisely in the failure of colonial authority to pin it down to a single agent, to secure it by naming it.

Even when colonial authority has named its agent, it still cannot secure it. One of the problems for colonial authority that emerges throughout the archive lies in the simple problem of finding a name for the man they had deemed to be guilty of the poisoning. Ah Lum's name is spelled differently, ranging from Alum to Allum to Ah Lum and so on, in almost every letter referring to the incident.[2] There is no stability to his identity from a colonial referent point. In that first report of the poisoning, Bowring's letter reveals its anxieties around the problem of naming in the marginalia. In his naming of Ah Lum as the primary culprit, Bowring admits his own ignorance of the baker's identity. Next to the sentence 'The principal, one Alum is said to have absconded to Macao' Bowring writes in the margin, '*merely a mythical name*' (PRO, CO, 129-62, at 94, my emphasis). Despite Bowring's desire to fix Ah Lum as the principal perpetrator, his own marginalia transport Ah Lum into the larger collective space of myth. Not only is his identity unfixable in the language of the colonial, but, despite the colonial desire for a single agent, Ah Lum's identity emerges into something larger.

The naming of the entire affair also reveals the way in which Ah Lum came to stand in for something larger than himself. The bakery poisoning in 1857 became known in the English-language newspapers in Hong Kong at the time as the Ah Lum Affair. In other words, the man who was deemed by the British court to be innocent of any knowledge of the poisoning nevertheless became synonymous with the poisoning. Why, in the popular colonial imaginary, did the event not become known as the E Sing Affair? How is it that Cheong Ah Lum comes to occupy a central place in the incident? Subsequent events suggest one answer. Taking the indignation of the English community upon himself, William Tarrant, the editor of one of the major papers at the time, the *Friend of China and Hong Kong Gazette*, sued Cheong Ah Lum for damages. Tarrant was awarded $1010, but Ah Lum left the colony before he could collect.[3] The judgment of the colonial court failed to converge with a decision that the English community had already made: that Ah Lum was the central agent in the poisoning. Tarrant's actions articulate the lingering accusation, the persistent desire for identifying, securing, and incarcerating a single agent. The naming of the affair exposes the colonial authorial desire for a single agent of history.

Long before Tarrant's actions, the Hong Kong attorney general's letter to the Colonial Secretary already exposes the failings of colonial governance. In a letter dated 20 January 1857, only five days after the poisoning, the attorney general, T. Chisholm Anstey, reveals the fissures that had begun to emerge within the colonial bureaucracy itself. He writes to W.T. Mercer, the Colonial Secretary:

> At a private conversation with His Excellency to which I understood myself to be invited, I had also this morning informed him that since last evening I have had cause to apprehend a failure of justice in the event of the poisoners being tried in the Criminal Court. The common jurors of Hong Kong are not generally men of affluent circumstances, and it is believed that most of the houses of business are in debt to their own Compradors or Shroffs. These latter again are strongly of the party, or under the influence of the miscreant Allum [*sic*], a man of wealth and, of course, a mon-

eylender. Placards having been posted everywhere calling *his friends* to his assistance, the Compradors and Shroffs have generally responded to the call, and they are going about to the European houses asserting violently *his* innocence, and the duty of the Court to set him free. One European so influenced may defeat the course of justice by simply becoming a juror, should chance so determine.

I simply informed His Excellency: I did not advise him: I continued of the opinion expressed in my letter of Sunday last the 18th instant that it was not for *me* to advise whether a Court Martial should be appointed to try cases of this kind during the present crisis: eminently desirable as many think it, and much as the general enforcement of Martial Law is unquestionably required.

I shall however obey His Excellency's desire that no information be laid before him that is not reduced to writing and addressed to the Colonial Secretary; although I cannot help fearing that the present awful crisis will not be best provided for by a general adherence to His Excellency's wishes in that respect, on the part of persons, like myself, who are anxious not to lose time in communicating the intelligence of the hour. (PRO, CO, 129, at 112–14)

While Bowring and Mercer held to the importance of a considered administration of justice, missives such as Anstey's reveal the shortcomings of adhering to process and protocol. The urgency of Anstey's letter and his impatience with the Colonial Secretary's insistence upon due process exposes the colony's own lack of faith in the process of colonial governance in a moment of crisis.

For the attorney general, the miscarriage of justice was preferable to an appearance of governmental weakness. Anstey felt that Ah Lum's acquittal would not only cause a lack of faith among the colonial community but would also produce contempt in the Chinese community. As Norton-Kyshe notes, Anstey regretted that the case ever went to trial at all because he was fully aware of the inadequacy of the evidence against Ah Lum. To the jurors, Anstey said,

We have rather hastily apprehended these men; we found no evidence that would have justified a Magistrate to commit them, so we manage to waive that process; and now that we have rather forced a trial, you must give us a conviction to save our character. *Better to hang the wrong men than confess that British sagacity and activity have failed to discover the real criminals.* (Quoted in Norton-Kyshe, 1: 417, my emphasis)

The attorney general's fears pushed the alibi of empire to its limit. The resulting five to one majority vote acquitting Ah Lum becomes a testimony to both a faith in the power of colonial governance on the part of the jurors, and failure of that colonial governance as an expression of the popular colonial belief that Ah Lum really was the culprit.

Anstey's letter also divulges a kind of second level of poisoning. The average jurors of Hong Kong, he notes, are generally compromised by their debts to Chinese merchants. 'One European so influenced may defeat the course of justice by simply becoming a juror, should chance so determine' (PRO, CO, 129, at 114). Only one compromised juror, Anstey suggests, poisoned by his relationship to the moneylenders of the colony, could annul the entire judicial process. Of course, what was so offensive about Ah Lum was not just that he owned a bakery that had, until that point, supplied all the bread for the colony, but that he was also a Shroff. The *Oxford English Dictionary* defines a Shroff as '[a] banker or money-changer in the East; in the Far East, a native expert employed to detect bad coin.' In other words, according to Anstey, Ah Lum is also a principal in the economy of the counterfeit. Members of the colony are indebted to him and to his friends not only for capital, but also for the entire process of the *exchange* of capital. Moreover, trade in the colony is an exercise in capitalist exchange, as well as an exchange that occurs in translation. Colonial traders depended upon local intelligence to differentiate between good and bad coin, real and counterfeit currency. The very notion of shroffing depends upon and implies the pre-existence of an economy of the counterfeit, a place where distrust, suspicion, and anxiety already run rampant. In this sense, Ah Lum's culpability lies not only in the possibility of his role in the bread poisoning, but also in the way his role as a moneylender exposed the weaknesses of trade in the colony and the dependence of the British upon those whom they colonize. This dependency had poisoned the judicial process before it was ever put into action against Ah Lum.

The Ah Lum affair epitomizes the failure of languages of colonial management. At the moment when Ah Lum, the perceived principal actor in the incident, was acquitted, when no clear enemy could be established, the whispers of conspiracy and insurgency became rampant shouts of alarm. If the alibi of empire is the rule of law, the Ah Lum affair exposed its paucity. When the British colonial government officially claimed Hong Kong, it dealt with the existing population of about five thousand Chinese inhabitants of the island by declaring them subjects of the Queen of England. On 1 February 1841, Captain Elliot issued the following proclamation:

### TO THE CHINESE INHABITANTS OF HONG KONG
### PROCLAMATION

Bremer, Commander-in-Chief, and Elliot, Plenipotentiary, etc., etc., by this proclamation make known to the inhabitants of the island of Hongkong [*sic*], that that island has now become part of the dominions of the Queen of England by clear public agreement between the High Offices of the Celestial and British Courts; and all native persons residing therein must understand that they are now subjects of the Queen of England, and to whom and to whose officers they must pay duty and obedience.

The inhabitants are hereby promised protection, in Her Majesty's gracious name, against all enemies whatever; and they are further secured in the free exercise of their religious rites, ceremonies, and social customs, and in the enjoyment of their lawful private property and interests. They will be governed, pending Her Majesty's further pleasure, according to the laws customs and usages of the Chinese (every description of torture excepted) and by elders of villages, subject to the control of a British magistrate; and any person, having complaint to prefer of ill-usage or injustice against any Englishman or foreigner, will quietly make report to the nearest officer, to the end that full justice may be done. Chinese ships and merchants, resorting to the port of Hongkong [*sic*] for the purposes of trade, are hereby exempted, in the name of the Queen of England, from charge or duty of any kind to the British government. The pleasure of the government will be declared from time to time by further proclamation: and all heads of villages are held responsible that the commands are duly respected and observed. (Quoted in Norton-Kyshe 5–6)

The proclamation is in itself a rich text for the study of colonial rhetoric. The language of justice, protection and fairness recurs throughout this foundational text of colonial administration. If the British traders justified their presence on the island because of the enlightened juridical and legal management they brought to it, then the failure of this colonial management in the face of an unmanageable inscrutability represents a moment in the failure of empire.

Here we come to the course of expulsion. Could the colonial administration of Hong Kong deport thousands of people on the suspicion of criminality that could not be proved? More specifically, could they deport thousands of people on a suspicion of criminality that had no other grounding than that of race?[4] In the quasi-juridical response to the Ah Lum affair, we can see the beginnings of a discursive moment of criminal typing that begins with containment and ends with expulsion. This is the trajectory of the colonial response to the poisoning – deploying a notion of agency in its singularity in an attempt to arrest the rampant rumour of insurgency and the contagion of panic.

In my consideration of a postcolonial model of agency, I have drawn largely from the work of the Subaltern Studies group because they articulate an understanding of agency that is not based in the individual, autonomous subject of history. Instead, they propose the possibility of thinking about agency across collectivities. Ranajit Guha's discussion of rumour and the circulation of the chapati in 1857 Meerut, the belief in Thakur during the Santal Rebellion of 1855, and Dipesh Chakrabarty's insistence upon the existence of precapitalist working-class consciousness in the jute mills of colonial India all suggest models of agency that do not depend upon single agents of history.[5] As Gayatri Spivak notes in 'Subaltern Studies: Deconstructing Historiography,' 'Subaltern consciousness as emergent *collective* consciousness is one of the main themes' of the work of the Subaltern Studies group (14).

I understand this collectivity within Spivak's contention that the group's assertion of subaltern consciousness is a *strategic* one: 'Although the group does not wittingly engage with the post-structuralist understanding of "consciousness," our own transactional reading of them is enhanced if we see them as *strategically* adhering to the essentialist notion of consciousness' ('Subaltern' 15). Spivak's deconstruction of 'the opposition between the [Subaltern Studies] collective and their object of investigation – the subaltern – on the one hand; and ... the seeming continuity between them and their anti-humanist models on the other' (ibid. 20), enables an understanding of subaltern collectivity that is not simply the work of restoring subaltern subjectivity. I will take up Spivak's deconstruction with particular attention to her discussion of rumour later in this chapter.

Like the chapati, the bread from the E Sing bakery transforms an old and familiar symbol into a performative sign of conspiracy and insurgency; the bread of the E Sing bakery circulates as the sign of contagion, conspiracy and violence:

> The semiotic condition of uncertainty and panic is generated when an old and familiar symbol (chapati) develops an unfamiliar social significance as sign through a transformation of the temporality of its representation. The performative time of the chapati's signification, its circulation as 'conspiracy' and/or 'insurgency,' turns from the customary and commonplace to the archaic, awesome, terrifying. (Bhabha 202)

The colonial archive of the bread poisoning reveals yet another attempt to return this sign of violence and conspiracy to the register of the familiar and sensible. The chemist's report attempts to re-situate the terrifying sign of the poisoned bread into a narrative of the rational. The chemist of the War Department, F.A. Abel, examined four specimens of bread and reported that 'each of the specimens of bread was found to contain arsenic, which was proved to have been introduced in the form of arsenious acid (white acid of commerce)' (PRO, CO, 129, at 285). After a breakdown of the amount of arsenic found in each specimen, the chemist concludes the following: 'It may be observed that the quantity of arsenious acid contained in four ounces of the specimen of toast (no. 1) about 2½ grains has frequently been known to produce death when taken into the system' (ibid.). But an entire colonial community, including Bowring's wife and family, consumed this same bread and no one was killed. The result of the poisoning contradicts the chemist's own analysis. He fails to mention in his report that this may have actually been a case of excess, of too much poison to kill. Abel's scientific conclusion suggests an overreaching or overwhelming desire to name guilt and culpability despite the contradictions of the evidence at hand.

Although the chapati and the white bread of E Sing may not be historically contiguous, Bhabha's work offers a way of reading postcolonial agency in the Ah Lum affair. The poisoning of the E Sing Bakery bread occurred on the eve of the second Opium War. For a colony established on poison (opium), the valency of an act of rebellion that injects poison back into the daily bread of the colonizer must not be overlooked. It becomes a fitting metaphor for the eruption of otherness into the space of white domesticity. Attempting to contain the contagion of panic, the body politic of colonial Hong Kong convulsively expelled its foreign hosts. And yet, in that expulsion, there is a residual apprehension. Cheong Ah Lum's freedom functions as a conspicuous example of the inability of colonial symbolic management to safeguard the colonial community from the possibility of future contamination and malignancy. Despite the horrors of a day of endless retching, the body was unable to purge itself of all the arsenic. Despite the upheavals of mass deportations, the body politic of colonial Hong Kong could not purge itself of all its poisoning agents.

The white bread of colonial Hong Kong undergoes a violent reinscription and is transformed from an object of ordinary nourishment into one of poison and danger. In *Dissemination*, Jacques Derrida notes that this story of the origin of writing has been fundamentally misread because it relies on a translation of the word '*pharmakon*' that occludes the ambivalence of its meaning. Prior to Derrida's intervention, *pharmakon* had been translated as 'remedy.' Derrida argues that this 'translation by "remedy" can thus be neither accepted nor simply rejected ... Writing is no more valuable, says Plato, as a remedy than as a poison ... There is no such thing as a harmless remedy. The *pharmakon* can never be simply beneficial' (99). Thus, every antidote must contain within it another kind of poison. The power of the signs of insurgency lies in the understanding that nothing is safe from the violence of reinscription – at any moment, the potentially curative may emerge as poisonous and vice versa.

Understanding the sign of the poisoned bread through Derrida's reading of the *pharmakon* makes possible a reading of anti-colonial insurgency that is not mired in a positivist notion of agency. The 'victory' does not lie in the poisoning, but in the effects of ambivalence unleashed by this reinscription of the ordinary, of daily bread. In her reading of Guha's work on rumour in 'Subaltern Studies,' Spivak argues that rumour can be most usefully understood as a form of 'illegitimate writing rather than the authoritative writing of the law' (23). By the writing of the law, Spivak recalls for us Plato's association between 'speech and law, *logos* and *nomos*. Laws speak' ('Subaltern' 23). For Spivak, 'rumour is a relay of something always assumed to be pre-existent. In fact the mistake of the colonial authorities was to take rumour for speech, to impose the requirements of speech in the narrow sense upon something that draws its strength from participation in writing in the general sense' (24). Sidestepping the phonocentrism of taking rumour for speech and thus attributing to it an authority which it cannot have, and which it thrives without – 'rumour is not error but primordially (originally) errant, always in circulation with no assignable source' ('Subaltern' 23) – Spivak illuminates rumour as *pharmakon*. Understanding the power of subaltern reinscriptions thus demands attending to the poisonous as well as the curative effects of writing.

Let me turn then to another rumour, another inscription. The second meal: a Chinese Canadian restaurant today. Stepping through the doors, you will sit down at one of the booths. Opening the menu, you will come to sweet and sour pork.

The origins of the Cantonese name for sweet and sour pork, a staple of Chinese-Canadian restaurant menus, bear the slivers of a textual, nominal resistance. The real sweet and sour dish is all about bones, drenched in honey and vinegar and succulently crisp. When Chinese cooks on the railway made this dish for Europeans, one version of the story goes, they were chastised for stealing the meat and serving their superiors only the bones. The cooks then left the meat on the bones and renamed the dish *goo lo yok* in the village dialect, *gwei lo yok* in Cantonese, or, in a repetition of that now familiar derogatory term for white people, 'ghost man meat' in English. It was a little culinary joke with a rebellion in the ribs. On Chinese restaurant menus today, the words *goo lo yok* have no literal meaning but are a phonetic approximation of the village dialect – the original slur phonetically translated and defamiliarized in translation. This nominal resistance, this moment of postcolonial ribbing, has become so standardized that contemporary consumers of Chinese food never realize they are ingesting chunks of sly civility with every sweetly sour mouthful.

It is in this second meal that I want to look now at the residual of resistance in diaspora. What happens when the eruption of otherness occurs in the space of migrancy, when the native at home is transported and becomes the migrant, the diasporic subject? How do you read for postcolonial agency not just in the slenderness of historical narrative, as Bhabha asks, but also in the precariousness of migrancy? In Hong Kong, 1857, we have a narrative of containment and expulsion; in the narrative of sweet and sour pork, we have a semiotic virus that cannot be contained. Unlike the Ah Lum affair, where the lingering suspicions – the residual – followed the subjects of resistance, in sweet and sour pork the residual follows the object. Raymond Williams writes that

> the residual, by definition, has been effectively formed in the past, but it is still active in the cultural processes, not only and often not at all as an element of the past, but as an effective element of the present. Thus certain experiences, meanings, and values which cannot be expressed or substantially verified in terms of the dominant culture, are nevertheless lived and practised on the basis of the residue. (*Marxism* 122)

Williams distinguishes the residual from the archaic, noting that the archaic is 'that which is wholly recognized as an element of the past, to be observed, to be examined, or even on occasion to be consciously "revived"' (122). This understanding of the residual is one that recognizes explicitly its potential as 'alternative or even oppositional ... to the dominant culture' (122). The residue of sweet and sour pork opens up a reading of white anxiety that is not unrelated to the histories of Chinese migration. Following the object, sweet and sour pork, we can track the lingering unease of white authority and the incorporation of a nominal resistance that has spread throughout the Canadian cultural reality in the menus of the ubiquitous Chinese diner.

The story of sweet and sour pork shares with rumour some defining features. It has no basis in fact. It would be wrong to read it in any literal sense as a history of the evolution of a particular dish on the contemporary menu. It is not an unearthed artefact of food history, brushed off and translated. Its status as true or false is irrelevant, because the narrative's currency lies not in any claim it might have to historical truth value but in its circulation. The narrative's value lies in a retelling that suggests the existence of another register of emplacement, another temporality of enunciation. As Bhabha notes of the chapati, 'Whether we take the chapatis as historical "myth" or treat them as rumour, they represent the emergence of a form of social temporality that is iterative and indeterminate' (200).

The difference between the story of the poisoned bread of 1857 and the story of sweet and sour pork lies in their circulation. In the case of the latter, it is a myth or rumour that circulates in limited form – only among the Chinese-speaking diasporic community. This is a story that is twice-buried under the cover of another language, Toisanese under Cantonese under English. It does not circulate among settler colonialists and so its effects unfold differently than those of the poisoned bread. There is no contagious panic through which we might look for the agency of the Chinese subject. From the perspective of agency as a sign of resistance circulating through panic and rumour in the colonial community, the story of sweet and sour pork seems to have had no effect at all. A dead letter gathering dust, the sly civility of sweet and sour pork seems to have missed its destination. Its potential for agency seems to be annulled by the mistake of its address. This is not just the problem of language. In 1857 the problem of language was equally present. This is about a process of submersion that happens through incorporation.

As Williams notes, dominant culture deals with residual elements through incorporation. While 'a residual cultural element is usually at some distance from the effective dominant culture ... some part of it, some version of it ... will in most cases have had to be incorporated if the effective dominant culture is to make sense in these areas' (123). The narrative of sweet and sour pork suggests the possibility of a model of agency that does not effect expulsion but consumption and incorporation. Current models of postcolonial agency ultimately dwell upon the agency of the native. They do not translate entirely in the space of diaspora. Here, we are really talking about the migrant. And so I come to the meal that is leftover and the incorporation of the residual. However, incorporation is not without its risks.

Relating the circulation of the chapati in colonial history to the Freudian totem meal, Bhabha notes that 'it is the indeterminacy of meaning, unleashed by the contingent chapati that becomes the totem meal for historians of the Mutiny. They bite the greased bullet and circulate the myth of the chapati' (202). While Bhabha reads a totemic value in the chapati, a place that the narrative of colonial history must return to again and again for its own legitimating mythology, Diana Fuss observes that the narrative of the totem meal has a specifically colonial history. The subtitle of Freud's *Totem and Taboo*, 'Some Points of Agreement between the Mental Lives of Savages and Neurotics,' functions as a reminder that, as Freud's own preface to the book notes, the essays in the book 'represent a first attempt ... at applying the point of view and the findings of psycho-analysis to some unsolved problems of social psychology [*Völkerpsychologie*]' (xiii).[6] The story of the totem meal is first and foremost the story of identification with otherness through violent incorporation.

Situating the story of sweet and sour pork within an understanding of the problem of identification gives new meaning to the idea of 'eating Chinese.' In the Freudian story of the totem meal, the brothers of a clan contend with their fear and jealousy of the totem (who is the substitute for the father) by killing and consuming it. In so doing, the 'clansmen acquire sanctity by consuming the totem: they reinforce their identification with it and with one another' (Freud, 'Totem' 140). Afterwards, the brothers feel guilt and remorse and hold a memorial festival to allay their guilt. Fuss argues that there is an intimate relationship between cannibalism and identification where she 'uncovers the *violence* at the heart of identification. All active identifications, including positive ones, are monstrous assassinations: the Other is murdered and orally incorporated before being entombed inside the subject' (34). Although Fuss's interpretation is very compelling, the violence of identification would be more poignantly understood if we complicate her reading of the cannibalistic moment of identification. Fuss is a little misleading in suggesting that all acts of identification are monstrous assassinations. Freud's totem meal is not only about the repetition of the actual act of violence, the murder of the father, but is also the repetition that represses and preserves the desire for violence. In this sense, it is at once an enactment and a disavowal. This understanding of the double-edged nature of identification explains more satisfactorily how it works within the heart of a liberal project of the incorporation of otherness. The cannibalism that girds Freud's totem meal is more than a transparent 'colonialist construction of the Other as primitive, bestial, and predatory' (Fuss 36). It is also a clue to the desire for and repression of otherness in modern liberal states. In Hong Kong, 1857, the government could and did attempt to simply deport thousands of native Hong Kong inhabitants from the colony. In contemporary Canada, the repression and preservation of the desire for violence mediates the problem of the incorporation of otherness. The violence of identification is then more than just 'the primary means of gaining control over the objects outside itself; identification is a form of mastery modeled directly on the nutritional instinct' (Fuss 35). The incorporation of otherness enacts the cannibalistic scene while also simultaneously disavowing it.

In the context of identification, the idea of eating Chinese takes on the significance of a moment of violent incorporation with all of the cannibalistic connotations that accompany that moment of consumption.[7] However, eating Chinese in Canada is not simply a mastery of Chinese otherness driven by the nutritional instinct. It is a repetition of the cannibalistic scene where the desire for violence is both preserved and repressed. It is at once an enactment and disavowal of violence, achieved through the positivism of embracing otherness.

And yet this form of mastery depends upon a stabilized otherness. Keeping in mind that Freud's project in this meditation on the lives of 'these poor naked cannibals' is one of understanding the less well-developed members of his own contemporary society, the dependence of the totem meal, the scene of cannibalism crossed with parricide, on an absolute primitive other becomes especially paramount (Freud 2). As Fuss notes, Freud's account depends upon an understanding of the savage as being suspended in the timelessness of perpetual otherness: 'Freud relies upon the signifier of temporality to construct the racial Other in culturally ethnocentric terms, reading in the unconscious life of "primitives" the preservation of "the primeval past in a petrified form"' (35). This construction of otherness as without a history, as perpetually caught in an evolutionary stage prior to that of the European, is a familiar one in postcolonial theory. As Bhabha's work on the colonial stereotype in 'The Other Question' makes clear, stereotype depends upon a fetishized fixing of the racialized subject. Similarly, as documents such as the 1885 *Report of the Royal Commission on Chinese Immigration* reveal, there is a kind of timelessness, a perpetual sameness, read onto Chineseness in Canada.[8] The Chinese subject has always been, and will always be, Chinese.

Sweet and sour pork has always been on the menu. It has always tasted like this. It always will.

The story of sweet and sour pork poses a challenge to the narrative of the primitive and unchanging ethnic other. Its nominal resistance suggests that Chineseness in Canada, the construction of Chineseness in migrancy, has not only a history, but a genealogy: 'The totem meal, which is perhaps mankind's earliest festival, would thus be a repetition and a commemoration of this memorable and criminal deed, which was the beginning of so many things – of social organization, of moral restrictions and religion' (Freud, 'Totem' 142). We can understand the story of sweet and sour pork as having a kind of counter-totemic value. The story functions as one of the genesis of fake Chinese food. It would be the story of the creation of a Chineseness specifically for Western consumption and this Chineseness comes to stand in for Chineseness in general in Canadian culture. The story of sweet and sour pork suggests the creation and circulation of a Chineseness that is a substitute for the authentic, timeless, and unchanging other of settler colonial consuming desires. In this story of creation, the Chinese immigrant denies the white settler colonial subject the moment of identification, of violent incorporation, while appearing to provide it. The story suggests that the idea of 'eating Chinese,' with all the violence of appropriation and incorporation that accompanies it, is not quite eating Chinese at all. In thinking that he is eating Chinese, the settler colonialist will actually consume *goo lo yok*, white man meat, a version of himself, and will engage in a moment of symbolic self-cannibalism. Serving back to the settler colonialist his own excessive desires, the story deflects the violence of colonial identification and incorporation away from the Chinese subject and back towards the settler colonial one. This narrative suggests a way in which the Chinese migrant escapes the dialectic of self-otherness. Chinese migrants did not need whiteness or Europeanness to define themselves. Right from the beginning, there was another register of emplacement.

In the space between *goo lo yok* and sweet and sour pork, we can hear the doubled discourse of diasporic resistances. The doubled process of naming extends to the doubled language of the menu itself. The ambivalence of European authority surfaces in suspicions around the doubleness of the menu. Not only is there a Chinese chop suey menu juxtaposed with the Western one of hamburgers and milkshakes, but there is also always a lingering sense that the menu doesn't tell the whole story. Somewhere, past the swinging doors dividing those in the diner from those in the kitchen, there is the suspicion that there are dishes that are simply not on the menu. We've all heard the urban myth about how Chinese restaurants have one menu for white people and another for Chinese people. What the menu makes manifest is the latent suspicion that all is not self-evident. What is maddening about the menu is that it is at once explicitly readable and equivocally illegible. Along the margins of the menu lies the possibility of conspiracy, of another language, of a second menu.

Let us return to the materiality of sweet and sour pork. Imagine it – gooey, unnaturally red-orange, shiny with an aura of plasticity that could come only from that special combination of vegetable oil, rice wine vinegar, and a lingering sense of its inauthenticity. After all, we all know that this isn't *real* Chinese food. It is Chinese and not Chinese, at once impossibly full of ethnic meaning and yet strangely meaningless in that excess. In this materially ambivalent plasticity, let me explore further the relationship between rumour and history.

Describing the way in which rumour can bend and change according to the subjectivity of its transmitter, Guha proposes that

> rumour functions as a free form liable to a considerable degree of improvisation as it leaps from tongue to tongue. The aperture which it has built into it by virtue of anonymity permits its message to be contaminated by the subjectivity of each of its speakers and modified as often as any of them would want to embellish or amend it in the course of transmission. The outcome of all this is a *plasticity* that enables it to undergo transformations. (261, my emphasis)

In this plastic quality of rumour, in the way it changes shape while still retaining the trace of its original form, there is a sense of the materiality of rumour's memory – a sense of its materials memory. Borrowing the phrase from materials engineering, Richard Terdiman suggests that signs carry within them a quality not unlike that of the crease in a pair of Perma-press slacks. Bend them, fold them, and they will still retain the trace of their original shape. Terdiman notes that

> certain products and materials resume their shape after they have been deformed ... This property is termed 'materials memory.' It seems a process without a subject: it 'just happens.' This may be a useful notion for understanding the conservative character built into social existence and practice by the sorts of mechanisms Marx and Freud – among many others – have sought to account for. Such a concept would allow us to argue that the

knowledge of social process does not disappear, but (like the productivity of the worker reified in the tool) rather it seems to *migrate* to a different place, into a text different from the one we carry in our recollection. Such a memory forcefully produces the past in the present. (35)

In the aura of plasticity that attends the materiality of sweet and sour pork with all of its shiny red-orange artificiality, we might read for the production of the past in the present. In the lingering sense of its inauthenticity lies precisely the moment of the echo, of the materials memory of a sign that carries with it the memory of its production. The plasticity of sweet and sour pork carries within it an echo of an earlier resistance. Knowledge of that social process does not disappear and resistance does not simply end with the deportations and failed judicial processes. Rather, it resonates through history into a different text.

The story of sweet and sour pork destabilizes Chineseness in a nominal resistance that forces into the present the history of its production. Terdiman argues that '[w]e are not free to keep the past *past* – it colonizes our present whether or not we realize its encroachment' (46). The past of language continually infects its present, bouncing back through the memory of the production of its significations. The past of sweet and sour pork inexorably seeps into the present of its consumption; the history of coolie labour echoes in the plasticity of its red-orange sauce and colonizes the present of its consumption.

Signs carry within them the capacity for rememoration. It is not that the bread of the Ah Lum affair and the sweet and sour pork of contemporary menus are historically contiguous or causal, but that they offer one way of reading both the affinities and the distinctions between resistances in different historical moments and in different nation spaces. As Terdiman points out, the process of inscription and reinscription is one that is necessarily about history, about the contagious process of citation and re-citation. The poisoning of the bread in 1857 emerges as a violent reinscription of the ordinary into a sign of danger and insurgency. The story of sweet and sour pork embeds within its nourishing exterior a barb, a serving back to Europe-in-Canada a sign of its own excessive desire. As Derrida's theory of the *pharmakon* suggests, writing, or inscription, always carries within it the potential to be both poisonous and curative. Every remedy carries within it the potential for violent reinscription, for poison. In sweet and sour pork, the residue of arsenic remains in the story of its production. Guha's thinking on rumour anticipates the way in which agency thrives on continual citation. 'The additions, cuts and twists introduced into a rumour in the course of its circulation transform its message (often just minimally) by such degrees as to adjust it to the variations within a given ideology or mode of popular expression and by doing so broaden the range of its address' (Guha, *Elementary* 261). The agency of Guha's text thrives on contamination. In the story of sweet and sour pork, we can locate a citation that thrives on the traces of old poisonings.

In both colonial Hong Kong and the Chinese diaspora in Canada, we have an example of agency without a singular agent of history. The affinity between subjects of colonial Hong Kong and diasporic subjects in Canada lies precisely in the frustration of the colonial and settler colonial desire for identifiable and knowable agents. However, these two subjectivities diverge when we give full recognition to the different material circumstances that contour their daily existence. There is a difference between resistance under a colonial regime, wherein the entire colonial community can be poisoned with a single batch of morning bread, and resistance under a liberal state as a migrant subject. Within the difference between a colonial regime's response to the unknowability of anti-colonial agency and Europe-in-Canada's response to diasporic agency lies the difference between expulsion and incorporation. In the diaspora, the precariousness of migrancy forces a different kind of engagement with power than that of anti-colonial resistance.

Unlike in colonial India, in diaspora, there are not always rebellions or other large, identifiable acts of resistance to which we can point. Part of the work of this chapter is to explore the possibilities of collective forms of agency within small acts, those acts that may have quietly become a part of our everyday lives while still retaining the traces of oppositionality. Robin Kelley's reading of black resistance on public transit in post–Second World War Birmingham, Alabama, offers one way of reading for agency within the everyday. Noting that most black working-class resistance 'has remained unorganized, clandestine and evasive,' Kelley suggests that 'examples of black working-class resistance in public spaces offer some of the richest insights into how race, gender, class, space, time and collective memory shape both domination and resistance' (56). Kelley examines a range of tactics, from using the bus as a 'moving theatre' (72) to blaming the 'unreliability of public transportation' as 'a plausible excuse for absenteeism, for stealing a few extra hours of sleep, for attending to problems or running errands – all of which were standard resistance strategies, or purely strategies for making ends meet, waged by household workers' (70). This attention to the small resistances that take place in public spaces suggests one way of reading for agency in diaspora.[9]

Tracking the residuum of sweet and sour, we find that there is another language of emplacement – that of the migrant. The agency of sweet and sour pork cannot be symbolically managed, not only because it occurs in a foreign language, but also because it asserts a different register of emplacement altogether. In delivering back to Europe-in-Canada a sign of its own excess, Chinese cooks on the railway also produced a narrative of resistance that would circulate throughout the Canadian culinary landscape; it is a resistance that becomes a part of the Canadian body politic in the meal that is consumed and incorporated.

In the final part of this chapter, I will consider more closely the connections between the agency of the poisoned loaves of the E Sing bakery and that of the naming of *goo lo yok*. There has been a slippage between the postcolonial and the diasporic that is a symptom of something more than just a categorical confusion. It is a symptom of postcolonialism's ongoing concern with what Stuart Hall, echoing Ella Shohat, has marked as the productive tension of the 'post' in postcolonialism (253). That is, the tension between a postcolonialism that is the study of the aftermath of colonialism, and one that focuses on going beyond colonialism in terms of a theoretical and epistemic shift. Within the productivity of this tension, the diasporic subject emerges. At postcolonialism's limit, which Hall presciently notes as a process wherein the postcolonial is always under erasure, where its very undecidability must be read as the strength of its interventionary work, diaspora emerges as one way of understanding the subjects of colonial displacement.

Postcolonialism's repeated turn to the diasporic subject is an expression of its desire to follow the subjects of colonialism's oppressive histories outside of the space of European colonialism and into the sphere of its aftermath. Some of postcolonialism's harshest critics have focused on the breadth of its embrace. It has been accused of being its own colonizing force in terms of First World theoretical work mining the raw materials of Third World literature, of having no historical specificity, of being opaque and disconnected from true subjects of oppression, and of being too ambivalent about the terms of its own debate.[10] In some ways, postcolonialism could be seen as travelling too easily without the specificity of local referents. But it travels because it is concerned with following the subjects of colonial oppression after the ostensible end of that oppression – both in the sense of aftermath, and in the sense of going beyond.

Postcolonialism travels into the space of diaspora because colonialism is a dislocating force.

While it seems more obvious to understand Chineseness in terms of diaporic formation, it is equally important to think through the relationship between Chineseness and postcolonialism. In the postscript to the chapter 'Against the Lures of Diaspora' in *Writing Diaspora*, Rey Chow addresses the problem of thinking of Chinese identity within a postcolonial frame. For Chow, this problem is one of the situation of Chinese intellectuals in the West as well as that of the limitations of postcolonial theory. Pointing to the experiences of peoples living in Hong Kong, Macau, and Taiwan, Chow notes that China 'was never completely "colonized" over a long period by any one foreign power, even though the cultural effects of imperialism are as strong as in other formerly colonized countries in Asia, Africa, and Latin America' (118). Although Chow is preoccupied here with the responsibility of Chinese intellectuals abroad to those in China, this chapter also, while incidentally foreshadowing the increased interest in diaspora studies to come, gestures to the gap in theorizing the politics of dislocation that diaspora studies can mediate. Chow's warning against diaspora is more precisely a warning against the desire of 'third world' intellectuals in the West to claim minority positions while masking their own 'hegemony ... over those who are stuck at home' (118). However, if we shift our understanding of Chinese diasporic subjectivity away from that of Chinese intellectuals in the West and towards those who are stranded in the West with none of the privileges with which the intellectual arrives, the space of critical diaspora studies might be something to explore rather than avoid.

In exploring these two stories of food, rumour, and resistance, I suggest that there is something to be said for embracing the lures of diaspora and understanding diasporic subjects as those who have been displaced by the effects of colonial oppression. This is not a preoccupation with victimhood. Rather, it is a recognition of the inescapable histories of traumatic dislocation from which modern diasporas have emerged. Colonialism and imperialism in their direct form have been responsible for the vast majority of nineteenth- and twentieth-century displacements of peoples from the south to the north, from the postcolony to the metropole.[11] I acknowledge Stuart Hall's important observation about the kind of presumptuousness that lies at the heart of assuming that all diasporic trajectories are uni-directional: 'The notion that only the multi-cultural cities of the First World are "diaspora-ised" is a fantasy which can only be sustained by those who have never lived in the hybridised spaces of a

Third World, so-called "colonial," city' (250). However, I want to dwell on the problem of diaspora as one of the limits of postcolonial and minority discourse theory. Because the term diaspora must retain its resonances with the dislocations of oppression, we must untangle it from the concerns of transnational migrancy in general.

The recent resurgence of the term diaspora in the Western academy has arisen out of a profound perplexity around the cultural spaces and products of peoples who have been displaced by oppression and violence. If the term diaspora is to retain its potential as a space of powerful critique, it cannot float away from the constitutive sorrows of dislocation.

Reading for agency in the precariousness of migrancy, I want to highlight the ways in which the state of migrancy is framed by social and political precariousness. It is not that all migrants exist in a precarious state, but rather that migrancy carries within it the potential for precariousness. This is a precariousness marked by race, gender, sexuality, and class. What stands out for me in this marking is the way in which the words 'Go home' resonate more for some communities than for others. For some, the injunction to go home carries with it a profoundly different capacity for pain, humiliation, and political disempowerment than it does for others. In the context of the Chinese diaspora, I am focusing on a diaspora marked most explicitly by race but inescapably defined by issues of sexuality, class, and gender. As the history of race riots and race-based legislation such as the head tax illustrates, the Chinese Canadian community has been attacked primarily on the basis of its Chineseness, even though issues of sexuality, class, and gender – especially evident in the promulgation of the perception of a degenerate bachelor society that has taken jobs away from upstanding and hardworking white men – are crucially imbricated in the targetting of Chinese immigrants.[12] Writing of the way in which racism perpetuates the exclusivism of racialized diasporic communities, Vijay Mishra notes in 'The Diasporic Imaginary' that 'as long as there is a fascist fringe always willing to find racial scapegoats for the nation's own shortcomings and to chant "Go home", the autochthonous pressures towards diasporic racial exclusivism will remain' (426). Mishra describes the sense of 'familiar temporariness' that marks what he has called the old Indian diaspora, the diasporic community that is the legacy of indentured labour in the West Indies (426). In this idea of a familiar temporariness we can begin to read for the kind of precariousness that lies within racially marked diasporic communities. A fourth- or fifth-generation Chinese Canadian might still be asked to 'go home' in a way that the fourth- or fifth-generation white Canadian will never be.

In the story of sweet and sour pork, I established a reading for agency where success is measured not so much in capital accumulation but in the challenges posed to colonialism. Rather than reading for agency within the terms of success defined by contemporary global capitalism, Chinese diaspora studies need to read for resistances that upset the colonial order and its legacy. A study of the Chinese diaspora with a more rigorous assessment of the relationships between colonialism, postcolonialism, and the diasporic community foregrounds the history of diasporic trajectories and offers a way of reading for the agency of the dispossessed in dislocation.

As a brief history of migration in the case of the Chinese diaspora community in Canada shows, immigration to Canada is marked by the effects of European colonialism as well as relations with Japan and Russia, most significantly due to the Opium Wars and the series of unequal treaties that China was forced to sign as a result of the wars. Between 1838 and 1900, China was in unequal trading relations with Britain, France, Germany, Austria, Japan, the United States, Italy, and Russia. The penetration of foreign capitalism undermined China's own economic integrity and accelerated its breakdown. The enormous taxation pressures brought about by the unequal treaties, in combination with poor harvest yields and an increase in popular unrest, led to a number of rebellions in China – including the Taiping Rebellion of 1850–64 and the Boxer Rebellion of 1900. These instabilities and hardships were, at least in part, triggered by colonialism. Moreover, Canada's desperate shortage of cheap labour led to an indenture system that was responsible for the vast majority of Chinese immigration to Canada in the late nineteenth and early twentieth centuries.[13] Of course, Canada was not the only destination for Chinese indentured labourers. Slavery was abolished and banned in British colonies in 1834. As a result, indenture was the next solution to labour shortages in the British empire. While the ship the *Caribbean* landed in Victoria with three hundred contract Chinese labourers in 1858, yet other ships were crossing the Pacific and the Atlantic carrying indentured labourers from Asia (mainly China and India) to sugar plantations in the West Indies, railroad work all along the western coast of both the Americas, farms in Australia, and mines in South Africa.[14]

The history of Chinese diasporic trajectories is thus intimately linked to the history of colonialism. As Jenny Sharpe notes, 'The designation of postcolonial as an umbrella term for diaspora and minority communities is derived in part from an understanding of decolonization as the beginning of an unprecedented migration from the former colonies to advanced industrialist centers' (182). However, as the trajectory of Chinese indenture labour shows, diaspora begins not only with the end of colonialism but also with its instigation. The nineteenth and twentieth centuries marked the mass exodus of dispossessed communities who were bound by indenture. In 'Diasporas Old and New' Gayatri Spivak argues that diasporic scholarship must continue to be vigilantly attentive to the old diasporas of indenture and slavery and seek out their connections with contemporary diasporas of the dispossesed rather than simply celebrate the achievements of the new diasporas of savvy transnational capitalists. At issue in separating the old from the new is not only the futility of forgetting, but also a denial of the constitutive effects of colonial traumas.

The public space of the small town Chinese restaurant opens up the possibilities of resistances that may not have a record in the colonial or settler colonial archive, but that are nevertheless present. This chapter suggests that postcolonial models of agency enable a reading of diasporic agency that is dispersed, without a single agent, hero(ine), or authorial presence. I have also argued that reading for diasporic agency demands a different, altered model than that of postcolonial theory. The postcolonial model of agency offered by Bhabha and connected to the work of Ranajit Guha does not entirely translate to the space of the diaspora. Agency looks different depending on whether you are a native or a migrant. In both the narrative of sweet and sour pork and the story of the poisoned loaves in Hong Kong, 1857, agency is dispersed. There is no single historical agent who poisoned the loaves at the E Sing bakery; there is no single historical agent who renamed sweet and sour pork. And yet, the migrant agency that emerges in the story of sweet and sour takes a different form. In that form, I come to what is left over: the meal that is incorporated. I suggest that in diasporic space, the model of agency functions less on panic than on the incorporation of the residual. Nevertheless, the relationship between the postcolonial and the diasporic is an intimate one. The challenge of a diasporic reading of agency lies in looking for the productivity of that intimacy. The diasporic cannot forget the history of colonial displacements. From the acerbity of rice-wine vinegar, I hope our tongues have found their way to honeyed ginger, to the culinary joke in the nominal resistance of eating Chinese in diaspora.

*Chapter Two*

# On the Menu: Time and Chinese Restaurant Counterculture

Almost nobody does it anymore. If you take the slower road south down the middle of Alberta from Edmonton to Calgary, following the old rail line, you will cut across Main Street, Olds, Alberta, where you might stop for lunch at the A & J Family Restaurant (figure 3). In 1915 you would have stepped across the railway platform (the railway stopped running a long time ago but the station is still there, empty and abandoned) and ordered a hot lunch at what was then known simply as the Public Lunch Counter (figure 4).

There is a long history to the small town Chinese Canadian restaurant. Work on Chinese diaspora communities in Canada has tended to focus on representations of Chinese immigrants in large urban centres such as Vancouver and Toronto. While locations such as Vancouver's Chinatown continue to be crucial sites for exploring Chineseness in Canada, relatively little attention has been paid to the more disparate but nonetheless persistently present communities of Chinese people in small towns across Canada. This chapter explores the small town Chinese Canadian restaurant and traces the possibilities of Chinese diasporic agency in the text of the menus. Taking a slower path, along the abandoned rail lines that carry in them the echo of a history of indentured Chinese labour,[1] and stopping in at the restaurants that are inevitably located near now empty train stations, I hope to recover the bond between slowness and memory embedded within the Chinese restaurant menu.

I want to situate my reading of the menus as an intervention against two broad displacements that I see happening in Chinese diaspora studies specifically as well as in diaspora studies more generally. First, the spatial metaphor of diasporic mobility risks displacing the temporal challenges that diasporic subjects pose to western European narratives of

3   A & J Family Restaurant, Olds, Alberta, 1999. Courtesy of the author.

progress. Second, the idea of the metropolitan trajectory has been taken too literally and mistaken for a trajectory of metropolitan migration. Let me begin by addressing this latter displacement, which will lead to my discussion of the former.

Diasporic agency has been conceived almost exclusively within an urban focus. The difference I want to highlight here seems like a straightforward one – diasporic populations are not always urban in the locations of their settlement. Particularly if we pay attention to the old diaspora of indenture and slavery, we can see that the urban space is simply not the only place where diasporic subjects ended up. In 'Rethink-

4   Public Lunch Counter, Olds, Alberta, 1911, Courtesy of Glenbow Archives.

ing Diaspora(s),' Khachig Tölölyan argues that the '*nation's* aspiration to normative homogeneity is challenged not just by immigration but also by various forms of cultural practices and knowledge production, *especially in major urban centers* and in the arts and humanities departments of many North American and Australian universities' (4, latter emphasis mine). Tölölyan's subsequent observations in the article about the need for rigorous attention to the ways in which diasporic critical practice may in fact collude with the very forms of hegemonic power that these critical practices see diasporas as challenging are crucial for future thinking on

diaspora as a critical category.[2] However, his emphasis on the urban migrant betrays an exemplarizing of metropolitan trajectories. Tölölyan's
discussion gestures to a wider tendency in current diaspora discussions
that naturalize and emphasize the diasporic as a particularly urban formation. Writing about Martin Delany's experience in England, W.E.B.
DuBois's time in Germany, and Richard Wright's encounter with France,
Gilroy argues that black literary traditions do

> not fit unambiguously into a time-consciousness derived from and punctu-
> ated exclusively by changes in the public, urban worlds of London, Berlin
> and Paris. Writers, particularly those closest to the slave experience, repudi-
> ated the heroic narrative of western civilization and used a philosophically
> informed approach to slavery in order to undermine the monumental time
> that supports it. (197)[3]

I want to hang on to Gilroy's important observation regarding an alternative temporality that challenges a European national imaginary, but I also
want to pause on these 'urban worlds of London, Berlin and Paris.' For
Gilroy, one of the strongest arguments for diasporic agency lies in reading diasporas as challenges to hegemonic nation state formations.

Diasporas have been read as social formations that contest the integrity
of the European nation state. Tölölyan, for example, observes that just as
the nation state has begun to encounter limits to its hegemonic desires,
diasporas have emerged in intellectual discourses as exemplary communities of this particular transnational moment (4). Building on his work
in *The Black Atlantic*, in *Against Race* Gilroy argues that 'consciousness
of diaspora affiliation stands opposed to the distinctively modern struc-
tures and modes of power orchestrated by the institutional complexity
of nation states. Diaspora identification exists outside of and sometimes
in opposition to the political forms and codes of modern citizenship'
(124). Although *The Black Atlantic* has undergone a number of important critiques,[4] Gilroy's exploration of a counterculture of modernity
and, connected to that, his insistence on an alternative temporality of
diasporic cultural expression have been ground-breaking interventions
in diasporic thinking. In *Against Race*, Gilroy holds that diasporas allow
for the emergence of complex subjectivities that work against forms of
nationalism:

> Valuing diaspora more highly than the coercive unanimity of the nation,
> the concept [of diaspora] becomes explicitly antinational. This shift is con-
> nected with transforming the familiar unidirectional nature of diaspora as

a form of catastrophic but simple dispersal that enjoys an identifiable and reversible originary moment – the site of trauma – into something far more complex. (128)

And yet, within the complexity of this explicitly antinational social formation, the worlds of London, Berlin, and Paris remain as the birthing places of the black literary culture.

By insisting on the urgency of a turn to examining a non-metropolitan diasporic subject, I am not arguing for a fantasized idyllic notion of a rural subjectivity. As Raymond Williams deftly illustrates, 'the country and the city are changing historical realities' (*The Country and the City* 289) and it would be a mistake not to see the larger narratives within which a fantasized conception of the metropolitan and the non-metropolitan are situated. In Williams's study, the changing meaning of country life is related to the changes in city life, and these changes need to be traced within the larger story of the progress of capitalism. Making the connection between agrarian capitalism, plantation colonialism, and neo-imperialism, Williams observes, 'What the oil companies do, what the mining companies do, is what landlords did, what plantation owners did and do' (293). And within this story of the advance of capital, there is also the story of the dislocation of peoples.[5] The usefulness of the analyses in *The Country and the City* has little to do with who lives in the country or the city or even what the country or the city might be, but with what those concepts stand in for and how they are used. Following from this conceptual focus of Williams's work,[6] I want to assert a conceptual rather than demographic argument. While it is true that many Chinese immigrants in Canada did settle and continue to settle in non-urban locations, my turn to the small town Chinese restaurant as a crucial locus for reading diasporic agency lies in my sense that a spatial reading of diasporic agency (which is related to a demographic reading) has eclipsed a temporal one. The presence of the diasporic other in the heart of European and North American metropolises – a presence that takes up space in cities such as London, New York, or Vancouver – is a spatialized vision of disturbance that does not always take into account the ways in which diasporic populations might, as Gilroy has so presciently argued, challenge the singular and homogeneous temporality of European and North American progress.

Turning to the non-metropolitan migrant enables a more specific exploration of temporal agency. It is my contention that turning to a more differentiated and specific idea of diasporic arrival enables the exploration of a diasporic temporality that not only interrupts what Homi Bhabha, in 'DissemiNation,' identifies as the nation's narrative time, but poses an alternative to it. I am not suggesting that rural life contains an intrinsically slower temporality than that of the urban. That would be part of the progressivist narrative wherein cities are the sites of bustling activity and rural spaces are the locations of the idyll and the pastoral. Rather, I am suggesting that in differentiating and specifying diasporic arrival, in seeing the relationship between old and new diasporas rather than treating them as distinct, we can locate a temporality that not only interrupts the homogeneous empty time of the narrativized nation, but is also alternative to it. What I mean by slowness then is this other register of temporal experience. However, as I will discuss more fully in the final section of this chapter, I also see this alternative temporality as engaging oppositionally with the dominant narrative of temporal progress, of slowing it down by insisting on the presence of the past in the present.

To return now to the first displacement, the displacement of a diasporic temporality onto spatiality, locations such as Chinatown become exemplary sites. Displaced, racialized subjects move into the city and assert their otherness by building communities within communities, cities within cities, and disturbing the balance of homogeneous whiteness on which the metropolitan rests. In a number of excellent discussions of Chinatowns in North America,[7] the conceptualization of Chinatown as an ethnic enclave emerges with surprising consistency. While there are some variations, these texts inevitably circle back to the boundedness – either self-imposed or enforced from without – of the urban Chinese communities.[8] Because they represent a dispersed and yet ethnically and racially coherent population, or give the impression of one, Chinatowns have become a convenient spatial metaphor for the Chinese diaspora in North America. The metaphor mistakes the space of Chinatown as *the* space of the Chinese diaspora. The prevalence of the assumptions within this spatial metaphor overshadow the potentially disruptive temporality of diasporic communities.

The mistaking of Chinatown as the space of the Chinese diaspora lends itself too easily to a liberal multiculturalism where the spatial presence of otherness enhances rather than disturbs the liberal state. It is not just that non-urban populations are left out in the assumption that Chinatown is an urban microcosm of China itself, but that this perception of the microcosm, the miniaturization of a racialized culture, neutralizes it as an oppositional site.[9] This assumption reveals more than just the museumization of a cultural space. It also uncovers the paradoxical trajectory of assimilation that enhances dominant culture's sense of its own inclusive superiority. Chinatown is an accepted part of the urban landscape and provides a space of consumption and amusement. It is not that there is no agential potential in Chinatown, but that the overwhelming emphasis on Chinatown as a spatial metaphor for the Chinese diaspora risks occluding other forms of agency emerging in other locations. In not looking for the kinds of oppositional work that might be happening outside of Chinatown, we risk mistaking a spatial presence for an agential spatial haunting. The idea of the enclave suggests a model of assimilation that never has to engage with the ways in which Chinese diaspora populations have done more than just occupy space in Canada, but have fundamentally challenged and, as I will discuss, constituted Canada's own notion of itself.

In contrast to Chinatowns, the small town Chinese restaurant is anything but an enclave. Although equally pervasive in terms of its dissemination across the Canadian landscape, it suggests a different kind of incorporation – one that is much more precarious if only because of its relative isolation. And yet, in that precariousness, these restaurants produce what I will call a countercultural space, a space of alternative temporality expressed through the culture of the restaurant counter. Rather than being a city within a city, as Chinatowns imply, they suggest a different model of negotiating otherness wherein the incorporation of otherness becomes a moment of serving back to Europe-in-Canada its own images, desires, and fantasies.

Sometimes abandoned where rail line contracts ended,[10] sometimes voluntarily seeking out locations for new work, a significant number of early Chinese migrants settled in non-urban locations, in small towns and villages throughout Canada. These migrants have no place in a metropolitan migrancy. They do not perform a return to the center. Rather they engage in a form of emplacement. Through texts such as the menus of small town Chinese restaurants, we can trace some of the ways in which they participate in the scripting of their incorporation into the body politic of Canada.

In the latter half of this chapter, I will explore some of the ways in which Chinese cooks and restaurateurs create and then contain the particular text of nationhood on the menus of small town Chinese restaurants. The homogeneous empty time of the Chinese restaurant menu emerges from the hands of Chinese restaurateurs as a subversive text that defines and delineates the idea of Canada for Canadians. In this sense, I locate the agency of Chinese diasporic subjects in Canada not in an impossible return to the metropole, but in the engineering of a mechanics of incorporation. The naturalization of the Chinese restaurant in the landscape of small town Canada attests to the way in which Chinese migrants have embedded particular forms of knowledge and practices, disseminating a vision of what 'Canadian' and 'Chinese' mean through the text of the restaurant menu.

By exploring the culture of the counter as a counterculture, I am focusing on the ways in which Chinese diasporic subjects transform the position of servitude into a space of the serving back, a space where the subversive potential of serving percolates to the surface. The counterculture of my project clearly is not the counterculture of *The Black Atlantic*, although I am indebted to the space Gilroy has made by making the problem of time a central one for conceptualizing diasporic agency.[11] The counterculture of this project is grounded in the long smooth counter that runs along the length of the restaurant separating the server from the served. Across that shiny expanse, the menu will be passed back and forth, a text that not only mediates the separation between server and patron, but is also read over and over again, presented over and over again – a simple, pedestrian exchange that carries within it the possibilities for something more.

While Gilroy's discussion of the disruptive and alternative temporality of black expressive counterculture dwells on an outer-national agency, one that transcends the borders of the nation state, this chapter explores a reading of agency within the host nation. Rather than reading the agency of the menus within the boundaries of Canada, I want to understand this agency within the larger parameters of a diasporic rubric. In this sense, the subversion of the menus needs to be read as informed by the dislocations of colonialism as well as the continuing difficulties of negotiating the assertion of otherness within a predominantly white cultural space and within the legacy of dislocation. As I have discussed in the previous chapter, a reading for agency that is conscientious of the precariousness of migrancy calls for an attention to the ways in which the agential has become entrenched within the everyday.

In turning to Chinese restaurant menus as countercultural texts, I want to come back to the argument I began in chapter 1 and further elaborate my reading of agency in terms of incorporation. For Gilroy, black music functions as a means by which the 'living memory' of the past oppression carries into the present. In the Chinese restaurant menu, I read a strategic incorporation that is not about assimilation, but is in fact its opposite. Small town Chinese restaurants are a sign not of assimilation but of dissimulation. If, as I have argued, sweet and sour pork served back to Europe-in-Canada a sign of its own excessive greed and embedded into the dish a nominal resistance, how can we read the resistances that are embedded within the menu itself?

The menu textualizes the food that is served. As Rebecca Spang notes in her historical work on the rise of the contemporary restaurant, the menu is a representational text: 'Sharing the name "menu" were two linked, but rarely identical, entities: the food a restaurant served and its bill of fare. The first resisted duplication and could be described only imprecisely, but the physical object called the *carte* – product not of the variable kitchen but of the reliable printing press – was infinitely reproducible and easily evoked' (Spang 184). There is always already a difference between the food on a menu and the food that is actually served. More importantly, the reproducibility of the menu provides a precise and reliable account of one aspect of the restauarant's representation of itself. Spang highlights the gulf between the menu and the food that might actually be available, on or off the menu, at any particular restaurant. While I will return later in the chapter to these issues of the mechanical reproduction and the menu as a highly representational text, for now, let me simply ask, What, then, does the Chinese restaurant menu represent?

The menus I will discuss in this chapter span a century of Chinese immigration to Canada. I read them as texts produced and reproduced within the social and political pressures of what it has meant to be marked as Chinese in Canada over the last century. From outright exclusion to restrictive immigration laws to a policy of official liberal multiculturalism, the menus in this chapter must be read as texts that have had to engage with the socio-political reality of being Chinese in Canada. The earliest menu is from 1923, the year that the Exclusion Act came into effect. Then there is the Diamond Grill menu from the 1950s that marks a period immediately after the end of exclusion. The contemporary menus are taken by following an old north–south Albertan rail route that no longer exists. They reflect the legacy of nearly two decades of official multiculturalism in Canada. As with all ephemera, the restaurant menus have come to me partly through archival research, but also through the inevitable idiosyncracy of word-of-mouth, happy accidents of discovery, and the generosity of collectors. The menus that I present in this chapter are by no means a complete or coherent archive. In my dream world, I would have a set of menus following the rise and persistence of a single restaurant. Lacking this dream menu collection, and despite the loose historical trajectory I have traced above, my reading of the menus is necessarily symptomatic rather than comprehensively chronological. These menus are not precise representations of the time of their existence, but rather are suggestive of historical moments and the history that I read them against. It is as an intervention within the nation state's desire for a homogeneous and progressive narrative of emergence, and the assertion of an alternative temporality, a particular form of slowness, that I want to situate the menus as texts of diasporic agency.

In his book of poetry about his father's restaurant in Nelson, British Columbia, *Diamond Grill*, Fred Wah writes that 'maps don't have beginnings, just edges. Some frayed and hazy margin of possibility, absence, gap' (1). Reading the menu as a map to an alternative discourse, this chapter explores three margins, three spaces of possibility, that work together to produce the agency of Chinese migrants – an agency that emerges not in a haunting of the metropolitan centre, but in the persistence of the pedestrian, the slow embeddedness of everyday life.

**Canadian or Western Food: Inventing Canadian Food**

What is Canadian food? Is Canada a nation devoid of a national food culture? One of the most curious features of the small town Chinese restaurant is its matter-of-fact definition of Canadian food. Boldly ignoring any sort of existential crisis about the definition of Canadian culinary culture, Chinese restaurants have gone ahead and named Canadian food for Canadians.

Nowhere else is Canadian food more consistently defined than on the menus of small town Chinese Canadian restaurants. Although dishes such as tourtière, Atlantic seafood chowder, or Beaver Tails are arguably more 'Canadian' than the hamburgers and French fries that are typical of the 'Canadian' portion of the Chinese Canadian restaurant menu, this menu specifically names a series of dishes as Canadian or Western. More than that, 'Canadian' is often used interchangeably with 'Western.' I want to suggest that one margin of possibility for locating Chinese diasporic agency in Canada lies in the way in which Chinese cooks and restaurateurs name and define Canadian and western for Canadians. The question is not so much what exactly is Canadian about hamburgers and fries, but what it means for this version of Canadianness to circulate with such persistence through the Chinese restaurant. After all, what does it mean that the Chinese restaurant has become a defining locus of Canadian food culture?

In his essay 'Steak and Chips' in *Mythologies*, Roland Barthes gestures towards a way of reading the semiotics of food and national culture. For Barthes, an 'item of food sums up and transmits a situation; it constitutes an information; it signifies' ('Psychosociology' 21). Reviewing the story of General de Castries's first meal after the armistice in what is now Vietnam, Barthes associates chips, *les frites*, with Frenchness:

> Chips are nostalgic and patriotic like steak. *Match* told us that after the armistice in Indo-China '*General de Castries, for his first meal, asked for chips*' …
> The General's request was certainly not a vulgar materialistic reflex, but
> an episode in the ritual of appropriating the regained French community.
> The General understood well our national symbolism; he knew that *la frite*,
> chips, are the alimentary sign of Frenchness. (*Mythologies* 63–4, emphasis
> in original)

Barthes's description of the Frenchness of *frites* links the alimentary sign not only to French culture, but also to a moment of French colonialism and nationalism. Chips function in this story to signify and consolidate French power on foreign and colonized soil. Even in Indochina, the general will have his steak and chips. As Keya Ganguly notes in her consideration of the diasporic and postcolonial politics of food, 'Not only does Barthes's parodic take on alimentary investments expose the patriotic zeal about food matters to be ideological in the same way as are political pamphlets or advertisements; more pointedly, he highlights something singularly "mythological" with respect to the French for which we can find no equivalent within Indian culture, diasporic or otherwise' (*States of Exception* 125). Ganguly's reading of the mythological import of the French fry emphasizes the possible role of food in the iconography of ideology and power. Observing the 'basic, muscular, efficient' imagery that chips signal, Ganguly argues that 'unlike effete "exotic cooking," steak and chips connotes something of a work ethic; like their imperial counterparts elsewhere, the French know how to get down to the business of ruling … Whereas the commonplace about food is that one eats to live, it appears that the Frenchman eats to rule' (126–7). And yet a few decades after the French general's meal in Indochina, when the idea of French food became ironically synonymous in the West with the effete exoticism of haute cuisine,[12] on the contemporary Chinese Canadian restaurant menu, *les frites*, French fries, have somehow become an integral part of what is understood as Canadian.

In placing the French fry, what had been no less than a singularly mythological symbol of French colonial power, under the category of 'Canadian,' the Chinese restaurant menu does more than simply gesture towards an increasingly homogenized fast food culture. The French fry's migration from French national symbol to being a staple of what is labelled Canadian on the Chinese restaurant menu gestures towards one way in which Chinese restaurateurs serve back to Europe-in-Canada their own ideas about westernness. The interchangeability of 'Canadian' and 'Western' on the menu is neither accidental nor innocent. The collusion between Canadian and Western situates the idea of Canada within the terrain of whiteness, something that stands in stark opposition to the plural and multicultural visions of Canadian nationalism that have been such a significant part of post-1970s Canada. Of course, the idea of western is a relative one both geographically and ideologically. But in the case of the menus, what is Canadian is not only associated with a trajectory of western European culture, it is also explicitly not Chinese. The back of the Club Café menu situates the 'Western Favorites' directly across from 'Suggestions for Chinese Dinner.' The Bacon Cheeseburger is all that the combination '(A) Dinner for 1: Pineapple Chicken Balls OR Sweet and Sour Shrimps With Chicken Fried Rice 6.00' is not. As the set-up of the menu suggests, Chinese food is not only the antithesis of 'Western' food, it will never be western. Separated by the law of the conjunction where a 'Chinese & Western Smorg' could never plausibly be collapsed into 'Western Smorg,' the logic of a westernness that depends upon the Chinese on the other side of the conjunction emerges as a repetition of the logic of exclusion.

In the accepted view of Chinese immigration in Canada, critics have pointed to the ways in which the head tax and exclusion laws indicate a legacy of legal racism whereby the Canadian state defined itself over and against Chinese.[13] That is, Canada is not Chinese. This idea of the need for Canada to maintain its national homogeneity through the legal exclusion of supposedly non-assimilable racialized groups is not new. What is different about the menus is that they repeat a racist rationalization of their own exclusion.

Remembering that it is Chinese cooks and restaurateurs who have developed these menus, there are two ways to read this embedding of Canadian racist rationales of exclusion. The first would be that these Chinese immigrants have internalized the rationale of racism and this internalization has emerged in the production of the menu. This is a painful reading that suggests that the work of institutional racism has been thorough in producing subjects that will act within the realms of their own inferiority. In sociological work on race, this is what has been identified as the damage hypothesis, where the damage done to racialized subjects over a period of time produces an 'inferiority complex' or the idea of 'white preference.'[14] However, I am not sure that this is the only or the most productive way of reading what appears to be the repetition of the rhetoric of racial exclusion on the Chinese restaurant menu.

My reason for this lies in my sense that the crucial work of grieving and thinking through the effects of racial damage is an internal – both in the sense of being internal to a racialized community and internal to the racialized individual – investigation. I will return to considerations of damage, grief, and loss in the final chapter of this book. For now, in this specific consideration of the menu, I will stay within the realm of a more externalized negotiation where the menus are a means through which Chinese Canadian subjects have negotiated the precariousness of being both minority and residually migrant. Within this negotiation, let me read the Chinese restaurant menu's presentation of whiteness in Canada somewhat naively and then move to what I hope will be an enabling reading.

Let's take it as a given that menus are about attracting business. Given the isolated existence of small town restaurants, where there tends to be only one in every town, this business is invariably white. The logic of the menus is then primarily that of attracting white consumers. Within this simplistic narrative of consumer demand, we can trace the embedding of a highly aware and agential representational praxis that is all about negotiating and alleviating the perceived threat of their otherness. These menus are texts of survival. For example, the 1950s Diamond Grill menu, the first menu in my archive where Chinese food appears, exists against the backdrop of the end of exclusion in 1947.[15] The menu's echoing of the logic of racist exclusion whereby Chinese is not Canadian needs to be read within a rubric of a highly self-conscious self-positioning. Inhabiting the precarious space of diasporic subjectivity means that there is necessarily a moment when you anticipate what is expected of you, of your body as it moves through space, of your language as you communicate to others, of your vision of the host country where you should be grateful for a space within reach of the comforts of advanced capitalism in the First World. The establishment of a Canadian menu that is explicitly not Chinese is an act of agential self-positioning.

Chinese cooks served back to Europe-in-Canada a narrative of Canada's own national emergence. Returning to where I began in this section, let me now suggest that Chinese cooks have stepped in and named a national food culture for Canadians by negotiating the presentation of their own continuing exclusion.

The history of the menu, Spang observes, is intimately related to that of the novel and the newspaper. Following from that relation, the menu needs to be read as a formal manifestation of print culture closely tied to the narrative of a national imagined community. Along with Benedict Anderson's linking of the novel and the newspaper, the menu can be thought of as a textual form that helped to consolidate a particular idea of national culture. Like the novel and the newspaper, the menu benefited from the rise of mass print capitalism in the eighteenth century. Spang suggests a close connection between conceptions of French culture and the French restaurant menu. Drawing on the doubled meaning of *la carte* – the map and the menu – Spang notes that the menu provided a tangible, bound, iconic space in which to imagine the space of the nation (192–3). The *carte*, the map, the menu, remains with us as one of the primary means by which food is represented, textualized, as a metonym of the boundaries of the nation.[16]

The menu as we now know it – a printed object, often folded in quarto or as a small booklet, with a list of the restaurant's offerings and the prices next to them – is intimately related to the history of European literary innovation. Exploring the development of the restaurant through print culture, Spang traces the changes in eighteenth- and nineteenth-century French menus with the innovations in French literary production:

> The shape and appearance of menus changed considerably during the nineteenth century, but each new format was shared by every place that was 'a restaurant.' The menu's layout consistently mimicked the century's typographic innovations: first a single large folio, packed with columns of closely printed type; then a small booklet, leather-covered and bound with silken cord; then again a single sheet, hand-decorated with languid goddesses and stylized flowers. Thus, while the early menus looked like the newspapers of the Consulate and the First Empire, mid-century menus resembled fat realist novels, and those of the Belle Époque, poster art. The menu kept pace with the era's literary productions because it was itself a sort of literary product, the restaurant's most marked – and marking – generic innovation. (Spang 189)

In the imaginary community of a dining public, the production of the menu as a text whose typography and form adopted an increasingly stable structure helped to stabilize the restaurant as a distinct industry. The introduction of a printed menu marked one of the most significant moments in the invention of the Western restaurant. In eighteenth-century France, the printed menu distinguished the restaurant from other public eating establishments such as inns or cafés, and standardized what would become an industry. 'Before restaurants could be distinguished from one another, they first had to be separated from all other eateries, and the highly standardized menu structure did just that, making a number of businesses into a specific sort of cultural institution' (Spang 188–9). Although the eighteenth-century French restaurants of Spang's study are far removed from the Chinese restaurants of this discussion, both institutions nonetheless share a name and a genealogy. The menu, like the novel, reflected the changes in European typographic traditions.

Through the form of the menu, Chinese diasporic subjects re-code Canadian settler colonial discourse. A formal consideration of the menu gestures to the way in which Chinese restaurateurs have seized a specifically European, French in this case, restaurant convention and used it as a means of reproducing and disseminating Chineseness while defining the idea of Canada for Canadians. Spang's connection between the menu and the novel brings us back to some of the earliest work in postcolonial studies, wherein the empire wrote back to the centre by seizing imperial tools.[17] The postcolonial novel wrote back to the metropolitan novel, the generic literary form that consolidated an entire European literary tradition in the eighteenth and nineteenth centuries. The diasporic Chinese menu functions also as a seizure of a form of cultural representation.

However, the standardization of burgers and fries as typical offerings on the Canadian side of the Chinese Canadian restaurant menu is a relatively recent occurrence. Turning to a menu from the 1950s, we can see that hamburgers and French fried potatoes are a very small part of a multitude of non-Chinese food offerings. Unlike contemporary menus that mark the categories of Chinese and Canadian or Western explicitly, the Diamond Grill menu of the 1950s does not name its non-Chinese dishes as Canadian or Western. The non-Chinese food offerings are plentiful and diverse, going far beyond hamburgers to include seemingly more sophisticated dishes such as 'Lyonnaise Potatoes,' 'Fresh Cracked Crab en Mayonnaise,' 'Lobster à la Newburg,' and 'Waldorf Salad.' In contrast, the Chinese food offerings almost seem like an afterthought, tacked on at the end of the menu, after the listing of the beverages and just before the Fountain menu. Small town restaurants operated by Chinese people did not always serve Chinese food. In the 1920s, when New Dayton was a thriving small town that had not yet been swallowed up by Lethbridge, Charlie Chew's New Dayton Café did not serve any Chinese food at all (figure 5).[18] Even though the proprietor's name was clearly emblazoned on the front of the menu, and thus New Dayton Café as a restaurant was operated by a Chinese migrant, like the Diamond Grill it does not declare itself to be a Chinese restaurant, much less a Chinese and Canadian one. Moreover, there is almost no consistency between the 1923 menu of the New Dayton, the 1950s menu of the Diamond Grill, and that of contemporary restaurants such as the Club Café or the Parkview. The westernness of the menu constantly shifts, reinventing itself throughout the period of this sample.

In the menus that we have, from 1923 to the present, the food offerings under the category of Canadian or Western serve back a narrative of Canada's development through various forms of capitalism. On the relatively simple short-order and fountain menu of the New Dayton Café the interests of early Canadian agricultural and railway interests dominate the offerings. The phone number is a single digit and the bill of fare is equally basic. The New Dayton menu consists largely of canned food and simple sandwiches. The most exotic or foreign-sounding offerings are not Chinese dishes but rather the Mexican-inflected items: Chili Con Carne and Tamales. Long before the incursions of the fast food's Taco Bell (where you still can't get a tamale), in 1923 New Dayton, a town that no longer exists, you could get a tamale in small town southern Alberta. These Mexican influences on the menu are not surprising when you keep in mind the trajectory of migrant Chinese labour. Not only did they come across the Pacific, but also up from the mines and railways of California.

Compared to the simplicity of the New Dayton, the Diamond Grill's vision of a short-order menu is lush and sophisticated. The wealth of the Diamond's western food offerings reflects the boom economy of post–Second World War Canada. The Diamond Grill's four-page menu is crammed with offerings. The number of menu items alone is staggering compared to the New Dayton menu. There are twenty-five kinds of 'Diamond Grill Choice Steaks and Chops,' twenty-five kinds of 'Eggs or Omelettes,' twenty-nine kinds of 'Sandwiches,' and over forty-nine fountain menu offerings. Reflecting the increasing prevalence of manufactured food, the breakfast offerings list a number of brand-name cereals that are still with us today and connected to some of the largest multinational food producers in North American – Rice Krispies, Grape Nuts, All Bran, Shredded Wheat. The modernity of the Diamond Grill

# New Dayton Cafe

Phone 4

# MENU

### C. L. CHEW,

New Dayton,    Alberta

---

**SOFT DRINKS** 10 Cents

Lime

Lemon

Orange

Coca Cola

Iron Brew

Root Beer

Strawberry

Canada Dry  .15

# Short Order Bill of Fare

## BREAKFAST

Bran Flakes with Milk ... .15
Corn Flakes ... .15
Shredded Wheat ... .15
Hot Cakes and Syrup ... .25
Toast and Tea or Coffee ... .15
French Toast with Jelly ... .45
Hot Milk Toast ... .25
Cream Toast ... .35

Canned Soup ... .30

Eggs and Omelettes ... .50

Ham and Eggs ... Bacon and Eggs
Poached, Fried, Boiled

Steak and Chops ... .50
Steak, Pork Chops, Rib Steak, Hamburger Steak
Fried Fish Sausage

Canned Pork and Beans  Canned Salmon
Canned Sardines  Tamales
Chili Con Carne

Extra with Steak, Fried Onions ... .10

## SHORT ORDERS

T-Bone Steak ... .75
Sirloin Steak ... .65
Pork Chops Breaded ... .60
Canned Crab Meat ... .65
Canned Veal Loaf ... .55
Canned Spaghetti ... .55
Canned Oysters ... .60
Canned Shrimp ... .60

## PASTRY

Apple Pie ... .10
Raisin Pie ... .10
Mince Pie ... .10
Cream Pie ... .10
Sauce Fruit ... .10

## BEVERAGES

Coffee, per cup ... .10
Tea, per pot ... .10
Glass of Milk ... .10
Cream, per glass ... .20

## SANDWICHES

Combination ... .30
Ham and Egg ... .25
Cold Ham ... .15
Cheese ... .15
Fried Ham ... .20
Sausage ... .20
Hamburger ... .20
Egg ... .15
Denver ... .30
Sardines ... .25

## ICE CREAM AND SOFT DRINKS

Plain Ice Cream ... .15
Marsh Mallow ... .20
Strawberry ... .20
Pineapple ... .20
Butter ... .20
Chocolate ... .20
Maple Walnut ... .25
Whole Cherry ... .25
Orange-Grape ... .25
Banana ... .25

### SPECIALS

David Harum ... .35
Merry Widow ... .55
Banana Split ... .40

### ICE CREAM SODA

Lemon ... .15
Cherry ... .15
Pineapple ... .15
Strawberry ... .15
Chocolate ... .15

### SODA SPECIALS

Egg Nog ... .15
Cold Lemonade ... .15
Hot Lemonade ... .15

Toast with Sandwiches is Extra

Coffee or Tea is Extra with all Sandwiches.

5   New Dayton Café menu. New Dayton, Alberta, 1920s. Courtesy Provincial Archives of Alberta.

is distinctly steeped in the economic shifts and changes of 1950s North America.

Finally, on the contemporary menus, the Canadian or Western food items, reduced largely to variations of hamburgers and fries, are the culinary embodiment of late capitalist streamlined efficiency. As Ester Reiter's work on the politics of fast food demonstrates, the hamburger signals an entire economic shift. Reiter notes that the growth and development of the fast-food industry in Canada, following the patterns in the United States, marks a major shift towards the commercialization of domestic labour. The production of the hamburger in North America is part of a growing oligopolic model of industrialization that is premised on a notion of 'the interchangeable worker.' It signals a change in the organization of domestic labour wherein more and more North Americans dine out for the sake of dining (Reiter 165). Moving from the issue of labour to that of culture, David Bell and Gill Valentine connect fast food to an increasing homogenization of culture wherein 'the line between dependability and monotony' is a fine one (135). In culinary terms, the hamburger exemplifies a late capitalist economic situation wherein flexible labour and the homogenization of a particular global culture are indicators of new regimes of capital accumulation.

Turning back to the Chinese restaurant menu, the reduction of the non-Chinese items on the menu to variations of hamburgers and fries suggests that the menu reflects the changes in Canadian economic development without actually changing the ways in which the restaurant actually operates. Retaining the essence of the 'mom and pop' businesses that Reiter notes as the precursor to the invasion of the franchised fast-food industry in Canada, the restaurants take up the changes in the industry but do not fall into the destructive rhythms of the fast-food industry, where labour is increasingly so unskilled as to be interchangeable. The hamburger and fries may be iconic of the fast-food industry, but their appearance does not necessarily change the rhythm of the Chinese restaurant's long-established short-order formula. Chinese cooks adapt and adopt the menu, but are outside of the rhythm of typical fast-food production. This difference in the temporality of the Chinese restaurant is something that I want to return to in the last section of this chapter. Here, what I want to emphasize is the absorptive power of the Chinese restaurant menu. The menus adopt fast food under the rubric of 'Canadian' food and adapt to shifting culinary desires while sustaining a sense of the Chinese restaurant's coherence and consistency. Maintaining the Chinese restaurant as an institution on the main streets of small towns, the restaurant menu moves from tamales to Potatoes Lyonnaise to hamburgers, serving back to Canada culinary icons of its own economic shifts.

Like a novel progressing through the empty national time of Canadian nationhood, the Canadian menu grows into itself. In the clocked and calendrical temporality of Canada's surfacing into nationhood, the story of national emergence can be read in the simultaneity of its progressive shifts from the simple short-order and fountain menu of the New Dayton, to the full and impressive selection at the Diamond, and then to its streamlined modernity at the Golden Wheel.

## Chinese Food: Reproducing Chineseness

Let me begin my consideration of the Chinese food on the menu by taking for granted that the Chineseness of the Chinese restaurant menu needs to be read as highly constructed. Despite the promises of 'authentic Chinese food,' let me assume that the construction of Chineseness on the menu is one that is acutely self-conscious and at least partially aware of the ramifications of its constructions. I hope to shift the weight of the discussion away from questions of authenticity and towards the problem of the dissemination of particular narratives of 'authentic Chinese food.' Rather than asking whether or not sweet and sour pork or chicken chop suey might qualify as 'real' or 'fake' Chinese food,[19] the question then becomes what I take to be a more pressing one: How does the Chineseness of the menu circulate? What does the menu as a text of counterculture reveal about the way in which some diasporic subjects have negotiated their otherness in the precariousness of migrancy?

In this section I want to look at the ways in which Chinese cooks and restaurateurs produce and define a particular kind of Chineseness for Euro-Canadian consumption. If, as the preceding section has argued, they produce and define a Canadianness that explicitly excludes the category of Chinese, what of the representation of Chineseness on the menus? The current critical canon on the representation of minority and postcolonial subjects falls into two general camps. On the one hand, oppressed subjects are subjected to stereotypical representations and on the other those subjects represent themselves. Either you are represented by power or, in the agential casting of the question, you take power and represent yourself. In Asian American literary criticism, for example, this has emerged in the conjoining of two lines of arguments: Through mechanisms such as immigration and labour laws, US citizenship defined itself over and against Asian identities;[20] and in the cultural work of Asian Americans – and here literature has perhaps the most substantial body of critical reflection behind it – Asian Americans represent themselves.[21] This agential-self representation is generally cast in terms of countering damaging stereotypes and fighting for a vision of Asian American identity that is free of ideological racism. Yen Le Espiritu summarizes this double movement, observing that

> categories of difference, race and gender relations do not parallel but intersect and confirm each other, and it is the complicity among these categories of difference that enables U.S. elites to justify and maintain their cultural, social and economic power. Responding to the ideological assaults on their gender identities, Asian American cultural workers have engaged in a wide range of oppositional projects to defend Asian American manhood and womanhood. (106–7)

In Asian Canadian critical work, similar kinds of arguments have emerged. Exploring the work of anthologies, Lien Chao observes that the publication of Asian Canadian anthologies such as *Inalienable Rice* and *Many-Mouthed Birds* signify 'the collective and social advancement and cultural development of contemporary Chinese Canadians in society' (166). In 'Tang Ao in America,' Donald Goellnicht notes that the 'familiar … stereotype of the Chinese laundryman or waiter' must be understood in conjunction with what had been the less familiar knowledge of the role of Chinese labourers in building the Canadian railway (198). Similarly, Glen Deer argues that 'the diversity of Asian North-American writers must always be re-asserted against the stereotypes of the public imagination' (14). The issue of negative stereotypes of Chinese Canadians is a continuing general concern in Maria Ng's essays 'Chop Suey Writing' and 'Representing Chinatown: Dr. Fu Manchu at the Disappearing Moon Café.' Roy Miki closes the 'Asiancy' chapter of *Broken Entries* with a hopeful call for Asian Canadian self-representation, wherein 'writers from a diversity of subject-positions can develop the conditions in which social justice can be achieved through language free from the tyranny of hegemonies of all kinds … where writers of color, including Asian Canadian writers, can negotiate their (non-totalizable) specificities – without looking over their shoulders for the coercive gaze of homogenizing discourses' (123). Miki's hopefulness looks forward to a space where Asian Canadian writing is free from the coercions of a backward glance. Miki's backward glance forcefully echoes Louis Althusser's famous turning back towards power, the interpellation of the subject by the policeman's hailing (Althusser 174). Perhaps, however, we might read for an agency within that backward glance that exceeds the project of countering negative stereotypes.

Remembering that there is another language of emplacement, another register outside of anglophone Canada's hailing of the Chinese subject, perhaps, there is a mode of self-representation wherein the coercions of the backward glance are anticipated and produced within the mode of that anticipation. This anticipation is partly Judith Butler's point in *The Psychic Life of Power*. The paradox of interpellation is that, in order to be interpellated, individuals must already recognize themselves as subjects to be interpellated. Catching Althusser on the very temporal progression he depends upon but then attempts to discount,[22] Butler asks, 'What, prior to the subject accounts for its formation?' (117). She then proceeds to point out the paradox of interpellation:

> Althusser begins 'Ideology and Ideological State Apparatuses' by referring to the reproduction of social relations, specified by referring to the reproduction of social skills. He then distinguishes between skills produced in the firm and those reproduced in education. The subject is formed with respect to the latter. In a sense, this reproduction of relations is prior to the subject who is formed in its course. Yet the two cannot, strictly speaking, be thought of without each other. (Butler 117)

Where Butler's analysis then turns to the problem of desire, my analysis pulls this problem of the prior into one of racial formation. That is, the question of what it means to hail a racialized subject elicits the knowledge that, prior to the subject's formation, there is a distinctly different body of knowledge already circulating for that subject. In the production of Chineseness on the restaurant menus, I read a representation of Chineseness that situates the project of 'representing ourselves' within a highly strategic mode.

In the previous section, I argued that the Chinese restaurant menu serves back to Europe-in-Canada a narrative of its own nationness. That is, the menu's bold declaration of what Canadian food is presents to Europe-in-Canada a tradition, however obviously invented, of its own. Following from that, I argue that the Chinese portion of the menu complements the Canadian one by serving up a highly self-conscious stereotypical Chineseness that nonetheless produces anxiety through the mechanical reproduction of the menu.

Unlike the western dishes on the menus, the Chinese dishes have changed relatively little since their first appearance on the 1950s Chinese Canadian restaurant menu. The contemporary menus' offerings of Chinese food may be more numerous than those at the Diamond Grill, but they read as merely variations on the same reliable basics that the Diamond Grill offered. Turning to the back of the menu to the 'Diamond Grill Special Chinese Dishes,' you will encounter Chicken Chop Suey and Rice first on the list. At the Diamond, you could get one kind of chop suey. At the Golden Wheel, there are five to choose from – Vegetable, BBQ Pork, Chicken, Beef, and Shrimp. Different, and yet basically the same. The menu mechanically reproduces a particular stereotype of Chineseness.

Although chop suey is a dish that has become iconic of inauthentic Chinese food, it can be revealing to consider it as a sign of Chineseness under negotiation through reproduction. The Diamond Grill menu explicitly names chop suey as Chinese. In that naming, the menu textualizes Chineseness, providing a medium through which Chineseness can be reproduced and disseminated. As Spang notes, menus develop in dialogue with one another – one restaurant will copy another's. In this process of pilfering and printing, a standardized restaurant cuisine emerges.

> As restaurateurs (and café-keepers) copied and reused menus, they disseminated a specialized terminology to a wider and wider audience. Insofar as very similar texts, if not exactly the same dishes, were available in a wide variety of eateries, names could spread semi-independently of that to which they had once referred... The menu, by fixing names and titles, both addressed the fantasy and further created the expectation of identity and uniformity. Eaters were not meant to be uniform, but the eaten was, and if it was not, then differences ought to be understood and apparent, capable of being erected into a taxonomy. (191–2)

The print menu has helped to standardize what we have come to know as Chinese food. The menu develops dialogically with one menu echoing the offerings of another one in an entirely different location. The menu is not only a record of displacement but also one of emplacement – it puts into place a kind of Chineseness which persists through the dissemination of the menu.

The standardization of Chinese dishes produces a soothing sameness in the representation of Chineseness on the menu. Just as you can walk into any small town in Canada and expect to find a Chinese restaurant, you can sit down at any one of these restaurants, open the menu and find chop suey. Chop suey's representation of Chineseness produces a fixity and stability in the Chineseness in Canada. Meditating on the colonial stereotype, Homi Bhabha notes in 'The Other Question' that one of the hallmarks of racial stereotypes is that of a fixity of representation: 'The stereotype is not a simplification because it is a false representation of a given reality. It is a simplification because it is an arrested, fixated form of representation that, in denying the play of difference ... constitutes a problem for the representation of the subject in significations of psychic and social relations' (75). The Chineseness represented on the menu functions within a persistent kind of stereotypicality. In the glowing artificiality of the red sauce for sweet and sour pork, there is a phantasmatic fixity to the representation of Chineseness on the menu. Walking into the Parkview Restaurant in Thorhild, Alberta, a diner could reasonably expect to eat the same Lemon Chicken that they would eat at the Golden Wheel in Ponoka, Alberta. The expectation of a kind of sameness, a regularity to the experience of the menu speaks not only to the rise of the Chinese restaurant as an institution, but also to the institutionalization of a kind of standardized Chineseness disseminated through the menus of Chinese restaurants across the landscape of western Canada. Looking at the menus across a span of geographical space, they *are* remarkably similar. They are organized the same way, they have the same categories of food items (appetizers, soup, chop suey, chow mein, egg foo yong and so on). They are structured along the lines of similar culinary expectations.

However, unlike colonial texts, the menus are texts where the fixing occurs by those who are stereotyped. The Diamond Grill menu, for example, fixes and names the category of Chinese. The menu institutionalizes the category of Chinese through items such as chop suey and chicken chow mein. This standardized sameness creates a language of Chineseness which functions as a different textualization circulating within Canadian culture. At once at the margins of culture, disparately spread out over vast geographies and away from urban centers, the consistency of the menus nonetheless asserts a pervasive Chineseness which departs from the definitions of Chinese perpetuated in Canadian law.[23]

As Bhabha usefully argues, a critique cannot be located at the level of whether or not good or bad stereotypes are being perpetuated; rather, it needs to be centered around the process of subjectification itself (75). In that sense, it would not be enough simply to say that an apparatus such as the restaurants produce counter-stereotypes which challenge the 'negative' ones of a Euro-Canadian regime. And yet, in the case of the stereotypical Chineseness produced by Chinese restaurateurs on the menus, Chinese diaspora subjects are producing and perpetuating Chinese stereotypes. These are not necessarily 'positive' stereotypes that have been put into circulation. In fact, the images in circulation eerily echo the projections of the dominant culture. In that sense, they are actually serving back to power precisely its own projection. The unsettling moment happens not in the production of a stereotypical trope (fake Chinese food, the Chinese cook) but in the reproduction of the eerily familiar coming from the other.

There is an excessiveness to the representation in the Chineseness on the Chinese restaurant menu. It is so simple, so uncomplicated, so palatable in that it is exactly what whiteness might expect of Chineseness. This staging of difference contests the ambivalence of colonial power because it exploits that ambivalence. And so the sameness. 'The process by which the metaphoric "masking" is inscribed on a lack which must then be concealed gives the stereotype both its fixity and its phantasmatic quality – the *same old* stories of the Negro's animality, the Coolie's inscrutability, or the stupidity of the Irish *must* be told (compulsively) again and afresh, and are differently gratifying and terrifying each time' (Bhabha 77). Yet, it is the Chinese diasporic subject who re-tells the same old story. It is the subject of settler colonial dominance who facilitates, through the space of the restaurant and the text of the restaurant menu, the compulsive return to the stereotype. It is comforting because it anticipates projected desires. It is exactly what you ordered, what you wanted, given back to you. It fulfills the colonial hunger for itself; they consume their own projection.

The menu stabilizes a kind of Chineseness which offers its consumer the possibility of a reassuring uniformity not only in the Chinese food on the menu, but also in the Chineseness which Chinese food signifies. Chinese restaurant menus present a comforting, palatable Chineseness that can be reproduced and disseminated through the institution of the restaurant. The Diamond Grill menu presents eight unassuming 'Special Chinese Dishes' – items such as Chicken Chop Suey and Rice, Chicken Noodle, Chinese Style, Egg Fooyong and Sweet and Sour Pork Spare Ribs and Rice. The Chinese portion of the menu is very small compared to the restaurant's offerings of more than twenty-five different egg dishes, thirty different sandwiches and thirty-two sundae options. The Chinese food on the menu does not challenge western ones for representational space on the menu, nor does it challenge the non-Chinese diner in terms of its content. The Chinese food items on the Diamond

Grill's menu have become standard fare at Chinese restaurants across the prairies. While the contemporary menus have more options, all of the dishes that the Diamond Grill offered are still there. The uniformity of Chinese food on the menus suggests the creation of a uniform Chineseness that could be reproduced, disseminated and identified.

At the same time that the menu names and makes knowable a palatable Chineseness, it also troubles the possibility of fixing an authentic ethnicity. Inherent in the notion of reproduction is the problem of the original. While the menu allows for a mediated form of cultural contact, it also complicates the idea of an authentic or original Chineseness. The apparatus of mechanical reproduction in the printing of the restaurant menu mocks attempts at authenticity. Walter Benjamin argues in 'The Work of Art in the Age of Mechanical Reproduction' that mechanical reproduction challenges the idea of authenticity: 'From a photographic negative, for example, one can make any number of prints; to ask for the "authentic" print makes no sense' (224). As Eduardo Cadava notes, Benjamin refers not to the fact of reproduction, but to the possibility of reproducibility: 'technical reproduction is not an empirical feature of modernity … Rather, it is a structural possibility within the work of art' (42). While Benjamin's critique relates specifically to the work of art, and not to constructions of race and ethnicity, his analysis of authenticity bears upon this discussion. Benjamin saw in photography the potential deconstruction of '[t]he presumed uniqueness of a production, the singularity of the artwork, and the value of authenticity' (Cadava 44). Rey Chow argues that

> we need to extend Benjamin's conceptualization, a conceptualization that is ostensibly about objects – works of art and their mechanical reproduction – to human beings. Once we do that, we see that in our fascination with the 'authentic native,' we are actually engaging in a search for the equivalent of the aura even while our search processes themselves take us farther and farther away from that 'original' point of identification. (Writing 46)

Chow makes a useful connection between the aura of the original work of art and that of the authentic racial other. Because my use of Benjamin is limited to the reproduction of Chineseness on the small town restaurant menu,[24] his analysis of the condition of reproducibility is particularly apt.

It makes no sense to ask for authentic chop suey. We already know that it is a copy of something that is outside the margins of the menu.

Any number of chop suey dishes can be produced, but no one is more authentic than another. The reproducibility of Chineseness embodied in the restaurant menu frustrates the construction of a knowable authentic Chinese subject at the same time that it offers up a palatable Chineseness that gives the impression of knowability. As Benjamin observes, reproducibility endangers the authority of the object.

> The authenticity of a thing is the essence of all that is transmissible from its beginning, ranging from its substantive duration to its testimony to the history which it has experienced. Since the historical testimony rests on the authenticity, the former, too, is jeopardized by reproduction when substantive duration ceases to matter. And what is really jeopardized when the historical testimony is affected is the authority of the object. (221)

The reproduction of Chineseness on the menu jeopardizes the authority of the Chinese food on the menu to stand in for Chinese – it puts into question the possibility of knowing Chinese authoritatively through the Chinese food on the menu.

In naming Chineseness for the Euro-Canadian community, Chinese food on the restaurant menu brings to the surface the uneasiness of attempts at knowing and identifying otherness. Chow writes of the possibility of the native's gaze reflecting back on the colonizer in the colonial gaze:

> Contrary to the model of Western hegemony in which the colonizer is seen as a primary, active 'gaze' subjugating the native as passive 'object,' I want to suggest that it is actually the colonizer who feels looked at by the native's gaze. This gaze, which is neither a threat nor a retaliation, makes the colonizer 'conscious' of himself, leading him to his need to turn his gaze around and look at himself, henceforth 'reflected' in the native-object. (*Writing* 51)

Similarly, Eleanor Ty argues that the authors in her study of Asian North American literature 'disrupt visible signs dealing with the expectations of being Asian Americans or Asian Canadians ... They reciprocate the gaze and destabilize the set of meanings commonly associated with their Asian bodily features' (11). The menu functions on this order, delivering or serving up a palatable Chineseness at the same time that it jeopardizes its own authority as a text of Chineseness. Chinese food on the menu betrays the version of Chineseness that white communities can consume, revealing more about whiteness than Chineseness. More than that, Chineseness on the menu tells us about how Chinese diaspora subjects negotiate the reproduction and dissemination of Chineseness.

The menu attests to a self-conscious and utterly aware production of fictive ethnicity. It functions as a reminder that the racialized other herself might also produce an inauthentic and imperfect Chineseness as a strategy of resistance. The legacy of the menu suggests that Chinese diaspora subjects exploit the menu's capacity for the reproduction of a cultural space in order to produce an ethnicity that can be made palatable and frustrates the desire for an authentic Chineseness.

**Slowness and Alternative Temporalities**

In this final section, I want to consider the ways in which Chinese diasporic subjects do not simply insinuate themselves into the dominant discourse; rather, as the history of legal exclusion suggests, they are constitutive of it. They emphasize the roots of Canada's national emergence in the routes of diasporic agency.

Unlike many of the non-Chinese items on the Diamond Grill menu, chop suey retains its place on contemporary Chinese Canadian restaurant menus. The white or western items feel antiquated and anachronistic. We know what Chicken Chop Suey or Sweet and Sour Pork Spare Ribs might be. On the other hand, a Love Me Special fancy sundae or a Manhattan Sandwich feel foreign, as though they belong to another time or space. This stability of the Chineseness of the menus across time stages the disjuncture between the historical shifts in whiteness and that of Chineseness.

The progressivist reading of this disjuncture would be the dominant one of European progress – whiteness changes, advances and develops more rapidly than Chineseness. Extending this reading towards a liberal multiculturalism, you might even say that as whiteness advances and becomes more tolerant, it allows for an increasingly visible Chineseness on the menu. Each menu successively contains more and more Chinese dishes. The New Dayton menu of 1923 offers no Chinese dishes at all. The Diamond Grill menu of 1951 offers eight and contemporary menus such as the Club Café or the Parkview reverse the Diamond Grill's proportions of Chinese food, offering mostly Chinese food and only five or six Western Chinese. What might be the meaning of this increasingly visible and overt Chineseness on the restaurant menus? I want to caution against the temptation to link the increasingly visible Chineseness of the menus with the political liberalization or opening up of Canadian immigration policy. On the surface, this link would seem to make sense. In 1923 Canada passed what became unofficially known as the Exclusion Act – a change to the *Chinese Immigration Act* that made Chinese immigration into Canada virtually impossible. In 1947 Canada repealed the act, allowing for limited Chinese immigration. In 1988, Canada passed the *Multiculturalism Act*, an attempt to officially acknowledge cultural difference and pluralism in Canada. Accordingly, it would make sense to think of the increasing Chineseness of the restaurant menus as following the trajectory of these changes to Canadian immigration policy.

However, this reading would presume a linear and causal history of increasing tolerance. This is, of course, the story that Canada tells itself about its own history of racism (the story goes something like this: we were bad before but we are learning, we are becoming more enlightened and more tolerant, and we are getting better now). It is a story that follows a liberal notion of progress as well as an easy historicist notion of history's linearity that is deeply problematic in terms of its objectification and dismissal of the past.

Let me propose that the Chineseness of the restaurants is not just outdated, but it is *out of time*. In his discussion of the problem of the writing of minority histories, Dipesh Chakrabarty challenges Fredric Jameson's injunction to 'always historicize': 'historicizing is not the problematic part of the injunction, the troubling term is "always." For the assumption of a continuous, homogeneous, infinitely stretched out time that makes possible the imagination of a "always" is put to question by subaltern pasts that makes the present, as Derrida says, "out of joint"' (111). The heterogeneity of the time of the Chinese restaurant menus challenges the continuous empty one of European history. Within the outdatedness of the restaurants, we can read a form of diasporic resistance.

The first lines of the menu read: 'Diamond Grill, Nelson's Newest and Most Modern Restaurant.' From the perspective of the twenty-first-century reader, the Diamond Grill's claim to be modern seems quaint and yet antiquated. And yet, contemporary small town Chinese restaurants are also seen as being quaint and outdated. The Diamond Grill's antiquity relates to the antiquity of contemporary restaurants such as the Club Café in Innisfail (figure 6) or the A & J in Olds. They are old, relics. There is a sense that very little has changed. On contemporary menus such has those of the Club or Golden Wheel, the Chinese food offerings are largely elaborations of the Chinese dishes at the Diamond – different kinds of chop suey, chow mein, egg foo yong, and so on.

Compared to the cosmopolitan bustle of twenty-first-century China-

6 Club Café, Innisfail, Alberta, 1999. Courtesy of the author.

towns of Vancouver and Toronto, these restaurants seem old-fashioned and out of step with the changing pace of new immigration patterns and new immigrant identities. This quality of being out of step brings us back to Homi Bhabha's theory of the time lag or belatedness of racialized subjects.[25] It is what Gilroy has marked as the counterculture of modernity and 'the living memory of the changing same' (*Black Atlantic*, 198). From the perspective of history, this belatedness would be what Chakrabarty has called the time knot of subaltern history – that is, the idea of a plurality of times existing together or the disjuncture of the present with itself (109). Whether we read the discordant time of the restaurants as belated or disjunctive, it contains an alternate or different temporality that challenges the desire of late-modern capitalist formations to write them out of the present. This is more than just the story of survival. This is about slowing down and occasionally br(e)aking the relentless flow of late modernity's desire to hurry away from that which it has marked as non-modern. 'It is the function of the *lag* to slow down the linear, progressive time of modernity to reveal its "gesture," its *tempi*, "the pauses and stresses of the whole performance"' (Bhabha 253). The menus assert a slowness in the construction of Chineseness that poses a challenge to the speed of a supposedly new global order that insists on its own newness.

As I noted earlier in this chapter, by slowness I do not mean the characterization of time in non-urban space as idyllic and somehow slower than that of the metropolis. In reading small town Chinese restaurant menus, my goal has been to explore a diasporic temporality and the idea of the time lag. There is some sense of a connection between speed and modernity (think, fast food) that these menus challenge. As Reinhart Koselleck observes, there is an intimate relationship between speed and European modernity. He argues that in the period from 1500 to 1800 'there occurs a temporalization (*Verzeitlichung*) of history, at the end of which there is the peculiar form of *acceleration* which characterizes modernity' (5, my emphasis). Koselleck recounts Robespierre's famous 1793 speech on the Revolutionary Constitution, in which he declared: 'The time has come to call upon each to realize his own destiny. The progress of human Reason has laid the basis for this great Revolution, and the particular duty of hastening it has fallen to you' (cited in Koselleck, 7). In contrast to Luther's era, where 'the compression of time is a visible sign that, according to God's will, the Final Judgement is imminent, that the world is about to end,' Koselleck notes that 'for Robespierre, the acceleration of time is a task of men leading to an epoch of freedom and happiness, the golden future' (7). Robespierre's inauguration of the individual autonomous agent of history who would 'realize his own destiny' heralds an era where rational men should rush headlong into the possibilites and promises of a progressive future.

In many ways, Chinese diaspora criticism has also embraced a notion of a liberatory modernity, of a friendlier future peopled by modern subjects. In analyses that call for a move beyond a perceived idea of an outdated Chineseness, the desire for a certain freedom from the past is part of a larger goal towards a more agential understanding of the Chinese diaspora subject in North America. In her article 'Can One Say No to Chineseness?' Ien Ang argues that one of the central problems for Chinese diaspora studies is that of modernizing Chineseness and, at the same time, creating a modernity that is Chinese:

> Central to the intellectual problematic of cultural China is what one sees as the urgent need to reconcile Chineseness and modernity as the twentieth century draws to a close. There are two interrelated sides to this challenge. On the one hand, the question is how to modernize Chineseness itself in a way that will correct and overcome the arguably abject course taken by the existing political regime in China, a course almost universally perceived as wrong ... On the other hand, there is also the question of how to sinicize modernity – how, that is, to create a modern world that is truly Chinese and not simply an imitation of the West. (229–30)

Ang's call for modernizing Chineseness belies an investment in an idea of the march of historical progress wherein Chineseness needs to catch up to European modernity. Similarly, Aihwa Ong's *Flexible Citizenship* also invests in a sense of urgency around the need to separate old and new diaspora subjects. Ong argues for an agential view of modern Chinese transnationalists who 'subvert the ethnic absolutism born of nationalism and the processes of cultural othering that have intensified with transnationality' (24). This appeal for a consideration of a new migrant subjectivity divorced from the old one of indentured and migrant labour movements hopes to fend off contemporary racism by arguing against archaic representations of Chineseness that are not representative of contemporary Chinese diasporic populations. Similarly, in her discussion of racist stereotypes and Chineseness in Canada, Maria Ng surveys recent Chinese Canadian literature and asks for a movement away from what she understands as derogatory and stereotypical representation of Chinese Canadians. Ng suggests the need for a movement away from representations of Chinese Canadians that are too tied to the past:

> Although they represent a kind of reality of earlier immigrant lives, and although they are experiences that need to be recorded and remembered … a wider and more inclusive representation of Chinese Canadian lives is needed, not only to prevent the continuing impression of a nondifferentiated ethnic group called the Chinese but also to include and empower the lives of recent immigrants who are contributing to the Canada of the twenty-first century. ('Chop Suey' 184)

Ng's call for differentiation between the Chinese immigrant of the past and the new Chinese immigrant of the present assumes an understanding of Chinese immigrant subjectivity as one that has become progressively more sophisticated, more removed from the degrading positions to which earlier immigrants were relegated. In the 'immigrants who are contributing to the Canada of the twenty-first century,' there is a suggestion that the immigrants who contributed to the Canada of the nineteenth and twentieth centuries are outdated and no longer representative of the contemporary Chinese Canadian subject.[26] And yet, this desire to make the past past suggests that the history of Chinese immigration in Canada has followed a trajectory of increasing cosmopolitanism.

This desire risks relegating what might be considered old diaspora subjectivities to the dustbin of Chinese diaspora history rather than thinking through the ways in which these identities not only haunt modern diaspora subjectivity, but are also constitutive of it. Recognizing the constitutive role of the past, Chakrabarty suggests that 'difference is always the name of a relationship, for it separates just as much as it connects … One could argue that alongside the present or the modern the medieval must linger as well, if only as that which exists as the limit or the border to the practices and discourses that define the modern' (*Provincializing Europe*, 110). In differentiating the new diaspora from the old, the history of coolie labour migration lingers on the border of the cosmopolitan transnationalist entrepreneur. Vijay Mishra proposes the idea of a 'diasporic imaginary' as a way of thinking about the way in which old and new diasporas work together in the construction of diasporic subjectivity. He also warns of too easy a celebration of transnationality and deterritorialization. Cautioning against reading diasporas as '*the* ideal social condition,' Mishra suggests that essentialist narratives of homeland and exile will continue to haunt them so long as the specter of racist culture persists

('Diasporic' 426). Mishra's identification of the perseverance of racist culture is important for thinking about why attempts by new diaspora subjects, savvy and educated flexible citizens, cannot break through in a cultural space that will continue to question their right to full citizenship in the first place.

I do not want to glorify the old-fashioned or the outdated. Nor do I want to assert the Chinese cook or restaurateur as the ideal Chinese diasporic subject. However, I am doubtful of claims to the new, to something that too easily divorces itself from an ugly past of state-sanctioned labour exploitation and legalized racism. In her discussion of the problem of developing a materialist feminist historiography, Rosemary Hennessy argues that newness can function as a particular kind of conservatism:

> The conservative face of the new appears in its function as a mechanism whereby oppositional modes of thinking are sutured into the prevailing regimes of truth in order to maintain a symbolic order. The discourse of the new can serve to anchor emergent modes of thinking in traditional categories that help support rather than disrupt the prevailing social order ...
> In its conservative manifestation, the appeal to new-ness serves as the guarantor of repetition, an articulating instrument whereby the *preconstructed* categories that comprise the symbolic infrastructure of the social imaginary are sustained through moments of historical crisis by their dissimulation in the guise of the new. (103–4)

As Hennessy observes, the desire for newness can sometimes conceal a certain conservatism. Declarations of the agential exemplarity of the new diaspora risk re-entrenching the conventions of the old. In the premature requiems ascribed to small town Chinese restaurants, there is a sense that they are not only not representative of contemporary Chinese Canadian subjectivities, but also that they are moving towards extinction.

Part of this movement towards a premature requiem is tied to a pervasive narrative of increasing urbanization. In this narrative we will all eventually live in major cities, our food will come from mega-agricultural operations, and the small town will eventually die. I find this narrative suspicious. The air of inevitability has the imprint of one of European modernity's favourite narratives – progress, the march of time towards some sort of developmental utopia where, in this case, we will all be transnational cosmopolitans identifying more with our mega-cities than our national boundaries. The declaration of newness carries in it the desire for a divorce from what has been declared uncomfortably old and old-fashioned. Chinese Canadian restaurants are old. But they are not extinct. Chinese immigrants still work as cooks. Even though the Chineseness of Chinese Canadian restaurants doesn't seem to fit with the new image of savvy and educated Chinese immigrants, I want to hang on to the politics of their unsuitability. Rather than jettisoning their Chineseness as unrepresentative, I have tried to think through the way in which their lack of fit with what might be called new Chinese diaspora subjectivity reveals the repetition in the rupture of new diaspora subjectivity. It is not that Chineseness should be stable or that it is doomed to a cycle of being tied to coolie labour trajectories; rather, the restaurants suggest an alternate and simultaneous temporality that is out of step, that challenges the European narrative of linear progress. In reading against the grain of a history that wants to progress into a future of increasing liberalized tolerance with racism as an unfortunate spectre of its past, I am not suggesting that diaspora criticism should cling stubbornly to the racism of the past. Instead, I am hoping to make way for a reading of resistance that recognizes the kinds of strategies and negotiations that might be at work in negotiating the racism of the everyday.

The menus retain the traces of the culture of the counter, where the long shiny plastic expanse separating the server from the served is not always a singular line. Counters can circle back on themselves, but to move in between them you still have to feel for the modern in the anachronisms of the present. In a prose poem commemorating the two connected horseshoe-shaped counters at the Diamond Grill, Fred Wah writes:

> These two counters have been designed for maximum use of a small space and are laid out to perform one continuous unit running past the soda fountain and up to the till. The only door in this Arborite feedlot is really a gate between the first counter seat and the glass display case of the till and can only be opened by those of us who know how to operate its very modern latch, hidden so you have to finger it from the bottom. This café is the newest and most modern establishment in Nelson (before the new Greyhound depot) and, of all its doors, I enjoy this gate with the secret latch, this early instance of the power that comes from camouflage and secrecy. (33–4)

In the culture of the counter, the line separating the server and the served maintains the appearance of shiny Arborite solidity. But there is a secret latch, a modern latch, where you feel your way through the underside of the plasticity of rumour and memory to pass. This secret passageway is partly about the way in which the culture of the counter turns the sadnesses of servitude into a counterculture of agential self-positioning. It is also about the countercultural habit of pushing the smugness of the present up against itself. Wah's insistence on the modernity of the latch against the outmoded materiality of Arborite suggests that inhabitating the precariousness of migrancy depends on an understanding of what it means to live in the present while still feeling, sometimes blindly, for the past.

I recognize that it is not only the desires of middle-class ascendancy that might cause those in the Chinese diaspora to want to keep the past in the past, to be swept up in the giddy momentum of a triumphancy where we have, through the sacrifices of sweat and blood, achieved the small signs of gaining a toehold in a ruthless world of socialized racism – a house in a good neighbourhood, children with university degrees, a front lawn that does not have to do double duty as an extra vegetable patch. It is very tempting to fight to 'arrive' and then to turn and say, *I am not one of them. Don't confuse me with them.* These are not easy pasts. But declaring them to be in the past, rather than recognizing that the 'new' Chinese immigrant is just as likely to be a dishwasher at a Chinese restaurant or a garment worker as she is to be a member of the transnational elite, works precisely within a racist regime where the linear march of time and progress wants to situate the dispossessed simply as an unfortunate feature of the non-modern. The precariousness of migrancy means that the ugly head of racism will always threaten to emerge. The words 'go home' will continue to resonate. It is because of this that we need to find a way to move in slowness and embrace the constant intrusion of the past in the present. The secret bond between slowness and memory lies in finding a way to make peace with pasts that harbour pain and humiliation.

In considering the Chinese Canadian restaurant menu across space and time, I have been arguing for a way of reading the menu as a text that bears witness to the agency of Chinese Canadian diaspora subjects in their scripting of 'Canadian' for Canadians and their production of a Chineseness. These representations challenge the notion of authentic Chinese at the same time that they serve up a comforting and fixed Chineseness. They also challenge the progressive and linear time of European history. These menus stage the constructedness of Euro-Canadian time. Against the speed of an insistently globalized world order that denies the constitutive role of the past, the diasporic agency of slowness emerges in the time of the menu.

*Chapter Three*

# Disappearing Chinese Café:
# White Nostalgia and the Public Sphere

When I first began my research for this book, I was surprised by how much these restaurants meant to the people who frequented them. Small town Chinese restaurants were de facto community centres and gathering places when there was no other place to go. They were the places people went to for their morning coffee, or after the hockey game, or for a first date, or for sodas after school. The people who frequented them were not just customers, diners, or regulars. They were very much a part of the restaurant. As documentary filmmaker Cheuk Kwan discovered of 'Noisy' Jim Kook's New Outlook Café in Outlook, Saskatchewan, the restaurant's patrons became so much a part of the restaurant that Jim came to trust them with the keys to the restaurant so that they could 'open up in the morning and make their own breakfast. On their way out, they would just leave the money in a little box on the counter' (Kwan). The New Outlook Café gives a whole new meaning to the notion of being a 'regular' customer. It also offers a glimpse into the Chinese restaurant as a space of such intimacy for those it serves. What does it mean, though, for Chineseness to be so close to the heart of communities that are, for lack of a better description, so white?

This chapter takes up the space of the Chinese restaurant and the curious intimacy between its proprietors and its patrons. While the previous chapter proposes an understanding of diasporic temporality that frustrates the demands of historicism, I do not want to suggest an arbitrary separation between the axes of space and time. Rather, I want to take up the possibilities of the Chinese restaurant as a diasporic space. Despite the warmth and trust that Kwan captures in his filming of Jim Kook and his customers, I suggest that the relationship between Chineseness and whiteness in the space of the restaurant can be somewhat less benign

than the one that Kwan portrays. I recognize that there is much in the
way of genuine respect and affection that these restaurants elicit from
their patrons. Nevertheless, as Rey Chow suggests in 'The Fascist Longings in Our Midst,' idealizations are rarely, if ever, innocent.

In this chapter, I want to take up the small town Chinese restaurant as
memorialized by two of its more famous patrons, Joni Mitchell and Sylvia Tyson, both of whom have independently written remarkably similar
songs about Chinese restaurants in small towns. Together the Tyson and
Mitchell songs illuminate something of the darker side of the idealization of the Chinese restaurant and its role as an explicit space of otherness in small town Canada.

'Nothing lasts for long,' sings Joni Mitchell in 'Chinese Café/Un-
chained Melody.' Rather than nothing, the song itself suggests that there
are some very specific things that do not last for long. This chapter is an
exploration of white nostalgia and the desire to commemorate the Chinese restaurant while simultaneously marking its disappearance. Like
the wooden grain elevators that used to dot the prairie landscape, the
Chinese restaurant has been recast as an icon of a purer, more innocent
past. Unlike the wooden grain elevators, however, the restaurants continue to exist in most small towns. They have not disappeared, and yet
there is a curious acceptance of the forecast of their disappearance. The
attempt to situate the Chinese restaurants as a location of a hermetic
past is not unique to triumphalist narratives of Chinese immigrant ascendancy that I discuss in the previous chapter. This desire to keep the past
in the past also plays a role in the construction of whiteness.

I take up Mitchell's 'Chinese Café/Unchained Melody' and Tyson's
'The Night the Chinese Restaurant Burned Down' not only because the
songs are so strikingly similar in their narrative content, but also because
the representation of the Chinese restaurant in these two songs illuminates its peculiar role in the consolidation of a white subjectivity. The
first part of this chapter examines the narratives of loss and nostalgia that
pervade the songs, and reads these narratives within the context of the
classic *Bildungsroman*. In the second part, I suggest that there is a connection through the notion of loss between the *Bildung* narrative and Jürgen
Habermas's concept of the public sphere. I explore the ways in which the
Chinese restaurant functions as a public sphere in development, a sort
of 'proto-public sphere' if you will. I show that the public sphere is itself
a space that is predicated on colonialism and imperialism and argue that
the use of the Chinese restaurants in both the Mitchell and Tyson songs
is neither casual nor accidental, but revealing of what these songs sup-

press in their use of Chineseness. In the final part of the chapter, I return
to the question that launched this chapter, Why the Chinese restaurant
in particular? Why do both songs specifically identify the Chinese restaurant, rather than any other space of small town life, as the location
of these narratives? I argue that the Chinese restaurant in these songs
functions as a screen in both senses – it screens out and suppresses the
predications of white subjectivity at the same time that it serves as a space
of projection for that subjectivity. When I first came across the Mitchell
and Tyson songs, I was amused and struck by the oddity of their use of
Chinese restaurants. As my research progressed, it became clear that the
Chinese restaurants in these songs neither casual nor accidental, but are
in fact revealing of what these songs repress. They signal the ways in
which Chineseness, and the Chinese restaurant in particular, have been
instrumental in the development of a vision of small town life that occludes otherness at precisely the moment when it explicitly invokes it.

**Portraits of Development: The Artist as a Young Woman**

In 1982 Joni Mitchell released 'Chinese Café/Unchained Melody' on
the *Wild Things Run Fast* album. This song also became a standard and
was re-released on Mitchell's collection *Hits* in 1996. Similarly, Sylvia Tyson's 'The Night the Chinese Restaurant Burned Down,' which was released on compact disc in 1989, emerged in the aftermath of the height
of 1960s folk music.[1] Both songs have become standards in Mitchell's
and Tyson's respective music repertoires. Coming almost two decades
after the height of folk music's dominance of North American popular
music, it is not surprising that both songs are retrospectives written from
the perspective of a middle-aged woman who looks back onto a time
before fame, when the singers were small town Canadian girls dreaming
about adulthood in the local café, the Chinese restaurant. I want to read
these two songs together because they share a strikingly similar narrative
sung in a similar musical genre: both songs look back on being in the
café with a girlfriend ('Carol' in the Mitchell song, 'Maggie' in the Tyson
song); use sentimental love songs of the 1950s ('Unchained Melody' and
'Canadian Sunset') as musical intertexts; use the Chinese restaurant as a
location of the past; carry autobiographical resonances; and focus on the
dreams of girlhood and the outcomes of adulthood. Tyson's song opens
with the scene of two girls who were on the verge of breaking away from
their small town lives. She sings about the part-time job she holds with
her friend Maggie the summer that they finished school and the nights

that they spent singing with the local Legion Hall band. Unlike the 'girls coming home from the canning factory / Laughing and talking about their wedding gowns,' Maggie and Sylvia do not plan on staying in the town. The bridge of Tyson's song sets up the burning down of the Chinese restaurant as the catalyst for their departure. She and Maggie look at each other 'as if we'd been given a sign' and they catch the midnight Greyhound bus out of town on the night the Chinese restaurant burns down. The end of the Chinese restaurant signals the end of their girl-hood, the end of their time in 'a dying town.'

Similarly, Mitchell's song opens on the scene of two girls dreaming of bigger things and whiling away the time in the local Chinese restaurant. Mitchell and her friend Carol are 'in the middle' – they are middle class and middle-aged women who have memories of being wild teenagers. Mitchell's song spans the years of her adulthood, the giving up of her daughter for adoption and the movement from the wildness of 'the old days' to the maturing of their children and the looking back to a time when she and Carol dreamt on dimes, playing 'Unchained Melody' on the jukebox one more time.

Thematically, both songs are about the loss of girlhood, the passing of youth. The first part of the refrain in Mitchell's song, 'Nothing lasts for long,' emphasizes the preoccupations with middle age and the passage of time that characterize the final verse of the song. Mitchell sings of a girlhood friend whose own children have now grown up. She sees the resemblance between the way they look now and their mothers when they were the age of those kids who have grown up so fast that it is like 'the turn of a page.'

Similarly, Tyson's song closes with a verse on the passage of time. Even though it all happened a long time ago, she sings about how that night when the Chinese restaurant burned down could still seem so recent. The familiar lamenting of the trick of time, the way something that has happened so long ago can still seem as though it was only yesterday, opens up the appeal of the song to a sense of its universality in the third line, 'Like any other summer night in any other little town.'

However, the generalizing themes of the songs lie not only in their appeal to the arrival of middle-age reflectiveness, but also in their adher-ence to a classic *Bildungsroman* narrative structure. The object of loss in these two songs is not so much youth or girlhood as the *possibilities* of youth and girlhood, what Franco Moretti has identified as the 'subjective possibility' of the *Bildungsroman*: 'Unlike what occurs in the short story or in tragedy, the novelistic episode does not refer back to an objective necessity, but to a subjective possibility. It is that event which *could also not have taken place*' (45). While there are clearly important formal differences between folk songs and the typical 'novel of education' or 'novel of development,' as the *Bildungsroman* has been loosely defined in English literature, the narrative trajectory of the Mitchell and Tyson songs shares many of the defining characteristics of the classic *Bildungsroman*.[2] These songs are portraits of the artist/songstress as a young woman. They record the movement from youthful innocence to knowing maturity.

Returning then to the subjective possibility of the 'Chinese Café' and 'The Night the Chinese Restaurant Burned Down' as *Bildung* narratives, the foundational loss that both songs lament is a sense of potentiality that enables the narrative to go forward. At the heart of the *Bildung* narrative is the idea of loss that enables the consolidation of the liberal subject. Following Moretti, I suggest that this lost potentiality is rooted in a liberal notion of freedom and that the *Bildung* narrative is that of the renunciation of freedom for what Georg Lukács termed the 'immanence of meaning' (quoted in Moretti, 71). In exchange for pure freedom, what might result in anarchy, the liberal subject gains a sense of the meaning of the everyday events that make up a life – sitting in a café and listening to sentimental love songs, being middle-aged on Christmas morning and sitting on a girlfriend's lawn. As Moretti perceptively notes, the classical *Bildungsroman* promotes the *opposite* of the promises of the French Revolution:

> It indicates a way – the only way, in the world of the novel – to restore harmony within the ruling class: In short: the classical *Bildungsroman* narrates 'how the French Revolution could have been avoided.' Not by chance is it a genre that developed in Germany – where revolution never had any chance of success – and in England – where, concluded over a century earlier, it had opened the way to a social symbiosis that renewed itself with particular effectiveness at the turn of the eighteenth century. (64)

The *Bildung* narrative orchestrates the mediation between the desire for individual autonomy and the necessity of socialization in order to consolidate a rational liberal subject.

As Thomas Holt's study of emancipation in Jamaica reveals, there are only certain kinds of freedom that are permissible under liberal governance. Noting that the elite never trusted the working classes, much less emancipated slaves, to 'work three days if two days' pay would keep them a week,'[3] Holt suggests that 'seventeenth-century political economists never fully accepted the liberal premises, because they were unable to resolve the seemingly inherent contradiction between the ethic of liberalism and the labor needs of a capitalist economy, between individual freedom and social order and utility' (*Problem* 35). The practical application of liberal ethics meant that free subjects 'would be free to bargain in the marketplace but not free to ignore the market ... free to pursue their own self-interest but not to reject the cultural conditioning that defined what that self-interest should be' (ibid. 53). One is never simply a free subject; one must learn to want to be free in the right way. Harmony can be restored only when the bourgeois reader/listener accepts that the potentiality of absolute freedom must be given up for what Moretti terms 'the comfort of civilization' (16).

The opening lines of Mitchell's song perfectly encapsulate the function of the *Bildung* narrative as a mediating structure of bourgeois interests: 'Caught in the middle / Carol, we're middle class / We're middle-aged.' From the start, the song centres on coming to terms with being in the middle, of negotiating the disappointments of middle age and the demands of middle-class desire. What is gained, the stability of looking 'like our mothers did now / When we were those kids' age,' can come only at the expense of the wildness of 'rock "n" roll days.' Similarly for Tyson, the distance from the 'the girls coming home from the canning factory / Laughing and talking about their wedding gowns' articulates the sacrifice of girlhood dreams for the pursuit of self-realization as an artist. Mitchell's and Tyson's emphasis on their middleness situates their songs within the tradition of an Enlightenment valorization of the average. Writing of Walter Scott's penchant for 'constructing his [historical] novels around an "average," merely worthy and never heroic, "hero,"' Lukács notes that 'we find here a renunciation of romanticism and a further development of the realist traditions of the epoch of Enlightenment' (151). These stories of the development of the woman artist emphasize a connection to the folk. This is the ideological work of an enlightened narrative that coerces through its folksy inclusiveness. The *Bildung* narrative of the emergence of 'Joni Mitchell' and 'Sylvia Tyson' as folk music icons works overtime to underscore their middling ordinariness.

In keeping with the tradition of the women's *Bildungsroman* in particular, the Mitchell and Tyson songs consolidate a specifically female subjectivity. This gendered subjectivity is both middle class and middle aged. For Moretti, the bourgeois dilemma is between individual autonomy and socialization. That problem remains for Mitchell and Tyson. But these songs suggest that this dilemma is inflected by gender for middle-class, middle-aged, white women. These songs are about the woman who got away from the canning factory, the woman whose kids didn't grow up straight, who didn't end up with the manicured lawn of a middle-class home. Mitchell and Tyson narrate a gendered version of Moretti's description of the bourgeois liberal dilemma, that of feminist autonomy set against the socialization of womanhood, of the wildness of rock and roll days set against taking on the appearances of their mothers. As Moretti bluntly puts it, 'You would like such and such values to be realized? – fine, but then you must also accept these others, for without them the former cannot exist' (17). The women in Mitchell and Tyson's songs take the particularity of individual freedom over that of a collective social one. This choice is, as Moretti states, 'the *raison d'être* of the classical *Bildungsroman*: if the hero[ine] wishes to enjoy absolute freedom in a specific domain of [her] existence, in other sectors of social activity there must prevail instead complete *conformity*. Everyday life, we have seen, demands the *stability* of social relationships' (55).

A necessary exchange girds the promise of freedom. In the economy of liberal subjectivity, nothing is free – not even the pursuit of freedom, not the pursuit of freedom from small town marriage, a life at the canning factory or the five and dime, and singing standards at the Legion Hall on weekends.

Both songs occlude this necessary exchange through the narrative of loss. In this occlusion, it is not that the women in the songs give up the promises of a 1960s social revolution in exchange for individual freedom, but that the chance for that revolutionary potential is lost with the passing of the restaurant. 'Nothing lasts for long,' Mitchell laments repeatedly in 'Chinese Café.' As I will discuss in further detail later in this chapter, both songs associate the passing of the Chinese restaurant with the passing of the potential of the promises of 1960s idealism. In Tyson's song, this potentiality is burned away, incinerated. Mitchell is at once less graphic and more precise in the *Bildung* model, where '*non*capitalist work' is crucial to the development of the 'specific individual, and to the end of emphasizing [her] peculiarities' (Moretti 29). In Mitchell's song, the potentiality is lost to the incursions of capitalist greed. The second verse of 'Chinese Café' begins by recognizing that money from uranium mining has transformed the town by paving over parks, tearing landmarks down, and exploiting aboriginal land. Mitchell blames the short-sightedness of capitalist accumulation for the passing of the opportunity, for the loss of potentiality. Noting that Lukács and Georg Simmel agree particularly on the inability of the 'modern "personality"' to reach its goal in a professional occupation alone,' Moretti observes that 'those who devote themselves to a modern profession must give up their own personality' (41). In the classic *Bildung* narrative, work is too impersonal and objective as a means of allowing for the expression of the individuality and particularity of the artist.

In this second verse of 'Chinese Café,' Mitchell's assertion of artistic individuality comes in conjunction with its imbrication with the dehumanization of business. It is uranium money that puts up sleek concrete and tears the old landmarks down. Mitchell's juxtaposition of her individual artistic development against that of the impersonality of the machinery of capitalism echoes that classic text of liberalism, John Stuart Mill's defence of individuality in *On Liberty*. Mill writes:

> Supposing it were possible to get houses built, corn grown, battles fought, causes tried, and even churches erected and prayers said by machinery – by automatons in human form – it would be a considerable loss to exchange for these automatons even the men and women who at present inhabit the more civilized parts of the world, and who assuredly are but starved specimens of what nature can and will produce. Human nature is not a machine to be built after a model, and set to do exactly the work prescribed for it, but a tree, which requires to grow and develop itself on all sides, according to the tendency of the inward forces which make it a living thing. (123)

Mill's metaphor of the machine, when set against that of the tree, puts into play the now familiar trope concerning the need to defend the free and natural from the constraints of conformity. For Mill, the very definition of liberty and progress lies in the full expression of individuality.

Mitchell's situating of her own development outside the realm of soulless machinery of 'short-sighted businessmen' allows for an assertion of her individuality through the 'noncapitalist' work of being an artist. Similarly, in 'Come in from the Cold,' a song released in 1991, Mitchell disconnects her work as an artist from that of capitalist work and simultaneously emphasizes the potentiality of her development as an artist. Singing of the way in which artists believed that they had a purpose, she recognizes that, despite all the work she did 'for/ something better,' she was still 'bought and sold.' In the context of the *Bildung* narrative, Mitchell's references to slavery point to the contradictions of freedom for the liberal subject. Rather than needing an 'escape from freedom' (Moretti 64), Mitchell is a slave to liberty who slaves freely 'for / something better.' And despite, or perhaps because of, the freeness of her labour, she is nonetheless 'bought and sold.' Of course, it is her music that is the object of exchange. These lyrics disconnect her from the impersonality of capitalist work at the same time that they valorize the individuality of her artistic work. In 'Chinese Café,' uranium money not only lacks personality, it also generates a paving over of the particular – sleek concrete replaces old landmarks, parking lots erase little parks, and all of this is accomplished by robbing First Nations peoples again. Mitchell's emphasis on place in this list of things lost to capitalist greed emphasizes a belief in the possibilities of local places, the potentiality of the public space. 'Chinese Café' and 'The Night the Chinese Restaurant Burned Down' mourn the loss of this common public space.

## Structuring Nostalgia: Mourning the Public Sphere

I have shown that the Mitchell and Tyson songs revolve around the loss of a potentiality rather than the ostensible object of youth or girlhood. Let me turn now to explore what that potentiality constitutes. Although the narrative circulates around a singular subject, it would be a mistake to see the lament as an individualized one. What is lost is not the potentiality, the subjective possibility, of an individual subject, but something larger: a collective possibility. While the *Bildungsroman* narrates how the French Revolution could have been avoided, the loss that consolidates the individual subject is one that must be read within the larger collective horizon of possibility. In the general case of the *Bildung* narrative, we avoid the French Revolution through the narrative that asks us to give up the promise of the French Revolution. In the specific case of these songs, Mitchell and Tyson avert the promises of 1960s idealism through a narrative that mourns the loss of that idealism rather than celebrates its achievements, however they may be defined.

What is mourned in both songs is the thwarting of what comes after the women take the last Greyhound out of a dying town and the birth of rock 'n' roll days. Both songs end at the beginning of their departures from their girlhood lives, at the beginning of their careers. Poised at an end and a beginning, the songs narrate departures from the small towns, from fifties orchestral music, but what is lost is not these things themselves but the innocence and idealism of what these women left the small towns and fifties orchestral music *for*. That is, what is lost is not what came before or what came after the launching of their careers into stardom, but the possibilities of what came after *before* it could happen – the moment of potentiality mislaid. And it is not individual freedom that has been sacrificed, but the promise of the 1960s as a musical departure from the tightly orchestrated sentimentality of songs such as 'Canadian Sunset' and 'Unchained Melody.' It is a musical departure that gestures towards the promise of a political departure from the tightly orchestrated sentimentality of the 1950s post–Second World War world of weekends at the Legion Hall and marriage as the only escape from the canning factory and part-time jobs at the five and dime. The promises of 1960s North American counterculture are not explicitly raised in the Mitchell and Tyson songs, but they appear in the repudiation of the world the songs depict.

The world of both songs is infused by a musical genre that precedes the 1960s revolution in folk music in which both Mitchell and Tyson would be key players. Both songs make specific references to 1950s orchestral love songs, songs that were sung by male crooners backed by full orchestras. Mitchell refers directly to the intertext in the title of her song, 'Chinese Café/Unchained Melody,' and Tyson specifically links the Chinese restaurant with 'Canadian Sunset' in the couplet that closes both the first and the final verse of the song: 'And the radio was playing Canadian Sunset / The night the Chinese restaurant burned down.' The versions of 'Unchained Melody'[4] and 'Canadian Sunset'[5] that were most likely circulating in the 1950s would have been the orchestral ones. Although the Righteous Brothers' version of 'Unchained Melody' has become more prominent in recent years, the version that most likely would have been on the radio and in the jukeboxes in the fifties was the orchestral version recorded by Les Baxter. Similarly, Andy Williams's 'Canadian Sunset' was recorded with a full orchestra and was one of the biggest hits of his career. Its lyrics are analogous to those of 'Unchained Melody.' Like 'Unchained Melody,' the song opens with a statement of loneliness and longing, and revolves around what we might now think of as FM radio's penchant for songs about the theme of everlasting love (although, admittedly, not many contemporary Billboard songs evoke Canadian ski trails so romantically). It is a song about someone who had only bargained for a change of scenery with a weekend in Canada and finds love in that most unexpected of places – the cross-country ski trail. I am pausing on these two 'background' songs not only because they form another point of correspondence between the Mitchell and Tyson songs, but also because they signal broader relations between the Chinese restaurant, liberal subjectivity, and the *Bildung* narrative.

The citation of 1950s love songs does more than evoke the world of girlish dreaming that both songs describe; it also collapses the space of the Chinese restaurant with the music with which Mitchell and Tyson associate it. Mitchell's evocation of 'Unchained Melody' suggests that there is an intimate relationship between the Chinese restaurant and the music emanating from the restaurant's jukeboxes and radios. The semantics of the slash at work in the title of the song, 'Chinese Café/Unchained Melody,' discloses the metonymic relationship between the music on the jukebox and the space of the restaurant itself. The slash suggests a kind of interchangeability, an easy transition between one term and another. Balanced on either side of the punctuation mark are two terms, markers, signifiers. The relationship Mitchell and Tyson establish between the Chinese restaurant and the musical intertexts of their songs relegates the Chinese restaurant to a kind of pastness.

The Mitchell and Tyson songs are a lament for a space of commonality, both that of female companionship in the Chinese restaurant itself, and then the 1960s folk scene that comes after. The drama of the loss of the space of the Chinese restaurant (either through the finality of a fire or through the irreversible flow of time) unfolds and gestures towards the drama of the loss of the public sphere of the 1960s folk-music revival.[6] From the perspective of the Mitchell and Tyson songs, the public sphere of the 1960s is a goal rather than a realized space of public discourse. The songs are representations of a possible future. The object of loss in both of these songs is not just youth, and not just the restaurant, but also the possibility for an ideal space of commonality.

I want to read this lost space of commonality within the context of Jürgen Habermas's public sphere. Extending Moretti's reading of the subjective possibility of the *Bildungsroman*, I suggest that this potentiality takes shape in the concept of the Habermasian public sphere. The relationship between the *Bildung* narrative and the Habermasian public sphere is one that Habermas himself alludes to in *The Structural Transformation of the Public Sphere*. Early in the argument, Habermas takes up Goethe's *Wilhelm Meister* as an excursive example of the demise of the representative publicness that he associates with the absolutist state. As Marc Redfield suggests, *Wilhelm Meister* is perhaps *the* exemplary text of the *Bildungsroman* genre. Goethe's novel is Redfield's test case for arguing that the *Bildungsroman* genre, under scrutiny, 'threatens to disappear altogether. Even *Wilhelm Meister*,' he argues, 'has proved resistant to being subsumed under the definition it supposedly inspired' (41). Whether Goethe's novel inspired the genre or is exemplary of it matters less in my discussion than the concurrent use of the novel in Habermas's definition of the bourgeois public sphere. For Habermas, the failure of

Wilhelm's attempt at representative publicness, at being Hamlet, sets the stage for the ascendance of the bourgeois public sphere: 'Wilhelm Meister's theatrical mission had to fail. It was out of step, as it were, with the bourgeois public sphere whose platform the theatre had meanwhile become' (Habermas 14). In other words, Habermas locates within *Wilhelm Meister* the expression of a proto–public sphere, the public space that not only exemplifies the characteristics of anachronistic representative publicness, but also ushers in the new form of publicity that would constitute the basis of the Habermasian ideal. This use of a classic *Bildungsroman* text to demarcate the end of one kind of publicity and the beginning of another suggests, conversely, that the public sphere as an ideal space of rational commonality also plays a role in the *Bildung* narrative. The public sphere is that which is lost, the potentiality of the liberal subject thwarted and so mourned.

The temporal structure of the Mitchell and Tyson songs, the way in which they end poised at a beginning and begin by looking back from an endpoint, suggests that they mourn the loss of something that temporally straddles both the end of their girlhood lives and the beginning of their careers as stars of 1960s folk-music culture. They mourn the loss of a common space of public discourse that focuses on both the Chinese restaurant as a space of the potentiality of youth, and that which comes after, the 1960s in this case, as an extenuation of that space of potentiality. That is, the Chinese restaurant in these songs sets the stage for the events of the 1960s that lie beneath the surface of the music. Functioning as a proto–public sphere, the Chinese restaurant in these songs demarcates the end of one kind of public space and the emergence of another. Poised at the end of an era of orchestrated sentimentality and ushering in the beginning of another marked by the liberatory ideals of free love and free speech – what has been seen as a sexual and civil revolution[7] – the Chinese restaurant prefigures the public sphere of 1960s folk culture.

I have been reading Jürgen Habermas in a mistaken sense. But I do so in good company. In evoking Habermas's public sphere, I am evoking the contagious idealism of a public space of 'rational-critical debate' (Habermas 58) that could permeate the governance of a society. In 1961 Habermas published *The Structural Transformation of the Public Sphere*. The book was translated and published in English in 1989. Exploring seventeenth- and eighteenth-century English coffee-houses, French salons, and German 'learned *Tischgesellschaften* (table societies), the old *Sprachgesellschaften* (literary societies),' Habermas identifies a coherent sphere of public discussion among the bourgeoisie that began with literary criticism and then moved into the realm of politics (34). This bourgeois public sphere opposed the rule of the absolutist state through the use of rational discourse:

> The bourgeois public sphere may be conceived above all as the sphere of private people come together as a public; they soon claimed the public sphere regulated from above against the public authorities themselves, to engage them in a debate over the general rules governing relations in the basically privatized but publicly relevant sphere of commodity exchange and social labor. (Habermas 27)

Habermas's normative ideal became the English bourgeoisie of the late seventeenth and early eighteenth centuries in particular. In a section of the book entitled 'The Model Case of British Development,' Habermas outlines a series of events that produced the ideal conditions for the development of a bourgeois public sphere. These conditions include the rise of the textile, metal, and paper industry that resulted in a newly rich bourgeois class, the founding of the Bank of England, the elimination of censorship, which 'made the influx of rational-critical arguments into the press possible and allowed the latter to evolve into an instrument with whose aid political decisions could be brought before the new forum of the public,' and 'the first cabinet government,' which 'marked a new stage in the development of Parliament' (58). Notably, the English coffee-houses 'were considered seedbeds of unrest' (Habermas 59). For Habermas, the English coffee-house, similar to the French *salon*, became a centre 'of criticism – literary at first, then also political – in which began to emerge, between aristocratic society and bourgeois intellectuals, a certain parity of the educated' (32). Although the second half of the book traces the demise of the public sphere in the late nineteenth and twentieth centuries due to the increasing commodification of public opinion, it is often to the first half of the book, where Habermas describes the rise of the public sphere, that subsequent critics have turned. Indeed, as Craig Calhoun candidly notes in his introduction to a collection of essays published in honour of the publication of the English translation of the book, 'The second half of *Structural Transformation* is less satisfying than the first. If the early chapters succeed in recovering a valuable critical ideal from the classical bourgeois public sphere, Habermas ultimately cannot find a way to ground his hopes for its realization very effectively in his account of the social institutions of advanced or organized capitalism' (29). It is my argument that the public sphere could not fulfil its promise because it could only exist within a structure of nostalgia.

As Mitchell and Tyson's objects of loss, the restaurant and the 1960s idealism it suggests, together reveal the structure of nostalgia at work in the Habermasian public sphere. As the *Bildung* narrative tells us, loss enables the consolidation of the liberal subject. I have understood the loss in these songs not as that of its ostensible object, girlhood or youth, but rather as that of a potentiality. I would then suggest that this potentiality consists not of individual possibility, but of a collective or communal one, and that this sense of communal potentiality lies in an understanding of the Habermasian public sphere. These songs in their singularity open up the way in which the Habermasian notion of the public sphere is structured by nostalgia.

Before discussing this nostalgia, let me first trace the way in which Habermas's concept has travelled. His idealism has not remained bound to the bourgeois public to which he first attributes the public sphere. Although Habermas has been criticized for being too idealistic,[8] a number of writers continue to use the idea of the public sphere in its idealized state, and often with little or no reference to the specificities of seventeenth- and eighteenth-century Europe. When Nyan Shah refers to a 'subaltern public sphere' in his discussion of medical health practices in San Francisco's Chinatown, he is not referring to propertied bourgeois white men engaging in rational-critical debate, but to the possibility of a common discursive space outside the dominant systems of governance that challenges and resists governing regimes. When Akhil Gupta and James Ferguson write of a 'transnational public sphere' (48), they are referring to a space of geographically unbounded cultural exchange, largely through mass media. Similarly, when Shirley Lim, Larry Smith, and Wimal Dissanayake write of a 'transnational Asia Pacific public sphere' in their book *Transnational Asia Pacific: Gender, Culture and the Public Sphere*, they are referring to a public space of cultural commodity exchange that is, at least in theory, democratically accessible.

The public sphere has become, in these instances, a generalized space of oppositionality that functions through the laudable means of democracy and public participation. Like Shah's subaltern public sphere, the public sphere is not defined, but is instead assumed as something of a given. In the sense that the Habermasian public sphere has been closely related to the rise of literary criticism as an institution, Lim, Smith, and Dissanayake's volume can certainly be understood as part of a transnational Asia Pacific sphere. However, they argue that their essays 'focus on the vitally important public sphere in the transnational Asia Pacific region' (6), and this is another matter altogether. Rather than contributing to the public sphere through intellectual debate, the volume promises to focus on the public sphere, to produce the public sphere as an object of analysis. In this way, the editors of *Transnational Asia Pacific* mobilize a concept of the public sphere as something of a catch-all space for a diverse jumble of issues, including gender, cultural identity, public negotiations of meaning, and so on.

When I first began research for this chapter, I was surprised by the disjuncture between these almost casual uses of the phrase 'the public sphere,' and Habermas's own almost painfully particular use of the term. When the 'bourgeois' is dropped from 'the bourgeois public sphere' and all kinds of other adjectives are substituted in its place, including 'feminist,' 'transnational,' 'transnational Asia Pacific,' and 'subaltern,' the idealism of Habermas's portrayal becomes portable. These uses of the idea of the public sphere have taken the Habermasian ideal and left behind his critique: the demise of the public sphere in the twentieth century due to the increasing commodification of public discourse and what he sees as the devolution of the public sphere into public opinion.

Despite the historical specificity of the idea, it seems to me that what persists, the reason why the idea of the public sphere continues to resonate and be put to use in all kinds of ways that have little or nothing to do with seventeenth- and eighteenth-century Europe, lies precisely in its idealization. There is something so compelling in the idea that there might be a public space where people could come together and talk and write about artistic and political issues in the interest of a common, shared sense of goodness. There is understandable appeal in the idea of a place where rational debate and the rigour of convivial conversation prevails, a place that is outside of the state and the market, and yet still capable of influencing the directions of both.

And yet, this view of the public sphere in its idealized sense can only exist in the past. For Habermas, the ideal public sphere can only be located in the London coffee-houses of the seventeenth and eighteenth centuries. For Mitchell and Tyson, it can only be that which has passed by, that which can no longer be retrieved or recuperated. If Habermas is asymmetrical in his treatment of historical epochs, it is not because of a prejudice against twentieth-century public culture, as Calhoun suggests, but rather because the public sphere can exist only in an irretrievable past. It can exist only in a structure of nostalgia. What the Mitchell and Tyson songs reveal is the structural nostalgia that manages the predications and the contradictions embedded within the concept of the public sphere itself. This is why Tyson's song ties loss so intimately to the spectacular incineration of the Chinese restaurant. The space of potentiality, the promise of a public sphere of political and social change, can only be lost if it cannot be returned to. It can only be idealized if it no longer exists.

Although Susan Stewart's analysis of the workings of nostalgia has been criticized for its practice of reducing all things to narrative and its failure to attend to the materiality of its subject matter,[9] her reading is particularly accurate in the case of the Habermasian public sphere and its subsequent permutations, including the one alluded to in the Mitchell and Tyson songs. It is precisely because the nostalgia in this case is narratological, because it circumvents the material conditions of its own enablement, that Stewart's analysis works so well here. Her understanding of nostalgia accounts for the necessity of loss in the Mitchell and Tyson songs; Mitchell and Tyson's nostalgia is grounded in a sadness, a lament, for something that can only exist in narrative. As Stewart puts it:

> Nostalgia is a sadness without an object, a sadness which creates a longing that of necessity is inauthentic because it does not take part in lived experience. Rather, it remains behind and before that experience. Nostalgia, like any form of narrative, is always ideological: the past it seeks has never existed except as narrative, and hence, always absent, that past continually threatens to reproduce itself as a felt lack. Hostile to history and its invisible origins, and yet longing for an impossibly pure context of lived experience at a place of origin, nostalgia wears a distinctly utopian face, a face that turns toward a future-past, a past which has only ideological reality. (23)

The past that Mitchell and Tyson seek exists only in narrative, in the intertexts of 1950s love songs. 'Unchained Melody' and 'Canadian Sunset' are about longing, about hungering for something that itself can exist only in narrative. In that sense, both songs express a longing, a sadness that is without an object because they have already narrativized the object. These songs reveal the structure of nostalgia endemic to the Habermasian public sphere. The public sphere, in Habermas's ideal sense, can only exist as an ideal. And in that idealization, it can only exist in a past that is not only historically inaccurate, but, to echo Stewart's phrase, also hostile to history. The critics who attack Habermas for a lack of attention to history can only be right if historical accuracy was a goal of the conception of the public sphere in the first place.[10] One of the reasons why the idea of the public sphere has become so portable, appropriated so widely with so little respect for the historical specificity that Habermas himself insisted on, lies in its formulation in a structure of nostalgia. These songs are not nostalgic; Habermas is not nostalgic. Rather, nostalgia is structural to their idealization.

One person's utopia always seems to come at the cost of another's. Maybe this is why, in the First World, we still turn longingly back to the 1960s, why the Mitchell and Tyson songs struck a chord among such a large community of listeners and became so popular, even though we know that the folk-music revolution was largely one that catered to a generation of middle-class suburban white people. Perhaps the idealism of that decade's enmeshment of popular music with social protest and calls for cultural change – and the subsequent demise of that idealism – is best summed up in the unapologetically nostalgic title of Robert Cantwell's history of 1960s folk music, *When We Were Good*.[11] It is in the goodwill of Habermas's ideal that we can get some sense of the seeds of its undoing.

While it is not at all original to say that Habermas believes in the Enlightenment project,[12] let me point out that his choice to locate the birth of a radical common space of oppositionality in seventeenth- and eighteenth-century Europe belies a valorization of particular notions of reason and rationality. The story has to start somewhere and Habermas began with the late seventeenth century. He could have made the argument that the public sphere began with the commons of Peter Linebaugh and Marcus Rediker's description in *The Many-Headed Hydra*. But he didn't start there – and not because he was only interested in the bourgeois class and paid scant attention to those below,[13] but because the ideal public sphere is tied to a particular notion of rational discourse. As Terry Eagleton notes, 'Habermas believes, perhaps too sentimentally, that what it is to live well is somehow already secretly embedded in that which makes us most distinctively [*sic*] what we are: language' (*Ideology* 408). But it is this sentimentality around the liberating possibilities of rational discourse that belies a tremendous investment in, again to put it crudely, all the good things about the Enlightenment and, with it, all of the bad. I take up the public sphere in its mistaken, that is idealized, sense in order to highlight the ways in which Habermas's historically specific claim has engineered within its construction the failure to realize its potential. Habermas's analysis actually invites historically inaccurate appropriations because it never comes to terms with its predication on a system of exploitative labour production and its internal contradictions rooted in the desire to transcend the discriminations of class (and implicitly race and gender) while consolidating a ruling class in the process. Let me deal then with the predication and the contradiction of the Habermasian public sphere in turn.

One of the most exciting promises of the Habermasian public sphere lies in the suggestion that there could be, and indeed has been, a place where rational discourse between free and equal subjects could influence the course of civil governance. One of its biggest contradictions lies in the presumption of a space of discourse that discriminates solely on the bases of intellect and reason, but which actually works to consolidate discrimination on the bases of class, race, and gender. The space of critique is ostensibly open to all who would engage in it, but its criteria for inclusion occludes its ideological function as a means of renaming the white, male, propertied subject as the reasoned subject. This is, of course, Eagleton's argument in *The Function of Criticism*, where he notes that literary criticism, born in the coffee-house of Addison and Steele and their various contemporaries, began as a critique of the absolutist state but ended up creating a bridge between the aristocracy and the emerging bourgeois class. As a result, Eagleton suggests, the public sphere is insistently classless because it needs to bring together two previously segregated classes of society, the aristocracy and the bourgeoisie. It could not be classless for those without property because, as he wryly notes, 'only those with an interest can be disinterested' (Eagleton, *Function* 16). Of course, Habermas insisted that the public sphere of his discussion was a distinctly bourgeois one and that it never promised admittance to those without property.

The acceptance of a bourgeois public sphere that is so clearly self-serving belies the promise of potentiality. In other words, it is acceptable to maintain and protect a social order that revolves around the ownership of property and literacy as long as everyone *has a chance* to own property and become literate. In his discussion of the Kantian public sphere, from which 'the idea of the bourgeois public sphere attained its theoretically fully developed form' (Habermas 102), Habermas notes that the exclusion of those without property could be rationalized given the existence of subjective possibility. For Kant, and consequently Habermas, 'the propertyless were excluded from the public of private people engaged in critical political debate without thereby violating the principle of publicity. In this sense they were not citizens at all, but persons who with talent, industry, and luck some day might be able to attain that status' (ibid. 111). Echoing the potentiality bound up in the production of the *Bildungsroman*, the loss of potentiality becomes the precondition of the public sphere's constitution. It can only ever promise the possibility of access, and yet the withdrawal of that promise is actually the defining moment of its consolidation. The public sphere is necessarily exclusive, and this is why it can only exist in a structure of nostalgia. It can only exist in the loss of potentiality.

Habermas concedes that a public sphere that is not really open to the public cannot be rightfully called a public sphere: 'The public sphere of civil society stood or fell with the principle of universal access. A public sphere from which specific groups would be *eo ipso* excluded was less than merely incomplete; it was not a public sphere at all' (85). Habermas takes up in detail Marx's critique in 'On the Jewish Question,' a critique that is precisely about the contradictions of ideal equality in the public sphere,[14] but ultimately understands Marx as calling for a socialist public sphere in which the sphere of political deliberation would be extended to those without property.[15] In that sense, Habermas's sense of the demise of the public sphere lies within its expansion and the consequential dilution of its original focus. This diagnosis betrays a nostalgia for the good old days of a limited bourgeois public sphere. For Habermas, 'the *principle* of the public sphere, that is, critical publicity, seemed to lose its strength in the measure that it expanded as a *sphere* and even undermined the private realm' (140). Although the contradictions of the public sphere are clear to Habermas, his analysis still overlooks the literate and propertied community of his ideal public sphere engaged in the pursuit of literary criticism and the production of public opinion in the interest of maintaining their own hegemony.

The issues of inclusion and exclusion are not the same as the problem of the contradiction of the constitution of the public sphere. Theoretically, the public sphere could include everyone, so long as they had attained the minimum criteria for inclusion: property ownership and literacy. However, the contradiction lies in the function of the public sphere as a means of veiling class interests under the guise of rationality. You can be a part of the public sphere as long as you are a rational subject. The unnamed condition of this rationality, as Eagleton points out, is that of being a member either of the aristocracy or the bourgeoisie. Reading the enlarged or democratized public sphere of the nineteenth century through Marx, Habermas notes that 'under such conditions, then, the public sphere was also presumed to be able to realize in earnest what it had promised from the start – the subjection of political domination, as a domination of human beings over human beings, to reason' (127–8). This valorization of reason conceals a practice of discrimination meant to unite the ruling classes. The issue then is not so much about access – who is or is not possibly a member of the public sphere – but the rationalization of domination under the guise of reason.

The feminist critique of Habermas has argued that this use of reason is deeply gendered and that the public sphere, in Marie Fleming's words, 'actually presupposes gender exclusion' (119). Building from Carole Pateman's earlier critique, which argued that the oppression of women was constitutive of the public sphere,[16] Fleming notes that, in addition to the private and the public, Habermas turns to a third sphere of discourse, the intimate sphere. Where the public was concerned with the literary and the political, and the private with the economic, the intimate sphere relied on the notion of a patriarchal conjugal family. For Fleming, Habermas's description of the bourgeois use of public reason was not 'a continuation of the salon-based, rational-critical public debate. According to Habermas, bourgeois subjectivity was structurally tied to a concept of "humanity" that originated as a feeling of 'human closeness' in the innermost sphere of the conjugal family' (122). The bourgeois use of public reason rests then on an understanding of humanity based on the patriarchal conjugal family.

While I am compelled by the feminist critique of Habermas – in a general survey of the literature, it seems that feminists have been some of the most vocal critics of the Habermasian public sphere – I have also been struck by their recuperation of the public sphere as an end product of the critique. Feminists have engaged with Habermas's notion of the public sphere, but one of the most common themes of their critique lies in the argument for the inclusion of women as members of the public sphere and of the constitutive role of women in its formation. Although Fleming's critique of reason reveals the patriarchal function of that reason, she closes with the acknowledgment that 'women's historical claims to rights to inclusion and equality' in the public sphere are, despite its patriarchal foundations, nonetheless valid (134). Similarly, Joan Landes's study of the French *salon* demonstrated the integral role that French women played in the emergence of the eighteenth-century French public sphere. In her introduction to *Feminists Read Habermas* Johanna Meehan argues that Habermas 'provides a model of subjectivity and an account of the pragmatic presuppositions of discursive validity, against which actual political and personal relations and discourses can be measured' (2). For Meehan, 'Habermas locates the emancipatory moment of modernity, which Weber and the earlier members of the Frankfurt School missed, in the increasing reflexivity made possible by advances in communicative rationality and in its institutionalization in law and in political and moral discourses' (6). Reading Habermas's discourse model against Hannah Arendt's agonistic idea of public space and the liberal tradition of that space as public dialogue, Seyla Benhabib argues that the Habermasian 'discourse model is the only one that is compatible both with the general social trends of our societies and with the emancipatory aspirations of new social movements, like the woman's movement' (95).

I have discussed the feminist recuperation of the public sphere at length because the simultaneous critique and recuperation of the Habermasian public sphere can tell us a lot about the way in which this concept has circulated since its inception in 1961. It suggests that the concept has been very useful for subordinate social groups, such as the feminist community, who want to think through the possibilities of op-positionality through discursive means. It is also revealing of the way in which this sustained critique of the Habermasian public sphere from a coherent and well-theorized intellectual position, feminism, does not want to dispense with the notion altogether. Further, feminism's recu-peration of the public sphere manages to retain a notion of a 'public' that is variegated rather than homogeneous.

One of the uses that the feminist critique has for the Habermasian public sphere lies in its hopeful proposal of a space where women can push to become fully participatory critical subjects. It provides a way of imagining a feminist community that can influence the governing of civil society while strengthening the bonds of that community through rational discourse. I cannot help but notice that the feminist critique and recuperation of Habermas is still a largely white feminist project. By 'white feminist' I do not mean only that most of the women engag-ing in critical work on the public sphere might be white, but that the recuperation of the Habermasian public sphere belies an investment in the apparatuses of whiteness – reason and rationality – which have been used again and again to oppress non-white peoples. Let me be clear: I am struck by the strength and breadth of the feminist critique and do not want to take away from the important work it has done in demand-ing a reconsideration of gender and the roles of women in the public sphere. However, I am sceptical of the recuperation of a public space that continues to be premised on assumed notions of rational discourse. Where the *Bildungsroman* consolidates 'free' or liberal subjects who can participate in the Habermasian public sphere, the women's *Bildungsro-man* consolidates a gendered subject who can participate in the feminist public sphere. Both 'Chinese Café' and 'The Night the Chinese Restaurant Burned Down' consolidate a particular vision of female subjectivity within the public sphere of the 1960s and that of second-wave feminism. However, this consolidation occurs at the expense of a radical questioning of the contradiction of the public sphere – its use of reason as a tool for occluding the uniting of the ruling classes – and the material conditions upon which it is predicated.

We know from postcolonial critique that the rationalization of domination through the valorization of reason cannot be innocent.[17] What Habermas does not highlight, and what has not yet been explored in the discussions of the Habermasian public sphere, is that the bourgeois public sphere does not emerge from nothing. There are material conditions that enable its emergence, specifically, European colonialism and imperialism. Thinking through the lens of production and materialist inquiry, one of the central predications of the public sphere of Habermas's analysis becomes apparent in the aroma of the coffee that drifts through the air of the English coffee-houses, the sweet taste of sugar that tempers the bitterness of that coffee, the tea that had become cheap enough for the bourgeoisie to make a daily drink, the *chocolat chaud* available in the salons. Would there be a Habermasian public sphere without a plantation economy to enable a class of people to take part in the leisure of coffee-house culture, without the coffee, tea, sugar, and cocoa that were the quiet witnesses to the spirited rational debate of Habermas's vision?

In *Culture and Imperialism* Edward Said makes a similar point regarding the role of Jane Austen's *Mansfield Park* in the English literary canon: 'The Bertrams could not have been possible without the slave trade, sugar, and the colonial planter class ... Having read *Mansfield Park* as part of the structure of an expanding imperialist venture, one cannot simply restore it to the canon of "great literary masterpieces" – to which it most certainly belongs – and leave it at that' (94–5). Having considered the fact that the public sphere that Habermas idealizes could not have existed without a plantation economy supporting and enabling it, we cannot put aside the foundational predication of the public sphere on an economy of labour exploitation. The dependence of the European Enlightenment on the products of colonial expansion is a point that Fernando Ortiz made more than six decades ago in his ground-breaking anthropology of tobacco and Cuban society, *Cuban Counterpoint*. As Ortiz wryly notes,

It is as though [tobacco, chocolate, coffee, and tea] had been sent to Europe from the four corners of the earth by the devil to revive Europe when 'the time came,' when that continent was ready to save the spirituality of reason from burning itself out and give the senses their due once more ... the tobacco of the Antilles, the chocolate of Mexico, the coffee of Africa, and the tea of China. Nicotine, theobromine, caffeine, and theine – these four alkaloids were put at the service of humanity to make reason more alert ... Solace for the senses and subtle nervous stimulants, all arrived at the same time to prolong the Renaissance. They were supernatural reinforcements for those of revolutionary ideas. (206–7)

Ortiz's deployment of the image of Europe in a state of drugged and drunken stupor awakened by the mass importation of coffee, tea, tobacco, and chocolate underscores the necessity of colonial trade to the 'mental jousts that initiated the modern age in Europe' (Ortiz 206). His ironic method of animating commodities and personifying continents touches at the heart of the material conditions that made possible the lively exchanges at Button's, Will's, the Rotary Club, and the thousands of other coffee-houses[18] that constituted the Habermasian ideal public sphere. In his assessment of Habermas and the public sphere, Calhoun notes that 'Habermas is well aware, of course, though it is not a heavily developed theme, that the bourgeois public sphere was oriented not just toward defense of civil society against the state but also toward the maintenance of a system of domination within civil society' (39). However, it seems as though very little attention has been paid to the predication of the bourgeois public sphere on a system of domination external to civil society: of colonialism and imperialism. The ideal public sphere could only exist in a space of capital that rests on surplus value and commodity fetishism; it is supposed to be a free exchange of ideas, but the conditions of its freedom are underwritten by the 'unfree' spaces of exploitation, colonialism, and imperialism.

**Screening Chinese: Obstructions and Projections**

While I believe there are wide-ranging implications to rethinking the public sphere in terms of its predication on a plantation economy specifically, and on colonialism and imperialism generally,[19] I want to think through what it means for the lost public sphere of the Mitchell and Tyson songs. This predication suggests that the use of the Chinese restaurant in these songs is not innocent, casual, or coincidental, but revealing. It opens up for us the suggestion of a world beyond Maggie and Carol, beyond the five-and-dime and the jukebox playing 'Unchained Melody,' a world in which the Chinese restaurant is a barbed assertion of diasporic presence in the absence of any mention of diasporic subjects. I want to look at this predication in terms of how we can understand the Chinese restaurant in these two songs. To return to some questions with which I began this chapter, why are these songs set in the Chinese restaurant at all? Why not simply in a local diner? Why is it important to name the presence of something Chinese, only to relegate the Chinese restaurant to a 1950s sentimentality that seems to have nothing to do with Chineseness or Chinese subjects?

One way to make sense of the curious use of the Chinese restaurant in both the Mitchell and Tyson songs lies in Said's argument about *Mansfield Park*. Both songs clearly identify the Chinese restaurant or Chinese café as a central element through their references to it in the title of the song. Although the restaurant seems to be little more than a setting for the narratives in the songs, there is a strange contrast between the centrality of the restaurant in the song titles and the way Mitchell and Tyson collapse the restaurant with 1950s love songs. Here, the Mitchell and Tyson songs disavow Chineseness at the same time that they name it. This double movement of naming a space of otherness and then sidestepping it at the same time is not unlike Austen's treatment of Antigua. As Said notes, what is important about the relationship of Mansfield Park (both the place and the novel) to Antigua is the contrast between the texture and detail with which Austen treats the domestic world and the presumptive silences about the external world of the plantation. We never see Sir Thomas in Antigua in the novel, but his infrequent trips there are accepted as a fact of life at Mansfield Park. Noting the connection between the Antiguan plantation in *Mansfield Park*, the West African Rubber Company in E.M. Forster's *Howards End*, and the San Tomé mine in Joseph Conrad's *Nostromo*, among others, Said argues that

> if we think ahead to these other novels, Sir Thomas's Antigua readily acquires a slightly greater density than the discrete, reticent appearances it makes in the pages of *Mansfield Park*. And already our reading of the novel begins to open up at those points where ironically Austen was most economical and her critics most (dare one say it?) negligent. Her 'Antigua' is therefore not just as a slight but a definite way of marking the outer limits of what [Eric] Williams calls domestic improvements, or a quick allusion to the mercantile venturesomeness of acquiring overseas dominions as a source for local fortunes, or one reference among many attesting to a historical sensibility suffused not just with manners and courtesies but with

contests of ideas, struggles with Napoleonic France, awareness of seismic economic and social change during a revolutionary period in world history. (93–4)

It is precisely in the lack of reference, in the 'very odd combination of casualness and stress [that] Austen reveals herself to be *assuming* (just as Fanny assumes, in both senses of the word) the importance of an empire to the situation at home' (Said 89). Similarly, the lack of reference to Chineseness in the Mitchell and Tyson songs assumes the significance of Chineseness to these songs' consolidation of a white, female liberal subjectivity.

While Said's analysis identifies Austen's references to Antigua as revealing of the centrality of empire to domestic British life, let me suggest that Mitchell's and Tyson's references to the Chinese restaurant reveal the function of Chineseness in late-twentieth-century liberal subjectivity. The relationship is, in many ways, somewhat more obscure than that of Austen and Empire, but it is so because one of the functions of the Chinese restaurant in these songs is precisely to obscure the predications of the lost space of ideal community in the songs, the material conditions which enable its emergence as an ideal.

The Chinese restaurant also functions as a site of projection, a backdrop where Mitchell and Tyson can impose a *Bildung* narrative of their development as young artists onto the empty canvas of the restaurant. I suggest that the Chinese restaurant, and through it the presence of Chineseness, functions as a screen for white liberal subjectivity in both senses of the word – first, in the sense of screening out the unpleasantness of past exploitations and, second, as a screen for the projection of a coherent white identity. As Moretti recognizes, the work of the *Bildung* narrative lies in a commitment to 'a present that is "individualized," and is the constant work of *reorganization* of what has taken place, as well as a *projection* of what is to come' (44, my emphasis). In this work of reconfiguring the past and projecting the hope of consolidated subjectivity, the Chinese restaurant is crucially situated both as a useful obstruction and as a site of projection.

As a screening out of an unpleasant and unmentionable past, Mitchell and Tyson use the Chinese restaurant as a way of separating the past from the present. As I noted earlier, in these songs the restaurant *is* the space of 1950s sentimentality; by association, it becomes equivalent to 'Unchained Melody' and 'Canadian Sunset.' The collapsing of the space of the Chinese restaurant with that of a particular time period serves to

delineate specific epochs in the songs. The songs evoke two time periods, the time before the Chinese restaurant burned down (before Mitchell and Tyson left their lives of dreaming on dimes behind) and the time
after (the 1960s, the explosion and revival of folk music, and Mitchell
and Tyson's rise to folk-diva stardom).

In the sense that the memory of the Chinese restaurant functions as a
screen that capriciously separates girlhood from womanhood, the past
from the present, the use of the restaurant in these songs evokes Freud's
notion of the screen memory as working to suppress the emergence of
another memory. In 'Screen Memories,' Freud observes,

> Whenever in a memory the subject himself appears in this way as an object
> among other objects this contrast between the acting and the recollecting
> ego may be taken as evidence that the original impression has been worked
> over. It looks as though a memory-trace from childhood had here been
> translated back into a plastic and visual form at a later date – the date of the
> memory's arousal. But no reproduction of the original impression has ever
> entered the subject's consciousness. (321)

Mitchell's and Tyson's recollecting of themselves as 'objects among other
objects,' whereby they see themselves not from the perspective of young
women, but as an outsider would see them, suggests the way in which
this memory of girlhood, to echo Freud again, 'has been worked over.'
However, the screen memory does not block out the past per se, but the
predications that enable the consolidating narrative of loss, the *Bildung*
narrative.

The public sphere is predicated on, and indebted to, empire and colonial expansion. As I have argued, exploitative labour relations enable
the object of loss, the public sphere, in both songs. Circumventing this
predication, the public sphere can exist only within a structure of nostalgia, a nostalgia that, as Susan Stewart proposes, is narratological. It is not
just that the public sphere can exist only as a form of the past remembered in the present, but that this process of remembering is a highly
crafted narrative – it has been worked over. These narratives of loss that,
as we know from Moretti's work on the *Bildungsroman*, consolidate liberal
subjectivity, are indebted to the work of empire. As *Bildung* narratives,
the Mitchell and Tyson songs are materially indebted to the exploitation
of racialized labour, not just in the sense that there would not be Chinese restaurants in towns such as Fort Macleod and Chatham (Mitchell
and Tyson's respective hometowns) were it not for the vast importation

of Chinese labour during the height of railway-building (read empire-building) activity, but also in the sense that there would be no idealized object of loss, the public sphere, without surplus value produced by exploited labour.

Mitchell's acknowledgment of the exploitation of First Nations land in the second verse of the song diverts attention away from her own complicity in these exploitations, shifting the blame to the '[s]hort-sighted businessmen' who, to cite another song of Mitchell's, 'paved paradise and put up a parking lot' ('Big Yellow Taxi'). The nostalgic narrative of the loss of the public sphere consolidates the *Bildung* narrative. The portrait of Joni Mitchell or Sylvia Tyson as young women about to become artists is the story of what might have been, not what is. They are narratives that rest on the predications of the modal while professing to be narratives of a simple past. That is, under the guise of straightforward temporal narratives of maturation and development, these narratives depend upon the potentiality of publicity, of the unfulfilled and lost public sphere. Mitchell and Tyson put the Chinese restaurant to use as a screen against the predications of the modal in the aspiration towards the certainties of a singular march through personal history.

Not only do both songs screen out the predications of potentiality, they also screen out the experience of being looked on. The screen memory's positioning of the recollecting subject as an 'object among other objects' also reveals the necessity of screening out the memory of being the object of the gaze of the unreadable other, the 'inscrutable' Chinese gaze. 'Contrary to the model of Western hegemony in which the colonizer is seen as a primary, active "gaze" subjugating the native as passive "object,"' Rey Chow argues that 'it is actually the colonizer who feels looked at by the native's gaze. This gaze, which is neither a threat nor a retaliation, makes the colonizer "conscious" of himself, leading to his need to turn this gaze around and look at himself, henceforth "reflected" in the native-object' (*Writing* 51). That reflection becomes even clearer in the emptying out of the other. Mitchell's recognition of First Nations land claims and the 'paradise' that was paved for a parking lot belies a tendency to rhapsodize conveniently empty spaces. In both the Mitchell and Tyson songs, Chineseness is no longer inscrutable but is evacuated.

Let me close by suggesting how this attempt to reduce the Chinese restaurant to a mere backdrop does not succeed. Reading the attempt to relegate the Chinese restaurant to the background – to suggest that it is little more than a convenient and coincidental backdrop (as both these songs do in their evocation of the restaurant, only to collapse it with the space of 1950s sentimentality) – through the lens of postmodern cultural geography, we can see that space is not static. As we know from Henri Lefebvre, it is a mistake to view space as merely a backdrop for the drama of human events. In *The Production of Space*, Lefebvre argues that the understanding of space as a mere backdrop to the events of human history occludes the ideological implications of the use of space in the production of history. Noting that most of the major wars in history, including the work of empire, suppress an understanding of space as socially produced in favour of a historicist narrative of conquest and development, Lefebvre suggests:

> The space of capitalist accumulation thus gradually came to life, and began to be fitted out. This process of animation is admiringly referred to as history, and its motor sought in all kinds of factors: dynastic interests, ideologies, the ambitions of the mighty, the formation of nation states, demographic pressures, and so on. This is the road to a ceaseless analysing of, and searching for, dates and chains of events. (275)

In order to resist the abstraction of space from the social relations that produce and are produced by space, we need to reanimate the spatial. Doreen Massey proposes that we accomplish this by understanding space as imbricated with time: 'The point here however is not to argue for an upgrading of the status of space within the terms of the old dualism (a project which is arguably inherently difficult anyway, given the terms of that dualism), but to argue that what must be overcome is the very formulation of space/time in terms of this kind of dichotomy' (260). Taking up space as dynamic offers one way of reading the Chinese restaurant in the Mitchell and Tyson songs in terms of its productivity, in terms of the way it produces and shapes the narratives of personal history in these songs. Rather than being a mute and static backdrop to the events of these songs, the Chinese restaurant is a productive space of social relations. Its Chineseness cannot be excised from the space of white memory. I suggest that the presence of the Chinese restaurant in these songs asserts a diasporic spatiality that cannot be suppressed and that illuminates the ways in which diasporic space both produces social relations and is shaped by them. In the next chapter, I will analyse the workings of diasporic spatiality.

The suppression of Chineseness in the Mitchell and Tyson songs draws attention to the inconsistencies of their representation. Why is it important to name Chineseness, as both the Mitchell and Tyson songs do? As

I have discussed, it is not just that Chineseness itself is integral to white liberal subjectivity, but that the presence of Chineseness in these projects is a fissure that opens up for us the ways in which the colonial predications of liberal white subjectivity are mediated by a structure of nostalgia.

While this chapter has explored two songs in particular, the structure of white nostalgia is not unique to Mitchell and Tyson. Rather, the Mitchell and Tyson songs are symptomatic of more generalized longings in the dominant culture for public space of commonality and community. This public sphere, as the object of white nostalgia's longing, is enabled by otherness at the same time that it needs to be evacuated of that otherness. I am not saying that white nostalgia is unique to white people, but that it is a form of nostalgia that uses otherness as a screen. It is not simply that Joni Mitchell and Sylvia Tyson are indiscriminately nostalgic white liberals. Part of my interest in taking up their music and the public sphere lies in my sense of a broader investment that we have in these projects. As I was writing about Habermas's public sphere, I was struck by how much of our contemporary society continues to be structured around this notion of a free space of intellectual exchange. And clearly, in all kinds of ways, the role that musicians such as Mitchell and Tyson have in raising issues of social conscience throughout their careers has fortified the relationship between music and popular social protest. A responsible critique cannot just look for 'bad guys.' As Gayatri Spivak makes clear at the end of her discussion of Kant, 'although Shakespeare was great, we cannot merely continue to act out the part of Caliban. One task of deconstruction might be a persistent attempt to displace the reversal, to show the complicity between native hegemony and the axiomatics of imperialism' (*A Critique* 37). This displacement of the reversal might be the task not only of deconstruction, but also of critical projects concerned with the ideal spaces of community, the longing for averted potentialities. In dealing with our post-Enlightenment legacies, we must also come to terms with our complicity in order to see through the comfortable screens of nostalgic representation. However, not all nostalgias are the same. As I will discuss in my final chapter, it is also necessary to recuperate nostalgia from the forbidding strictures of sentimentality. But let me turn first to the problem of imagining diasporic space and conceiving diasporic spatiality. As the next chapter will show, the small town Chinese restaurant is, despite the challenges of displacement that have characterized diasporic culture, a testament to the power of diaspora to be a force of emplacement.

# Chapter Four

# Diasporic Counterpublics: The Chinese Restaurant as Institution and Installation

You walk in and consider sitting down at one of the orange Naughahyde booths, but then the shiny counter catches your eye. You will see a row of stools in front of it. Behind the counter, there is an old cash register, shelves neatly stacked with an assortment of teas and candy bars. The coffee machine is plugged in. A mixture of elaborate paper lantern–style lights and bright fluorescent tubes illuminates the space. There is a glass jar filled with fortune-cookie fortunes. Everything feels a bit too familiar, right but not quite right. You are not sure if you should sit down. Welcome to one of Karen Tam's Gold Mountain Restaurants (see figures 7a and 7b).

These restaurants are a series of installations that Tam has done from 2002 to the present. So far, she has installed more than ten of them across Canada. Even though some of them have been in art spaces in major urban centres such as Centre A in Vancouver and the MAI in Montreal, most of the Gold Mountain Restaurants have been in small cities and towns across the country. She has shown at the Alternator Gallery in Kamloops, British Columbia, the Southern Alberta Art Gallery in Lethbridge, the Forest City Gallery in London, Ontario, and so on. Each of the installations is different. Each has its own name, its own furniture and signs and menus. Each one is also similar despite, and perhaps because of, their differences. They bear a resemblance to each other. They are recognizable as a particular kind of restaurant. They are not just Chinese restaurants, but a specific genre of Chinese restaurant characterized precisely by their lack of cosmopolitanism. Describing how unhappy his father had been at a fancy Toronto dim sum restaurant, the *Toronto Star*'s Peter Goddard notes that 'he would have felt utterly at home in the Shangri-La Café, Karen Tam's installation at YYZ Artists' Outlet, which

7a  'Jardin Chow Chow Garden: A Division of Gold Mountain Restaurant.' Karen Tam. As installed at Expression's ORANGE event 'Como Como,' Saint-Hyacinthe, Québec, 2006. 15 × 8.5 × 4.3 m / 49 × 28 × 14 ft.

7b  'Shangri-la Café: A Division of Gold Mountain Restaurant.' Karen Tam. As installed at *YYZ* Artists' Outlet, Toronto, Ontario. 2006. 9.75 × 7.62 × 3.65 m / 32 × 25 × 12 feet

does nothing less than recreate the soul of every down-to-earth, old-style mom-and-pop Chinese restaurant across the country' (H7). Tam's restaurants tap right into the curious and idiosyncratic jumble of things that make the small town Chinese restaurant what it is. In the process of assembling the restaurant as an art installation, an art practice that, as Goddard notes, reaches back to Ed Kienholz's critique of everyday culture's disregard for the brutalities of the Vietnam War through *The Beanery* in 1965 in West Hollywood,[1] Tam also opens up the question of the restaurant as a public space of critique.

While I have focused on the contradictions inherent to the public sphere in the previous chapter, I do believe that the Chinese restaurant can function as a genuinely public space of interaction, dialogue, and connection. I want to consider precisely this possibility by examining Karen Tam's restaurant installations. Two of the central arguments of this book are, first, that Chinese diasporic culture emerges through interaction and, second, that old and new diasporas are crucially constitutive of each other. In this chapter, I argue that Tam's installations illuminate precisely both the ways in which interaction between and across cultural divides produces diasporic culture and the powerful presence of the old diaspora within the spaces of the new. In so doing, in transforming this institution of small town life into an installation within the cosmopolitan spaces of contemporary art, she animates the Chinese restaurant as a diasporic counterpublic.

As Michael Warner understands, it is not the mimetic but rather the transformative function of a counterpublic that distinguishes it from the dominant public culture: 'Counterpublics are spaces of circulation in which it is hoped that the poesis of scene making will be transformative, not replicative merely' (122). In the spirit of Warner's counterpublic, Tam does not simply recreate restaurants. She makes a space, albeit a temporary, contingent, and fragile one, that highlights the mutually transformative relations between communities, between cooks and customers, between Chinese and non-Chinese. In that the Chinese restaurant is not a purely oppositional space, Warner's notion of a counterpublic must be delineated from Nancy Fraser's idea of a subaltern counterpublic. He notes that 'Fraser's description of what counterpublics do – "formulate oppositional interpretations of their identities, interests, and needs" – sounds like the classically Habermasian description of rational-critical publics, with the word "oppositional" inserted' (118). Instead, Warner argues that 'counterpublics are "counter" to the extent that they try to supply different ways of imagining stranger sociability and its reflexivity; as publics, they remain oriented to stranger circulation in a way that is not just strategic but constitutive of membership and its affects' (121–2). Warner's recognition that counterpublics are more than subaltern groups with an agenda, or what he calls a 'reform program,' is especially salient to thinking about how diasporic communities are distinct publics that engage with dominant culture through specific modes of address that may or may not always be heard or understood (119). Diasporas do not always, and usually do not, have coherent political or even social agendas, but they nevertheless continue to make spaces in which there is a sense of a community beyond that of the diasporas themselves. Disparate and dispersed, small town Chinese restaurants create a space that is nonetheless constitutive of a recognizable public that persists in addressing strangers and the strangeness of dominant culture through an invitation to sit down, to open up the menu, to consume something familiar and different. Tam's installations distil this function of the restaurant and re-presents it to her audience as yet another space of 'stranger circulation' (Warner 122).

It is crucial that counterpublics remain neither hermetically insulated from larger, dominant public culture nor infinitely open to the incursions of that culture. The tension produced by the closed and yet open space of address is, at least in part, indicative of a counterpublic. Counterpublics do not merely speak to and among themselves. Nor are they addressing just any stranger. But there is always an outward address that forges a relation among strangers:

> Perhaps nothing demonstrates the importance of discursive publics in the modern social imaginary more than this – that even the counterpublics that challenge modernity's social hierarchy of faculties do so by projecting the space of discursive circulation among strangers as a social entity and in doing so fashion their own subjectivities around the requirements of public circulation and stranger sociability. (Warner 121)

Warner offers the example of a queer public as such a counterpublic. A diaspora might be another. While there are important differences between a queer public and a diasporic one, the latter is also nonetheless a public that is acutely aware of the tension of its existence in relation to a larger, dominant public. The focus on the question of power and dominance makes Warner's conception of the counterpublic especially useful for thinking about diasporas. He understands that the public sphere is not simply a strategy of domination through exclusion of those who are not white, propertied, and male. Merely extending membership to women, non-white people, people who do not own land, and so on, is not necessarily the way to make the public sphere more public. For Warner, 'the projection of a public is a new, creative, and distinctively modern mode of power' (108). Warner emphasizes they ways in which counterpublic life is an engagement with relations of power. This emphasis is particularly salient in understanding the formation of diasporic subjects and communities. As I have argued elsewhere, 'Diasporas are not just there. They are not simply collections of people, communities of scattered individuals bound by some shared history, race or religion ... Rather, they have a relation to power. They emerge in relation to power' ('Turn' 15). Diasporic counterpublics, I suggest, recognize the distinctly modern mode of power embodied in projection of a public even as they remain acutely aware of their subordinate status. The point is not for them to take over, but for them to articulate a distinct space of relation despite the horizons marked out by a dominant public culture.

In suggesting that the Chinese restaurant is a diasporic counterpublic space, I am distinguishing the idea of a diasporic community from that of a diasporic counterpublic. A counterpublic is a space of address. It is the creation of a world in which relations of power are always present but are also always under negotiation. It is a space that calls out to other members of the diasporic community through a mutually recognizable form of address – Chinese food – and invites the transformations of subjectivity that come out of the requirements of public circulation. The Chineseness of the Chinese food is always under question at these restaurants but it is this very uncertainty, the persistence of it, that is so productive of diasporic counterpublic culture. Chineseness in diaspora is not smugly certain of its authenticity, of its connection to some ancestral or originary root. That is a good thing. Small town Chinese restaurants demand what amounts to the experience of a perpetual double take. Is this Chinese or is it not? Isn't it just like that one in the other town, or is it not? Karen Tam's installations capture this experience and recreate it. Is this a restaurant, or is it not?

Tam's installations create a public space within a public space. She produces a restaurant inside an art gallery. Through this act of doubled publicness, she shows her audience how difficult it is to cross the divide across the shiny space of the arborite counter, through the swinging doors. It takes more than just sitting as a customer in the restaurant to fully experience its publicness. As the records of that experience in the Joni Mitchell and Sylvia Tyson songs of the previous chapter show,

.memorializing the Chinese restaurant from only one side of the counter risks occluding the significant contributions of the activities on the other side – in the kitchen, behind the cash register, at the coffee machine, spaces where one is more likely to be standing than sitting. It is not that the restaurant isn't a public sphere, but that its publicness is a mediated one. To get to the Chinese restaurant's true publicness, Tam suggests, one must simultaneously step away from and move further into the space of the restaurant. Her installations invite their audiences to do that. By taking the restaurant out of the restaurant and installing it into the space of the gallery, she allows her audience to step away from it even as they are asked to enter further into the restaurant by inviting them behind the counter to examine the cash register and, through the swinging doors, into the kitchen, even though they may not feel as though they should be there. Days Lee points out in a catalogue essay for *Gold Mountain Restaurant*, that Tam 'has noticed that people who have worked in a restaurant tend to go behind the counter to examine the cash register, the dishes, and the coffee machine. Then, they walk through the swinging doors to inspect the kitchen where often a stove, a deep fryer, and even a sink are installed. However, the non-Chinese are hesitant to explore these spaces' (40). As she tells Lee, she asks people who may have only experienced the restaurant as customers to consider 'what life was like inside' (40).

But Tam's installations are not simply mimetic creations with a pedagogical function. They pose questions rather than answer them. Françoise Belu argues that 'through her mimetic *mis en abyme*, Karen Tam temporarily mystifies viewers in order to show them, first of all, that the Chinese restaurants of North America are themselves mystifications' (16). These are mystifications with a function. They create the spaces of interaction and connection that produce diasporic culture. The installations extend this function by bringing together unlikely communities and provoking conversation across the space of the counter. As the documentation of the *Gold Mountain Restaurants* project on her website attests, Tam's installations draw a wide range of attendees into one space. People who had little interest in the abstractions of contemporary art are suddenly wandering in and out of her installations. Old-timer Chinese restaurant owners sit at a bench at the doorway to the restaurant. In a challenge to the idea of museums and galleries as sacrosanct spaces, school kids are eating their lunches there. Even the curators are doing it. In my own experience of attending one of her openings, I found that I was as likely to chat with a family member of Tam's or a former restaurant owner as with an arts administrator, artist, or curator. It is not just that Tam democratizes the space of the contemporary art gallery. It is also, and more importantly, that she makes the public space of the gallery more public by making it more private.

In this move to offer a kind of privacy within a public space, Tam reclaims what Lauren Berlant calls 'the intimate public sphere' (5). Writing of the way in which Reaganism made private subjects such as sex and family into a platform for public action, Berlant argues that 'the intimate public sphere of the U.S. present renders citizenship as a condition of social membership produced by personal acts and values, especially acts originating in or directed toward the family sphere' (5). Even though Berlant's critique shines a light on the ways in which conservative politics marshalled intimacy for its own agenda by making private acts and values a test of nationalism and patriotism – to the point where, decades after Reagan, the notion of 'family values' still has resonance as a public issue in the United States and Canada – there are also good reasons for wanting to wrest the private and the intimate back from conservative politics. For example, Kathleen Stewart's use of the idea of an 'intimate public' in her tracking of 'ordinary affect' alludes to a possibility of connection between strangers at a profoundly private level (39). Stewart writes of a sign taped to the railing of a bridge in Austin, Texas. Stewart describes it:

> At the top of the sign, two names, ANGELA AND JERRY, are slashed through with big black Xs. Below the names, the sign reads: RELATION-SHIP DESTROYED WITH MALICE, BY FEDERAL AGENTS & A.P.D. [Austin Police Department] FOR BELIEFS GUARANTEED UNDER U.S. CONSTITUTIONAL BILL OF RIGHTS. I MISS YOU ANGELA, JESSICA, & FURRY DOG REEF. It's signed ALWAYS, JERRY. Below the signature, the words YANKEE GIRL are encased in a pierced heart and the words PLEASE COME BACK are highlighted with a thick black border. (38)

This sign is a message, an open letter, to the world full of rage against the Austin Police Department and intense love for someone who had been taken away. For Stewart, that sign, like 'the graffiti written on train trestles, or ... the signs the homeless hold on the side of the road' is an 'ordinary affect in the textured, roughened surface of the everyday. It permeates politics of all kinds with the demand that some kind of intimate public of onlookers recognize something in a space of shared impact. If only for a minute' (39). Stewart uses Berlant's concept and recuperates intimacy in the public sphere from conservatism and suggests that it can be, even if fragile and temporary, a way of injecting the private into the public as a demand for a recognition, for justice, for something shared. Where the intimate public sphere of right-wing politics, as Berlant shows, makes the intimate a basis for eliminating difference as a condition of entry into public life (that is, if you have the right family values you are the kind of citizen who will matter), Stewart suggests that the intimate can also be the basis of insisting upon difference as a fact of public life. Private rage, private tragedies, private losses are, in Stewart's conception of an intimate public, the very material that binds a public together. While Tam's installations of Chinese restaurants more broadly are far less specific than the roadside signs Stewarts reads, they do suggest that the idiosyncrasies of private experience, the differences these experiences assert, have a place in making public culture.

The restaurant installations are intensely private by all kinds of measures. First, Tam is not reticent about her own personal, private experience with Chinese restaurants. In interviews, and throughout the material for her catalogue, she talks about growing up with the restaurant she considers her 'second home,' the Restaurant aux sept bonheurs in east Montreal (Lee 39). It was her attempt to document her parent's restaurant when they decided to sell it that was the catalyst for what would eventually become the *Gold Mountain Restaurant* project. In some ways, you could say that Tam has been recreating her parents' restaurant over and over and over again as a project of private memorialization. Tam's installations are also private in the ways in which they invite interactions with the art that are highly personal. 'Visitors to her installation,' Belu notes, 'can no longer confine themselves to looking; they are plunged instead into another world in which they must dwell' (17). They have to enter into the installation, confront the invitation to sit down, to go past the swinging doors into the kitchen. Further, the installations shy away from grand statements about art, or race, or society. 'Karen Tam practises a veritable social art that is diametrically opposed to general statements about society' (ibid.). In this movement away from the general, Tam's installations demand a more intimate, more specific social engagement. Finally, the restaurant installations also transform the public space of the gallery into the privatized space of a commercial restaurant. This transformation highlights one of the contradictions of public spaces such as art galleries: despite their public status, they often function like private spaces in that their claims to high culture limit those who might enter. On the other hand, Chinese restaurants, despite being private businesses, have often functioned as public gathering spaces.

This tension between public and private that runs throughout the installations makes possible a set of dialogues and interactions that are, according to Warner, one of the central characteristics of publics and counterpublics. He argues that public speech must be simultaneously personal and impersonal: 'Public speech can have great urgency and intimate import. Yet we know that it was addressed not exactly to us but to the stranger we were until the moment we happened to be addressed by it ... To inhabit a public discourse is to perform this transition continually, and to some extent it remains present to consciousness ... It gives a general social relevance to private thought and life' (77). Tam's installations create this effect of inhabiting the very public space of the restaurant while demanding a very private series of reflections. Visitors to Tam's installations shuttle constantly between the public address of the art and its invitations to the personal and the private. As Belu observes of these restaurants where no food is served:

> The practical goal – eating – that makes a person go to a restaurant is omitted here: no meals are served, and viewers logically come to ask themselves questions about the context. For it is up to them to get to 'the very marrow' by asking themselves questions about their relationships with others and, specifically, with those others who are the most different from themselves, the foreigners. Social art, which can operate only through singularity, is always participatory. (17)

In that they are hyper-real recreation of the restaurant as a public space, Tam's installations make the gallery more public by delving into the tension between publicity and privacy that marks the constitution of the public sphere. In so doing, these installations insist upon a series of interactions and connections that form a diasporic counterpublic.

It is not just the installations themselves that perform this function of interaction and connection, but also the process Tam engages in for each and every installation. *Gold Mountain Restaurant* is not a travelling exhibition in the traditional sense. Tam does not pack up the 'restaurant' into boxes after each show. It is not simply crated and then shipped to the next gallery. On the contrary, when each installation is taken down, the contents return to their various owners in the local community. Tam relies upon the generosity and the idiosyncratic possibilities of the objects that she finds within each host community in order to construct her installations. Each one is built to suit the specific space in which it will be housed. Each has its own specificity from the name to the furniture to the features that can be found. Some might have a counter. Some might have a deep fryer. Some might have booths. Some might not. They all share in the same process of construction and installation wherein Tam arrives at each site and enlists the help of local (sometimes retired) restaurant owners, artists, and random passers-by. As Sylvie Lachance, general and artistic director of one of the installation sites, in Montreal, arts interculturels, or MAI, observes:

> Due to the nature of the project, while *Gold Mountain Restaurant* was being set up, MAI became a veritable construction site, in addition to being the site of an exceptional encounter between the artist's immediate family and her extended family (Montreal's Chinese restaurant owners), the MAI team, the members of its visual arts selection committee, numerous Montreal visual artists and curators, and a striking number of curious passers-by who sometimes seemed confused and surprised to see MAI 'change hats' and go into something more profitable! A number of passers-by couldn't resist the urge to come up to the gallery while the installation was going up, to offer the artist their own 'relics' as souvenirs of their Chinese restaurant experiences. (6)

Lachance's recollection of Tam's installation going up indicates the ways in which Tam relies upon the involvement of a range of people from diverse communities. It echoes my own memory of the installation of the London, Ontario, version of the Gold Mountain Restaurant, the Old Silver Moon Restaurant installed in the Forest City Gallery in 2006. I remember feeling a distinct sense of panic (which Tam obviously didn't share) when she outlined her process and asked me if I knew of people who might have some old signs, chairs and tables, lights, props, and so on. Of course, there are such things in every town. But what if she couldn't find them in time? What if people wouldn't lend their things out? Of course, the artist knew better. Her installations come together every time, and every time they draw together a range of unlikely conspirators in the project of making contemporary art.

Tam's process, from the ways in which she assembles each restaurant installation to the range of spaces that her installations have migrated out into, echoes that of the development of the restaurants themselves. Chinese restaurateurs find themselves scattered across the country. They must construct a restaurant out of the materials they find. They rely upon a mixture of an existing network of business associations and local passers-by. Even though the installations resemble the restaurants, after stepping into one of Tam's restaurants, one could just as easily say that the restaurants resemble art installations. Tam draws a connection between the space of the contemporary art gallery and the space of the Chinese restaurant.

Inserting an 'old' space, the small town Chinese restaurant, into the 'new' space of the contemporary art gallery, Tam's Gold Mountain Restaurants also signal the constitutive relationship between old and new diasporic cultures. As I note at the beginning of this book, there is a crucial relationship between what Vijay Mishra and Gayatri Spivak refer to as the old diasporas of indenture and slavery and the new diasporas made up of middle- and upper-class transnational migrants who, in the case of Chinese diaspora discussions, have been documented by Aihwa Ong as the flexible citizens of the late twentieth and early twenty-first centuries.[2] I agree with Mishra that these categories of old and new are not simply heuristic devices. Rather, they usefully draw 'attention to the complex procedures by which diasporas negotiate their perceived moment of trauma and how, in the artistic domain, the trauma works itself out' ('Diasporic' 442). Throughout her installations, Tam quietly highlights the use of Chinese workers in the building of the Canadian national railway, the head tax, and legal exclusion through the use of playful insertions in the text of the 'menus' that accompany her restaurants, in the fortune cookie slips she gives away, and even on the paper towels that are part of the exhibit. As Belu observes,

> Anyone who reads the message that Karen Tam has inserted into one of the fortune cookies on exhibit – *One Chinaman died for every mile of track laid* – will readily grasp that keeping up morale was a necessity for these workers, who were contemptuously referred to as 'coolies' ... or 'choo-choos.' They will also understand that the image of a railway printed on a paper towel inscribed with the motto *We only roll between East and West* is not merely there for decoration, but fulfils a duty to remember. (16)

Tam's fortune cookies and paper towels are not only injunctions to remember the cruelty of the history of the exploitation of Chinese workers, but also, as Mishra suggests, a way of working out a moment of trauma in the diaspora through the domain of contemporary art. Tam injects the memory and the trauma of the old Chinese diaspora into the shiny newness of the space of the contemporary art gallery. In Tam's Gold Mountain Restaurants, the coevality of the old and new diaspora is not simply an idea, but an actual spatial manifestation. Further, Tam indicates that this temporary occupation of the art gallery by her restaurant is about the relationship not only between the old and the new, but also between the private and the public.

By placing a private business into a public art gallery, she highlights the contradictions and tensions that illuminate how Chinese restaurants function as a counterpublic space. 'Counterpublics are publics too' (Warner 113). The restaurants are public spheres that cannot fully claim to be public in the way that an art gallery can. They run counter to it not only in that they are private businesses, or in that they are racially and ethnically marked, or even in that they are more about food and eating than the kinds of conversation and rational dialogue that defines the Habermasian public sphere; but also in that they 'cannot afford that confidence' (Warner 110). Referring to an instance where a group calling themselves the She-Romps had invited the Spectator himself to attend one of their saucy gatherings, Warner observes the 'uneasy mix of mocking humour, male fear, and urbane scandal ... required for [the Spectator's] own confidence in a public composed of strangers' (110). Warner's identification of the difference between the counterpublic of the She-Romps and that of the world the Spectator inhabits as being not so much a question of gender or even clubbiness, but rather one of confidence, is richly precise. What differentiates the counterpublic from the public is not an identity category or even necessarily the question of membership more broadly. It is the question of a having a certain kind of confidence – confidence enough to claim to generality even when that generality is itself exclusive; confidence enough to take for granted that the forms of sociability practised in that space extend beyond its walls; confidence enough to assume that strangers who may not yet have entered that space may be addressed as members of the public nonetheless. Instead of hiding this lack of confidence, Tam's installations put it on display and illuminate the workings of a counterpublic space by exploiting an existing public space. She shows her audience how the Chinese restaurant is a public space where there is always an awareness of the limits of its publicness.

These limits to publicness raise the question of membership. Who, after all, is a member of the diasporic counterpublic that I am describing? This question of membership circles back to one of the central questions of diaspora scholarship: Who is diasporic? The debates over the constitution of diasporas, and over the definition of diaspora, have largely been about the problem of membership and belonging. Indeed, the flourishing of diaspora as a term for describing various populations of people has lead to sometimes heated discussions over the unseemly flexibility of the term. If, the disparagers of diaspora's capaciousness ask, everyone can be diasporic, what is left to distinguish the diasporic from the non-diasporic? As Stéphane Dufoix observes in his review of the question:

For some people, this flexibility is a sign of migration's diversity. For others, it is a betrayal of the word's meaning. In the first case, 'diaspora' means nothing more than the idea of displacement and the maintenance of a connection with a real or imagined homeland. In the second, the only real question is, Does this population deserve the name 'diaspora'? I have chosen not to choose between these two options – catchall or *private club*. Instead, I consider both extremes by showing that they belong to the history of the word. (2, emphasis mine)

It is this idea that diasporas might function as a kind of private club with its own codes of entry and membership that brings me to thinking about the relationship between diasporas and counterpublics. Where the classic Habermasian bourgeois public sphere functioned in many ways like a private club with very specific criteria for membership, its claim to publicness relied upon an anxious obscuring of those criteria. That is, even though it was very self-consciously a gathering of literate, propertied, white men, it found itself in a situation where those very features could not be acknowledged. Warner characterizes this situation as one of negativity and abstraction, where the bodily features that were specific to the subject of the bourgeois public sphere had to be negated and a utopia of self-abstraction put into place. In order for the literate, propertied, white man to claim universality, he must rid himself of those positive attributes that give him the privilege of the claim to self-abstraction.

Public discourse from the beginning offered a utopian self-abstraction, but in ways that left a residue of unrecuperated particularity, both for its privileged subjects and for those it minoritized. Its privileged subjects, abstracted from the very body features that gave them the privilege of that abstraction, found themselves in a relation of bad faith with their own positivity. To acknowledge their positivity would be to surrender their privilege, as, for example, to acknowledge the objectivity of the male body would be to feminize it. (168)

The problem for the public sphere is that it has specific membership criteria but is ostensibly open to everyone. This problem illuminates the issue of diasporic membership through contradistinction. Diasporas seem to function as the bourgeois public sphere's precise opposite. They have unspecific membership criteria (Is one diasporic only in the first generation of displacement? Does it matter whether the cause of dispersion was voluntary or involuntary? How closely must the relationship to the 'home' or 'origin' country be maintained for the subject of diaspora to still be diasporic?), but do not want everyone to be able to join. Diasporas appear to be defined by an excess of particularity without the limits that this excess should offer. Diasporas are not private clubs. Nor can they afford to shed their specificity.

And yet, this debate over membership forgets that diasporic culture does not emerge in isolation. Not unlike Tam's installations, diasporic culture is not something that can be packed in a suitcase before dispersion and then unpacked and installed into the space of arrival. It is not a self-evident object. It is, as I have been arguing in this book, forged out of the connections and interactions between diasporic and non-diasporic communities. Thus, the question of membership in diasporas is also a question of how diasporas project into the dominant public. Who is diasporic is as much a question of the spaces of origin as it is one of the spaces of arrival. Without arrival, and the kinds of negotiations and dialogues that are inherent to the process of arriving and figuring out how to fit in, how to survive, how to sustain some sense of cultural difference, there is also no diaspora. To return then to my earlier question – Who is a member of the diasporic counterpublic? – I suggest that it is made up not of the people who claim to be diasporic, but of the collections of people, diasporic and non-diasporic, who actively engage in the interactive and dynamic processes of the forging diasporic culture. It is not the Chinese restaurant workers who make up this counterpublic. It is the diners and the cooks who together constitute the diasporic counterpublic.

If, as Dufoix notes of Rogers Brubacker and Phil Cohen, some critics worry over the dilution of the idea of diaspora into a kind of definitional meaninglessness, then it might seem particularly worrying to claim that a diasporic counterpublic is made up of diasporic and non-diasporic members (33). Certainly Nancy Fraser's notion of a feminist counterpublic sphere and Thomas Holt's notion of a black counterpublic sphere would suggest that counterpublics are made up of very specific, identifiable groups. Fraser criticizes the use of the bourgeois public sphere as a normative ideal and poses the possibility of a multiplicity of competing and alternative public spheres, suggesting that there are 'subaltern counterpublics' which

> are parallel discursive arenas where members of subordinated social groups invent and circulate counterdiscourses to formulate oppositional interpretations of their identities, interests, and needs. Perhaps the most striking example is the late-twentieth-century U.S. feminist subaltern counterpublic,

with its variegated array of journals, bookstores, publishing companies, film and video distribution networks, lecture series, research centers, academic programs, conferences, conventions, festivals, and local meeting places. (123)

Fraser's concept of alternative/counter-public spheres and her example of the US women's movement as an alternative public sphere also suggest an investment in the idea of the public sphere itself.[3] This investment is an echo of Mary Ryan's understanding of the usefulness of the concept of the public sphere for the twentieth-century US women's movement. Looking at the women's movement in the United States in the nineteenth and twentieth centuries, Ryan contends that 'Habermas's construction of the public sphere had a singular advantage for feminists: it freed politics from the iron grasp of the state, which, by virtue of the long denial of franchise ... effectively defined the public in masculine terms' (261). Ryan traces the way in which women in the United States used the public sphere to gain access to public space and the 'tenacious efforts of women to subvert these restrictions [to full citizenship] and to be heard in public testify to the power of public ideals, that persistent impulse to have a voice in some space open and accessible to all where they could be counted in the general interest' (284).

Similarly, Thomas Holt's argument for a black public sphere, and the eventual publication of *The Black Public Sphere* by the Black Public Sphere Collective,[4] extending Bruce Robbins's and Nancy Fraser's arguments for thinking about a plurality of public and counterpublic spheres. Holt suggests in his afterword to the collection that

the notion of *a* public sphere, or spheres, can provide a powerful entry into the interrelatedness of matters that – within the disciplinary fragmentation of the academy's normal science – might appear disconnected ... Moreover, this rubric, which is theoretically a space defined equally by speakers and listeners, leaders and followers, material resources and discursive performances, might recast the stubborn tensions between structure and agency that burden so much of contemporary social theory. ('Mapping' 326)

Holt closes by recognizing that 'the black public sphere is partly the creature of the political economy of a global, advanced capitalist order, but in the past it has offered – and may yet again offer – space for critique and transformation of that order' ('Mapping' 328). The appropriation of the public sphere is not simply a case of 'using the master's tools,' but also one of the difficulties of complicity. As Houston Baker notes, there is a certain irony in using a concept that had been originally intended to describe the political organization of propertied white men who counted black people as part of their property (13). Baker, Holt, and other members of the Black Public Sphere collective put forward a compelling argument for thinking about alternative public spheres that reappropriate the Habermasian concept. However, because the world is not just black and white, because we cannot simply turn dichotomies upside-down, I wonder about the cost of the reappropriation. As Holt acknowledges, 'It must be remembered [that] the public sphere had a historically specific provenance and development: it cannot simply be mapped onto contemporary African-American lifeworlds' ('Mapping' 326). While the Collective's response to this problem has been to mark out a separate black sphere of experience, I wonder if we do not need to pause yet again on the historical contingencies of the bourgeois sphere and the ways in which its predications and founding contradictions might reveal further layers of complexity.

Warner's critique of Fraser's concept of a subaltern counterpublic sphere points out the limits of simply inverting the public sphere for subaltern purposes. Noting the feminist agenda that Fraser uses to distinguish the feminist subaltern counterpublic sphere, Warner asks, 'Why would counterpublics of this variety be limited to "subalterns"? How are they different from the publics of U.S. Christian fundamentalism, or youth culture, or artistic bohemianism? Each of these is a similarly complex metatopical space for the circulation of discourse; each is a scene for developing oppositional interpretations of its members' identities, interests, and needs' (119). Warner's suggestion that a feminist counterpublic might share the same attributes as a US Christian fundamentalist group exaggerates to prove the argument, but the argument is sound. The problem with understanding a counterpublic as a private club with a very specific set of membership criteria is not only that it mimics the very bourgeois public sphere that it aims to counter, but also that it does not recognize the publicness of its address. A counterpublic is not a club with a series of slogans that it shouts out into a world that will or will not listen. Rather, it extends a perpetual invitation to those who may not yet identify as members and may not yet feel that they might step into it. Like the She-Romps, they are aware that the power of dominant culture has placed them outside of the public sphere even as they continue to extend an open invitation to the Spectator to join them. Anyone could potentially become a member. Anyone could become the subject of its address. That is its power. If we take seriously Warner's proposal that counterpublics are not necessarily self-evident communities with political agendas, that they are much more nebulous and also more open than that, and if we take seriously that diasporic culture does not form in isolation, then it makes some sense that a diasporic counterpublic needs both diasporic and non-diasporic participants.

Thinking about diasporic counterpublics shifts discussions of diaspora away from classification and membership, and towards a recognition of the contingencies and dynamism of diasporic culture. Diasporic culture is contingent upon the conditions of dispersion and arrival. It cannot know in advance what it will be, just as people in diaspora cannot know in advance what kind of home they will make, what kinds of resources and communities they will find, what the forms of cultural survival will be and how they will flourish. The diasporic counterpublic recognizes how diasporas are communities that look both inward and outward.

Let me illustrate more clearly through the Chinese restaurant how a diasporic counterpublic is made up of both diasporic and non-diasporic members. As a gathering of diners and those who prepare and serve the food, it is a public that never fully claims universalism. It is too marked by race and too aware of its subordinate status. In this sense, it is not like the hockey rink or the community centre. But it is like them enough to make some claims to publicness. Its address is not merely to other Chinese diasporic subjects. That it is a business, a restaurant, necessitates an address that extends beyond the Chinese community. The restaurants are spaces where a range of people will, at least for a moment, be eating Chinese. Through the consumption and production of something that will be called Chinese food, a series of interactions and negotiations unfold. Even though the exchanges are mediated by capital, and perhaps even overdetermined by merchant–consumer relations, I suggest that there is something there that exceeds that a purely commerical relationship.

It is a relationship that produces a sense of a public that has a specific membership but is not closed or limited. What draws this public together is an ongoing agreement around the production and consumption of Chinese food. That food is mutually acknowledged as Chinese but, as my discussion of the menu in chapter 2 illustrates, it is also constantly changing, mutating and responding to ideas of Chineseness and Canadianness among both Chinese and non-Chinese people. The food represented on the Chinese restaurant menu is a textual testament to the basis of this public. It is not an agenda so much as it is an index of cultural interaction. The food that you will find at these restaurants, the easy juxtaposition of egg foo yong with beef dip sandwiches, would not exist without the unique coming together of Chinese and non-Chinese appetites in small towns across the country. Indeed, it is hard to find egg foo yong anywhere else and even the beef dip sandwich is hard to come by outside of a small town Chinese restaurant. Of course, because it is a counterpublic, there is nothing so blatant as a statement that the Chinese restaurant menu will represent Chineseness in diaspora. Given the diversity of Chineseness in diaspora, that would be an impossible claim to make. But the menu offers some sense that some kind of quiet, mutual pact has been made that the Chinese restaurant will be a gathering of a whole constellation of varying tastes and cravings that will come to constitute this institution of small town life. It is a counterpublic of culinary expression. Its discourse is not that of the rational dialogue and debate that characterizes the bourgeois public sphere, but it has a shared discursive sensibility nonetheless.

As crucial as the offerings on the menu are, a Chinese restaurant is not entirely about the food. It is also a physical space with it own architecture and interior. Tam's *Gold Mountain Restaurant* installations perfectly capture this specific physicality. Even though each of her installations is different, taken together as an entity, the Gold Mountain Restaurants evoke through borrowed and found materials the ways in which these restaurants form a particular genre of their own. It is not easy to identify the specific elements that constitute these spaces. Is it the prevalence of Naughahyde? The typography of the signage? The swinging doors? There is no prescriptive and coherent list of physical elements that mark these restaurants, and yet we know one when we see it. This combination of vagueness and reliance upon the unreliabilities of collective knowledge is suggestive of the problems attendant upon thinking about diasporic spaces more broadly. The originary spaces of diaspora are fraught with problems of definition and delineation. These are spaces remade through memory and some sense of what 'home' should and could be. Sometimes, there is a sense that this 'home' is itself more imaginary than the relationships that tether those in diaspora to it. With reference to the Jewish diaspora and Israel, Jonathan and Daniel Boyarin offer the idea of dispensing with a physical home entirely and ask whether or not a people need a land in order to be a people by suggesting that a people can 'maintain its distinctive culture, its difference, without controlling land, *a fortiori* without controlling other people or developing a need to dispossess them of their lands' ('Diaspora' 723). Despite the promise of such an idea, Jasmin Habib, in her research on the ways in which Jews in diaspora have sustained their connection to a notion of homeland, notes that the Boyarins' proposal is 'not an accurate reflection' of how the subjects of her enquiry 'envisioned their relationships or identifica- tions with Israel' (266). She argues that the Boyarins are mistaken in 'assuming that nationalism is territorially based' and thus 'miss the point that the relationship of diaspora Jews to Israel is *not* specifically limited to territory and that it is already about Jewish heritage or tradition' (266). This example of the problem of home and homeland for Jewish diaspora culture highlights the problem of a process of simultaneous displace- ment and emplacement with which diasporas are continually engaged. In many ways, diasporas are characterized by the lack of physical space, the loss of home and homeland. Further, in the spaces of arrival, diaspo- ras struggle with issues of isolation on the one hand and ghettoization on the other. In terms of the Chinese restaurant as a diasporic counter- public, I am aware that some publics need spaces but not all of them do. Thinking about diasporas in terms of publics and counterpublics makes the issue of space particularly poigant.

What does it mean to think of a public or a counterpublic in spatial terms? Warner's publics and counterpublics seem to have less to do with space than they do with texts. 'This essay,' he writes of his discussion of publics and counterpublics, 'has a public. If you are reading (or hear- ing) this, you are part of its public' (65). Even though Warner suggests that publics can be as ephemeral as the group of people who might be reading his book, or any particular book, at any given time, I am struck by how much the Habermasian bourgeois public sphere relied upon a very defined space. In the previous chapter, I wondered what these pub- lic spheres would have been without the supply of cheap coffee, tea, and sugar afforded to them by European colonialism and imperialism. Cof- fee, tea, and sugar aside, what would the bourgeois public sphere have been without the coffe-houses in which these beverages were imbibed? Even though the *Spectator* and the *Tatler* as publications addressed an au- dience beyond the immediate one of those at the coffee-house, they still relied upon the space of the coffee-house as the basis for their discourse.

Understanding a public as being tied to an actual space does limit the reach of its publicness – it is not a virtual entity that can extend far beyond the pages of a physical book or newspaper. But it also illuminates its materiality. What is the relationship between the eigteenth-century coffee-house and the papers associated with that space? In Habermas's view, the coffee-house was crucial as a place for rational critical dialogue and debate. The papers came out of the discursive action that unfolded in the physical space of the coffee-house, extending the sphere of its influence beyond the reaches of those who might actually have been there. In the case of Chinese restaurants, what unfolds is less defined and coherent. Within its counterpublic status, the restaurant is still a gathering place. Rather than binding through the bluster of aesthetic arguments among men of letters, where the coffee imbibed is incidental, at the Chinese restaurant the food is central and the conversation is itself incidental. And even though the coffee consumed in the eighteenth-century English coffee-house may have been a secondary consideration next to the lofty discussions of art and politics that defined the public sphere, as my discussion of Simon Ortiz's argument in the previous chapter suggests, coffee was also absolutely central to the development of the bourgeois public sphere. Conversely, even though the food may be that main attraction at a Chinese restaurant, the conversations and dialogues that occur at the restaurant are no less important to the function of the restaurant within the community.

As diasporic counterpublics, Chinese restaurants stage over and over again the delicate negotiations and interactions that constitute their publicness. They carve out a distinctly Chinese space within a landscape that would otherwise offer no reference whatsoever to their difference. At the same time, they remain persistently open to non-Chinese presence in the form of actual bodies within the restaurant and the catering to the tastes and hungers of these bodies in the form of the menu. The restaurants enact diasporic displacement in their overt claiming of difference, of Chineseness. And yet, the restaurants also attest to the ways in which Chineseness can be very much emplaced. They do offer their customers some sense, however problematic, of entering a space that is clearly not Euro-Canadian. It is a space that is identified as Chinese by both the Chinese and non-Chinese members of the community. What that Chineseness is, whether or not it is an accurate or authentic reflection of Chinese culture, is not the point. It is the very openness to interpretation, the very fact that these restaurants do not offer a static and authorial claim to Chineseness, that renders them as such fine counterpublic spaces. They do not constitute a republic of difference, but rather a counterpublic of uncertain and constantly negotiated differences. In this sense, they do not resolve the problem of home and homelessness for diaspora. Instead, they offer a crucial mediating space through which that problem can be staged and navigated.

Tam's installations stage and animate the Chinese resturant as a counterpublic sphere. By taking her audience to a place that they already know, Tam asks them to reconsider what they do know about Chinese-ness, about hunger, about what it means to make a place even when one is displaced. Walking into one of Tam's Gold Mountain Restaurants is as much an experience of mild dislocation (you are in an art gallery that has become a restaurant that has become art) as it is one of emplace-ment. Her restaurants, and the process through which she constructs them, show how, as Warner suggests, a public can be 'a poetic world making' (114, emphasis removed). Her restaurants illuminate how the Chinese restaurants that are her inspiration can be a transformative, not merely replicative, space of circulation. It is the circulation of identities and difference that makes Chinese restaurants such a rich site for the kinds of relationships and interactions out of which diasporic culture is forged. Diasporas and diasporic cultures are not static objects of study. Jasmin Habib critiques definitions of diaspora which suggest that it is 'a thing rather than a process or a relationship' (16). Even though many critics explore 'lives lived in a home away from homeland,' she observes that they fail to take up 'the very practices that define this continuing re-lationship to homeland' (17–18). Let me suggest, though, that the other side of these diasporic practices, how diasporic people sustain and create relationships to the places in which they have found themselves is just as important. This chapter is an exploration of one example of such a process. So much emphasis has been placed on the relationship to the spaces from which diasporas have been dispersed and yet so much of the work of diasporic cultural survival depends upon the relationships diasporic communities build in the spaces of arrival. As an institution of small town life, and as an installation in contemporary art galleries across the country, Chinese restaurants are a diasporic counterpublic. They invite you to come inside, take a seat, look around, wonder, talk to someone, eat something, and engage in diaspora.

# Chapter Five

# 'How taste remembers life':
# Diaspora and the Memories That Bind

This chapter takes up Fred Wah's embrace of the connection between taste and memory, and the idea that the body can experience something that extends beyond the boundaries of the individual subject. Diasporas are collectivities by definition. And yet, it is not clear what binds those in these collectivities. In the previous chapter, I examined how people in diaspora assert a sense of their presence in the spaces of arrival through diasporic counterpublics and how they forge relationships between diasporic and non-diasporic communities. In this chapter, I want to look at what it is that ties one person in diaspora to another. How do we think of these as agential connections rather than obligatory and restrictive attachments? In the articulation of the problem of the ties that bind, I am thinking of what David Scott calls 'the demand of diaspora criticism'[1] (127): that is, a way of thinking through these connections that is neither culturally nationalist nor completely deconstructed. This is not a question of identity politics – although there are certainly some compelling overlaps – but a question of community formation and transmission. In that sense, the demand of diaspora criticism is not so much the problem of how the individual diasporic subject belongs to the group, but rather how the group constitutes itself as a group, how does a diasporic community understand itself as such?

I will explore this problem through Fred Wah's writing on Chinese restaurants and the relationship between food, taste, hunger, and memory. In so doing, I will take a brief look at two critical discussions that are symptomatic of each other and suggestive of the overall issue in the question of diasporic community. In the first discussion, I will look at the ways in which much of the literary criticism on Wah presumes a transparency to race that precludes an engagement with the formal innovations of his writing. In the second, I will look at the debate on Chineseness that has become an increasingly significant preoccupation of Chinese diaspora studies. As I will show, both of these discussions remain tied to a historicist racialized subjectivity. Against this historicized vision, I suggest a way of thinking about diasporic community as constituted not in history, but in memory. It is here in memory, as a counter to history, that I will show how Wah illuminates Chinese food and the small town Chinese restaurant as productive of Chineseness in diaspora.

While this chapter focuses on Wah, I recognize that Chinese restaurants have a particular place in Canadian literature, particularly in W.O. Mitchell's *Who Has Seen the Wind*, and the work of Wayson Choy, Judy Fong Bates, Denise Chong, and Sky Lee. Choy, Chong, and Lee's books focus on Chinese restaurants in cities such as Vancouver. Although Mitchell and Bates do set their stories in small town Chinese restaurants, the restaurants in their writing function as a backdrop for human drama. Canadian literary representations of Chinese restaurants tend to use them as settings in which human drama unfolds. They are the places where the stories happen. What might it mean for the restaurants themselves to be understood a dynamic part of the story? In Wah's writing, the restaurant is incredibly alive – its doors swing open with a loud kick, the counters glisten, you can almost smell the browned that grease Shu, the cook, scrapes onto the plates as the final touch for the mixed grill. In turning to Wah's writing and the connections his writing draws between race, hunger, and diaspora, I hope to attend not only to the small town Chinese restaurant in Canadian literature, but also to how it reveals a construction of Chineseness in diaspora.

**Form and Content: The Dilemma of Wah Criticism**

Let me turn first to the dilemma of Wah criticism. Pamela Banting's attempt to grapple with the formal elements of Wah's poetry is enormously suggestive of the problem of thinking about experimental writing that takes on issues of race and identity. In her discussion of the genealogical implications of Wah's syntax, Banting argues that Wah's innovation in form precedes his innovation in content: 'While the content of his work is intriguing and its "themes" heartfelt and important, it is his notation that not only makes his work new and exciting but in some respects precedes the development of the content' (100). I disagree with Banting's analysis in that I see the grief and the longings of the poetry as a complicated intervention against historicism that is deeply imbricated with the complexities of the form of Wah's writing. What is more, her understanding of the content of Wah's poetry as divorced from its form facilitates Banting's privileging of the autobiographical rather than the tension between autobiography and fiction. This privileging leaves her criticism vulnerable to an exorbitant 'Chinese-ing' of Wah's writing. Attempting to theorize Wah's experiments with syntax in the context of his Chineseness, Banting argues that

> Wah's use of the indicative, the imperative and a pseudo-imperative mood, his omission of pronouns, his elision of standard grammatical particles, and his superadding of the functions of different parts of speech to a single word or word cluster, like his construction of a synthetic middle voice, translate not only the Chinese written character as a medium for poetry but some of the patterns of actual *spoken* Chinese as well. That is, Wah translates not just the paradigmatic model of the Chinese language; a phenomenological, oral/aural, 'lived' Chinese gets translated as well. This translation of Chinese ideogrammic and speech structures into English deconstructs the meta-discourse [Harold] Bloom isolates as attendant upon standard English syntax and 'undermaterializes' the phonetically-based English word, creating the conditions necessary for listening, in the same moment, to the Otherness of both English and Chinese. (108–9)

Banting's argument is both suggestive and yet disturbing in its desire to pin down the difficulty of Wah's syntax within what I can only take to be an imagined sense of 'spoken Chinese.' There isn't really any particular spoken Chinese – spoken Chinese exists more specifically within the world of dialect: Cantonese, Toisanese, Mandarin, and so on. In addition, Wah has written in response to another moment of racial identification, 'Well fuck! I can't even speak Chinese …' (*Diamond* 39). Banting's desire to locate the difficulty of Wah's writing within the assumed simplicity of being Chinese suggests one of the most difficult aspects of writing critically about Wah.

Similarly, Susan Fisher's 'Japanese Elements in the Poetry of Fred Wah and Roy Kiyooka' also presumes a transparency to the racialization of Wah's writing that betrays an ethnographic desire. Attempting to address Wah's experimentation with Japanese poetic forms such as *haibun* and *uta nikki*, Fisher's article seeks to uncover an 'appropriate way to link poetics and ethnicity' (94). Perhaps it is this preoccupation with appropriateness that leads Fisher to a conclusion that empties Wah's writing of a politics of race. Arguing that there is 'no special match between the themes of Asian cultural displacement that interest Wah and Japanese forms,' Fisher proposes that 'Wah's choice of Japanese models is awkward for any theory of ethnopoetics. Whatever aesthetic a Canadian-born person of Chinese ancestry might unconsciously absorb from the conversation of parents or grandparents, it is not a Japanese one' (100). Despite noting that Wah himself argues for the importance of challenging dominant racist culture through form and technique, Fisher concludes, 'There is in fact no particular "poetics of ethnicity"' (101). Her analysis reveals a desire for a theory of origins rather than an exploration of the way in which Wah uses the estranging possibilities of language as a means of challenging racist culture. What does it matter where Wah learned about *haibun*? Does the disjuncture between his ethnic self-identification (Chinese-Scots/Irish-Swedish) and the Japanese forms he adopts in his poetry really suggest that there is no relationship between race and aesthetics, no 'poetics of ethnicity'? Aside from an astonishing tendency to essentialize Wah's Chineseness, Fisher's conclusion suggests an arbitrary separation between aesthetics and race. It is sadly ironic that an article that is ostensibly about the intersection between race and formal innovation concludes with an utter evacuation of the politics of race in the discussion of Wah's formal challenge to the colonial inheritance of English literature.

Conversely, Cynthia Sugars's 'The Negative Capability of Camouflage' collapses the politics of diaspora with that of racial essentialism. While I agree with Sugars that 'Wah engages in a reinscription of conventional Canadian spatiocultural iconography,' her examination of 'the means by which which Wah effects this de-diasporization' through an emphasis on hybridity risks allowing for too much slippage between a nostalgic cultural nationalism and a desire for authenticity (30). Hybridity is not necessarily bad. Julie McGonegal recuperates hybridity by theorizing the hyphen: 'By suggesting the need to preserve difference while simultaneously developing points of commonality,' McGonegal suggests, 'hyphenation lends hybridity not only the conceptual but also the political edge that it presently lacks' (191). Sugars and McGonegal offer much more promising engagements with Wah's writing by examining how his poetry attends to the complexity of mixed race identity. Both of these essays engage in delicate and sophisticated ways with the problems of race and identity in Wah's poetry, but there is relatively little discussion of the poetry as poetry. McGonegal does discuss Wah's use of code-switching, but she reads it more as akin to Mary Louise Pratt's concept of the contact zone than as a poetic device. It is a wonderful reading, but it leaves me wondering if these same arguments could have been made about a novel or a collection of short stories. There seems to be a split in the criticism of Sugars and McGonegal where writing in complex and nuanced ways about racial identity does not necessarily allow for an engagement with race and poetic form. To engage with the ways in which race intersects with form would be to tread the difficult and ultimately unsatisfactory territory of Banting and Fisher.

Caught between a modernist poetic tradition that has sought in Asian poetic form some of its most vigorous sources of reinvention[2] and another tradition of reading minority literature for an ethnographic or sociological reflection of diasporic Asian identity, many of the critical approaches to Wah's work risk occluding the very challenges he has posed to the literary establishment. Two notable exceptions include Smaro Kamboureli's discussion of the politics of 'faking it' in Wah's writing and Iyko Day's discussion of Wah as an avant-garde writer. Kamboureli argues, 'Faking it, then, is a kind of writing whose generativeness must be heard twice over. Faking it, at least as articulated and practiced by Wah, keeps in sight the discursive means that have produced it while, at the same time, heralding a departure from them' (122). Day builds on this attention to the means of production in Wah's poetry and extends it into 'a consideration of an articulatory poetics and politics that reveal … the material and textual negotiation of the subject in ideology' (51). For Day, Wah's commitment to avant-garde forms signals his 'refusing to be commodified as an ethnic object of knowledge' (50). In *Black Chant* Aldon Nielsen traces the ways in which avant-garde black writing has been almost entirely ignored in favour of more 'accessible' literary forms. Disparaging a critical practice that has largely overlooked the writing of radical poets such as those in the Dasein Poets or the Cleveland Freelancers, Nielsen argues that 'the real cultural "avants" of America are not the sort of emissaries that our cultural ministries want to send out as an advance guard for the New World Order, and in representing our culture to ourselves we have too quickly settled for the representations of the modal average' (265). Similarly, Jeffrey Derksen sees a dangerous foreclosure of radical subjectivity in the failure of literary criticism to attend to the imbrication of form and content:

A sort of literary Darwinism in which people of colour or working-class writers, for example, are not in a historical context to utilize more disjunctive non-narrative poetics is in operation here. A prescribed need to enter into a validating history, to be self-actualized in a way that dominant groups will recognize, implies that writers of colour who continue along this path will evolve enough to use the complex literary devices that the dominant group has at its disposal. The weblike implication is that the writing of history will not change; it is accessible only through certain methods. Extended further, this signals that only the recognizable forms of subjectivity can enter history and there is no call for a radical redefining of a Western subjectivity. (73)

As Derksen argues, the desire for a recognizable ethnographic subject lies at the heart of criticism that seeks to separate the difficulties of Wah's formal techniques from the complexities of the content of his poetry. Further, Day notes that 'the appropriation of "marginality" by a traditionally white avant-garde also functions to legitimize a form of resistance that is the exclusive province of normative subjects of history' (40). Day's and Derksen's readings bring me to what I see as the central problem of the dilemma of Wah criticism – an unacknowledged reliance upon the historicism of racialized subjectivity.

Because this chapter hopes to intervene against the historicism of our present debates, let me briefly outline how I understand historicism and its relationship to the debates in Wah criticism. I take my understanding of historicism from Walter Benjamin via Dipesh Chakrabarty and Jean-Luc Nancy via David Scott. In *Provincializing Europe* Chakrabarty recognizes that historicism is a term with a long and complicated history of its own. Surveying the appearances of the term from Hegel to Ranke and then its more recent resurgence in the New Historicism that is often connected to Stephen Greenblatt, Chakrabarty suggests that

> we may say that 'historicism' is a mode of thinking with the following characteristics. It tells us that in order to understand the nature of anything in this world we must see it as an historically developing entity, that is, first, as an individual and unique whole – as some kind of unity at least in potentia – and, second, as something that develops over time ... The idea of development and the assumption that a certain amount of time elapses in the very process of development are critical to this understanding. Needless to say, this passage of time that is constitutive of both the narrative and the concept of development is, in the famous words of Walter Benjamin, the secular, empty and homogenous time of history. (22–3)

Taking up this assumption of a history as an extended storyline in the development of humanity, in 'Finite History' Jean-Luc Nancy argues that 'historicism in general is the way of thinking that *presupposes* that history has always already begun, and that therefore it always merely continues' (152). In addressing Nancy's challenge to go beyond history, David Scott nonetheless recognizes the hope of a historicist critique that looks for justice within the pages of history. There is a hope that 'the objective representation of what actually happened in the past' will 'lay to rest the falsehoods put about by chauvinists and allow us to arrive more rationally at a design for the present' (Scott 100). Nonetheless, for Scott, playing the 'game of "historicism," repeating with it the modernist dream, so naturalized since Hegel, so politically correct since Marx, that history can somehow redeem us, save us from ourselves' is a mistaken one (104).

The desire to situate Wah either in ethnographic terms or purely within the advances of avant-garde formalism betrays this reliance upon historicized racial subjectivity. On the one hand, there is the hope that we can be saved from erroneous understandings of what it means to be a mixed-race person of visible Asian descent by reading Wah. This is the historicist reading wherein there is a desire to 'get it right' by treating a text such as *Diamond Grill* as an objective sociological text. On the other hand, there is the plea for redemption in seeing Wah's progression as a writer within his formal innovations measured against the homogeneous empty timeline of the English literary tradition. This plea collapses in on itself when it tries to address his Chineseness by reverting to an unfortunate essentialism that evacuates Chineseness of itself. Wah is either so Chinese that his syntax echoes an imaginary spoken Chinese or he is not Chinese enough. Although Derksen does not situate this dilemma in terms of historicism, he is correct in identifying the problem of Wah criticism as lying within the difficulty of conceptualizing a racialized subject outside of the bounds of European subjectivity. It is within this reliance on historicism that we can see the dilemma of Wah criticism as symptomatic of the broader debate in Chinese diaspora criticism regarding, in Rey Chow's words, the theoretical problem of Chineseness.[3]

### Deconstructing Chineseness, Historicizing Nostalgia

The debate on Chineseness seeks to critically engage with racialized subjectivities by deconstructing Chineseness. It works against what has been a strong trend in Chinese diaspora studies towards the idea of a 'cultural China,' consolidated and put forward in Tu Wei-Ming's 1994 anthology *The Living Tree*. The collection as a whole argues for a particular understanding of Chineseness grounded in a stable notion of China as a centre of identification. Tu's introduction suggests that a notion of 'cultural

China' supplants the People's Republic of China as a locus of identification. Tu traces the rise of the idea of a cultural China as a movement that originates outside of mainland China, but he nonetheless reinforces China as a coherent social and cultural entity. The metaphor of the living tree continues to hold sway. In 1998 Wang Gungwu and Wang Ling-chi published a two-volume collection of essays, *The Chinese Diaspora*, that focused on the theme of *luodi-shenggen*, a term coined by Wang Ling-chi and his colleagues meaning 'the planting of roots in the soils of different countries' (Wang Ling-chi x). However, *The Chinese Diaspora*, a text that wants to become a definitive declaration of Chinese diaspora studies as a field, fails to acknowledge the cultural nationalism guiding the intellectual course of its project. Behind the organicist metaphor of the living tree and the subsequent theme of *luodi-shenggen* lies a devotion to the idea of China as an integral and coherent site of cultural belonging that takes for granted a coherent Chinese subject whose real home is not Canada or the United States or Australia, but an entity called cultural China. Against the claims of cultural nationalists such as Tu Wei-ming and Wang Ling-chi, writers such as Rey Chow, Ien Ang, and Allen Chun have tried to reposition the idea of Chineseness as a hegemonic form.[4]

Chow's introductory essay in *Writing Diaspora* explicitly connects the problem of race, what she has termed 'the myth of consanguinity' (24), with the problem of writing diaspora. Writing about the pressure to sinicize in pre-1997 Hong Kong, Chow gestures to the relationship between the metaphor of blood and that of belonging in diaspora culture:

> The submission to consanguinity means the surrender of agency – what is built on work and livelihood rather than blood and race – in the governance of a community ... Part of the goal of 'writing diaspora' is, thus, to unlearn that submission to one's ethnicity such as 'Chineseness' as the ultimate signified even as one continues to support movements for democracy and human rights in China, Hong Kong, and elsewhere. (24–5)

In this formulation, Chow juxtaposes blood and race against an understanding of agency. To submit to ethnic identification risks the loss of agential self-definition. While the particular historical and political context of Chow's discussion places this discussion of blood and race within the context of pre-handover Hong Kong, the goal of 'writing diaspora' also suggests that this discussion might be read beyond the Hong Kong Chinese community and into broader discussions of the Chinese diaspora.

My uneasiness with this understanding of blood, race, and belonging in diaspora lies in its situating of the theoretical problem of Chineseness as the problem of unthinking diasporic subjects who identify too naively with the idea of being Chinese. Within this understanding, Chineseness becomes a burden that the Chinese-identified subject must bear. Despite the long histories of racism where Chinese subjects continue to have their Chineseness read onto them, the real problem of Chineseness, in this reading, becomes those who have submitted to the myth of consanguinity and surrendered their agency as racialized subjects in that submission. That is, it is the responsibility of the Chinese subject in diaspora to refuse the lure of submission to ethnicity. Clearly, fanatical ethnic identifications are both dangerous and repressive. There is a sense here, however, that the vast majority of people in the world who might identify as Chinese despite being physically and metaphysically distant from the geopolitical entity of China are themselves somehow duped by the compulsion of consanguinity.

Ultimately, this charge against falling prey to the myth of consanguinity, against becoming a dupe of cultural nationalism, is a charge against homesickness – the nostalgia for a home that does not exist except as fantasy. Chow asks rhetorically, 'What is "home"? To be nostalgic, we remember, is to be homesick ...' (*Ethics* 144). The deconstructionist response to Chinese diasporic cultural nationalism is not only against its essentialism but also against its reliance on a historical narrative that is mythical. Noting that our current understanding of China as a coherent national body emerged only with the Nationalist Revolution of 1911, Allen Chun argues that

> since the very idea of (a national) identity is new, any notions of *culture* invoked in this regard, no matter how faithfully they are grounded in the past, have to be *constructions* by nature. In the end, they conform to a new kind of *boundedness* in order to create bonds of horizontal solidarity between equal, autonomous individuals constitutive of the empty, homogenous social space of the nation in ways that could not have existed in a hierarchical, cosmological past. (114)

This cosmological narrative is also one that proclaims a particular form of continuity to Chinese history and tradition at the expense of recognizing the heterogeneous reality of China's population and the existence, not to mention repression, of ethnic minorities. Nostalgia engenders a homesickness that can only be for a home that does not exist. The charge against homesickness is then an injunction against submitting and clinging to a mythic past. This charge functions as an appeal to a notion of 'reality' without any stake in what that 'reality' might be.

In the context of diaspora, the condition of homesickness requires the fantasy of an idealized or authentic home as its object. Tracing the tendency of Chinese cultural production outside of China to mimic Western cultural movements, Chow observes that

> émigrés who can no longer claim proprietorship of Chinese culture through residency in China henceforth inhabit the *melancholy* position of an ethnic group that, as its identity is being 'authenticated' abroad, is simultaneously relegated to the existence of ethnographic specimen under the Western gaze ... In exile, Chinese writing ... is condemned to nostalgia, often no sooner reflecting or recording the 'reality' of Chinese life overseas than rendering Chineseness itself as something the essence of which belongs to a bygone era. (*Modern* 15–16, my emphasis)

Chow's observation situates diasporic homesickness within the workings of nostalgia as an ahistorical desire that seeks to produce authenticity. More than that, this is a position that Chow identifies as a specifically melancholy one, linking the condition of diasporic nostalgia with that of diasporic melancholia.

As Freud's 'Mourning and Melancholia' illustrates, the injunction against melancholy did not end with the Middle Ages.[5] Rather, its pathologization carried over into our contemporary period. However, there is a notion of historicist progression that girds Freudian melancholia. For Freud, 'the disposition to fall ill of melancholia' relies on a narcissistic identification with the object of loss whereby 'the narcissistic identification with the object then becomes a substitute for the erotic cathexis, the result of which is that in spite of the conflict with the loved person the love-relation need not be given up' ('Mourning' 250, 249). What differentiates mourning from melancholia for Freud is that the former is amenable to the passage of time, or the idea of progress: 'We rely on [mourning] being overcome after a certain lapse of time' (244). In contrast, melancholia cannot be cured over a lapse of time; it does not give up the object of its loss but rather 'regresses' in a narcissistic identification. Moreover, melancholia does not want to be cured. Diasporic nostalgia and melancholia are conjoined by a regressive inability to move forward in history.

Diasporic communities continue to be marked by a melancholic longing, a homesickness without a home. In a chapter from *Ethics after Idealism* entitled 'A Souvenir of Love,' Chow suggests that nostalgia can 'constitute a cultural politics of *self*-nativizing' (134). More specifically, nostalgia can pose a challenge to European temporality: 'If its romance with the past seems to offer a way of imagining identity that is alternative to the one imposed by the rationalistic, consumerist, high-tech world, nostalgia is nonetheless most acutely felt not as an attempt to return to the past as such, but as an effect of temporal dislocation – of something having been displaced in time' (147). However, Chow closes with a warning that nostalgia's potential as an agential force might be compromised by its necessary hostility to history: 'If nostalgia may be considered an alternative way of conjuring up a "community" amid the ruthless fragmentations of postcoloniality, the community being conjured up is a *mythic* one' (148, my emphasis). Even though Chow sees the potential of nostalgia for radically challenging European teleologies of time and progress, she closes by pulling away from that potential. The community that nostalgia offers, according to Chow, is ultimately a mythic one. Despite nostalgia's potential to challenge European temporality, for Chow the only alternative to European rationality and teleologically defined progress must be a mythical one. This investment in historicism is precisely the reason why the deconstructionist critique of cultural nationalism is so unsettling. Chow's historicism is symptomatic of the larger critique that has been marshalled against the living-tree concept in Chinese diaspora debates.

This mobilizing of a historicized Chineseness against the cultural-nationalist position feels peculiarly empty to me, not because it unmoors Chineseness from the grounding of a stable centre of identification – a necessary and urgent task – but because it displaces the pressing issue of the oppression of historicism. Even though the debate on Chineseness and Chinese identity would suggest otherwise, this debate is not about essentialism or anti-essentialism. In fact, the anxieties over identity politics have displaced the question that Tu's cultural nationalism, despite its homogenizing essentialism, posed in the first place: What is it that connects Chinese subjects in diaspora? What is it that produces that obscure yet irrepressible sense of and desire for belonging to a group larger than oneself? This is, of course, why the conception of cultural China is so compelling – it divorces the idea of China from the entity that is the People's Republic of China. The thing that is China with which Chinese diaspora subjects might identify has nothing to do with China as a nation-state and everything to do with a fuzzier sense of Chineseness. The displacement of the problem of conceiving of diasporas into a problem of race and essentialism does a huge disservice to the enabling alternative histories embedded within the cultural production of Chinese diasporic subjects. This critique mistakes the issue of *origins* with the problem of *genesis*.

We know from Walter Benjamin that origins are concerned, not so much with the problem of genesis, as with the dialectical process of emergence. In *The Origin of German Tragic Drama*, Benjamin writes:

> Origin [*Ursprung*], although an entirely historical category, has, nevertheless, nothing to do with genesis [*Entstehung*]. The term origin is not intended to describe the process by which the existent came into being, but rather to describe that which emerges from the process of becoming and disappearance. Origin is an eddy in the stream of becoming, and in its current it swallows the material involved in the process of genesis. That which is original is never revealed in the naked and manifest existence of the factual; its rhythm is only apparent to a dual insight. On the one hand it needs to be recognized as a process of restoration and re-establishment, but, on the other hand, and precisely because of this, as something imperfect and incomplete. (45)

This concept of emergence and the eddy in the stream of becoming is one that I will return to again in the remainder of this chapter because it articulates the problem of diasporic community and a way of thinking about this community outside of the oppressions of historicism's insistent march forward. Benjamin touches precisely on the problem of Chineseness in diaspora – the building and establishing of something at the same time that we recognize its necessary incompleteness. The compulsion to recognize the oppressions of the past – for example, the history of Chinese indentured labourers – becomes something that is conveniently rooted in the past without a sense for the ways in which those pasts re-emerge in the present of migrant labour. This is a complicity with a teleology of progress. However, if we let go of this teleology, of this historicist narrative of origins, what then are we left with? How do we conceive of communities that are not held together by cultural-nationalist narratives of progress?

The debate on Chineseness and its subsequent forbidding of nostalgia forgets that nostalgia contains within its grammatical genealogy a narrative of colonialism. From an etymological perspective, nostalgia enters the world through colonial passages. In 1756 the crew on Captain James

Cook's ship became so homesick that the ship's doctor named it as a pathology: nostalgia. The *Oxford English Dictionary* marks the first use of nostalgia in Cook's journal: 'The greatest part of them [i.e., the ship's company] were now pretty far gone with the longing for home which the Physicians have gone so far as to esteem a disease under the name of Nostalgia.' Nostalgia, then, has its etymological beginnings in English as a pathology that described a severe state of homesickness – a homesickness engendered by the work of colonial expansion.

As its etymological beginnings reveal, the nostalgia of our contemporary usage is deeply invested in the project of European colonization. In this context, nostalgia needs to be cured in order for the colonial project to continue. The crew must go on. Ships must continue to sail. Moreover, nostalgia must be cast as a disabling pathology because it interferes with the cosmopolitan project of the right of people – European people – to settle and be at home anywhere in the world. This claim to cool cosmopolitanism is constantly belied by the colonizer's desire to reproduce homeland in the colonial outpost. What is colonial architecture (any governor's mansion, spaces such as the Raffles hotel in Singapore or the Parisian-style opera house in Hanoi) if not one of the deepest expressions of nostalgia for a notion of Europe that can only exist in the colonies? In his classic portrait of the colonizer as nostalgic, Albert Memmi notes that

> the colonialist appears to have forgotten the living reality of his home country. Over the years he has sculptured, in opposition to the colony, such a monument of his homeland ... As though their homeland were an essential component of the collective superego of colonizers, its material features become quasi-ethical qualities. It is agreed that the mist is intrinsically superior to bright sunshine, as is green to ocher. The mother country thus combines only positive values, good climate, harmonious landscape, social discipline and exquisite liberty, beauty, morality and logic. (60)

Memmi accurately observes that the logic of the colonial fantasy of homeland also means the colonialist cannot go home. 'Indeed, the idea of mother country is relative. Restored to its true self, it would vanish and would at the same time destroy the superhumanity of the colonialist ... Why should he leave the only place in the world where, without being the founder of a city or a great captain, it is still possible to ... bequeath one's name to geography?' (61). And so the injunction against colonial homesickness must be pathologized and cured by the act of mourning and an adherence to a notion of adhering to an objective reality. The correct colonial administrative subject might be homesick, pathologically nostalgic, but he will 'get over it' and continue on with the business of colonial rule.

In the postcolonial era, this pathology is transferred onto the migrant subjects who have been displaced by colonialism. And thus, the immigrant diasporic subject's attachment to a sense of home that is stubbornly elsewhere becomes the antithesis of cosmopolitan globalism. These communities are declared ethnic enclaves. The desire to reproduce home is marked as charmingly naive and also potentially dangerous in its insularity, in its seeming refusal to engage with the scene of the present. In the homesickness that functions as a continual reminder of the unhomeliness of diasporic subjects,[6] this sadness is diagnosed as a pre-modern pathology that needs to be overcome – mourned and then released. The mark of a good or obedient diasporic subject would then be that of the cosmopolitan transnational who has mourned the loss of a home and let go of it, or, in the case of the Hong Kong entrepreneur who displays his multiple passports as the *de rigueur* accessory of the new Chinese transnational,[7] one who forgoes the notion of a homeland altogether. From the view of the cosmopolitan transnational subject, there is something obstinately old-fashioned and out-of-step in the sadness of diasporic subjects who have not let go, who persist in their melancholia, who refuse the curative effects of mourning. In the context of Chow's forbidding of nostalgia, Chinese diasporic subjects such as Wah risk being misdiagnosed with an overwhelmingly white nostalgia that denies the name of history to anything other than the Hegelian march of progress. As my tracing of nostalgia's etymology suggests, I locate a form of resistance in the refusal to mourn, to be cured of sadness. There is something coercive in the assumption that political rectitude would produce happiness.

### 'proprioceptive synapse: memory': Diasporic Community in Wah's Poetry

In Wah's poetry, grieving resists precisely the curative effects of mourning. It is a perpetual and recursive grieving that is closer to melancholy than mourning because the mourning remains unfinished. The expression of loss emerges in the interrogative gesture of so many of the poems – they are musings, questions that can have no answer because there is no one to answer them. The address of the second-person pronoun in his poems is almost always that of his father. The poems take on the feeling of an extended conversation that not only is never finished, but has never begun. 'Elite 9' (pronounced 'ee-light') from *Waiting for Saskatchewan* contains a series of questions that not only cannot be answered, but can only be asked because of the impossibility of an answer:

> When you returned from China via Victoria on Hong
> Kong Island and they put you in jail in Victoria on
> Vancouver Island because your birth certificate had been
> lost in the Medicine Hat City Hall fire and your parents
> couldn't prove you were born in Canada until they found
> your baptism records in the church or in the spring of
> 1948 when we moved to Nelson from Trail during the
> floods while Mao chased Chiang Kai-shek from the main-
> land to offshore Taiwan and the Generalissimo's picture
> hung in our house and on a wall above some plants and
> goldfish in the Chinese Nationalist League house down
> on Lake Street or when you arrived in China in 1916
> only four years old unable to speak Chinese and later in
> the roaring twenties when each time Grandpa gambled
> away your boat passage so you didn't get back to Canada
> until 1930 languageless again with anger locked up in the
> immigration cells on Juan de Fuca Strait or when your
> heart crashed so young at 54 as you fell from mom's arms
> to the dance floor did you see islands? (*Waiting* 69)[8]

Wah writes an extended, unanswerable question that hangs sparsely on the page and yet articulates an entire history of grieving and sadness. 'Elite 9' is studded with personal detail – the precision of dates, 1948, 1916, 1930, and the precision of geography, China, Victoria, Hong Kong, Vancouver Island, Nelson, Taiwan, Trail, Lake Street, Juan de Fuca Strait. While these details anchor the poem within a personal narrative of migration, they also suggest a connection to a larger narrative of migration. 'Elite 9' functions as an evocation of Benjamin's conception of origins as a stream of emergence. The disappearance of the text of origin, the birth certificate, emerges again in the baptism records. These are simply part of the larger stream, of a narrative that is bracketed by the 'languageless' anguish of unjust imprisonment, of islands of isolation and incarceration. The unpunctuated stream of Wah's unanswerable question restores and re-establishes a history of dislocation that, in Benjamin's sense, can only be 'imperfect and incomplete' (45). The question he closes with, 'did you see islands?' hangs imperfectly, incomplete, and almost unable to bear the weight of all the subordinate clauses that precede it.

Wah's foregrounding of the subordinate clauses in 'Elite 9' suggests the intimate imbrications of personal histories with public ones. In the catena of relative clauses that surge persistently, Wah highlights the superordinancy of the subordinate. He gives primacy to histories that have been relegated to the realm of the secondary. Further, the stacking of relative clauses also creates a series of incomplete thought loops, thoughts that begin but don't quite end, that recur around and through the question 'did you see islands?' The use of incomplete loops in 'Elite 9' brings me back to Wah's reconception of memory and resonates with Richard Terdiman's argument about modernity and memory: 'But once we admit the ways – whether subtle and subterranean, or entirely overt – by which this eerie domination of *now* by *then* can happen, then memory turns labyrinthine' (346). In this sense, the temporality of the poetry is not a simple circularity, but a more elliptical movement that hangs on the edge of the unfinished.

Within this labyrinthine memory, the incompleteness of private grief merges in the incompleteness of public grief. It is not that Wah's father 'represents' an entire community but that 'Elite 9' suggests a way in which the line that separates the personal and the public history is nothing more than a historicist construction whereby the personal is always subordinated to the larger narratives of historical progression. Wah's invocation of historical events that mark the trans-Pacific experiences of diaspora, Mao's rise, the Nationalist campaign, the incarceration of incoming Chinese immigrants on Juan de Fuca Strait suggests a relationship to an experience of dislocation that is at once private and public, personal and also communal.

The persistence of grief structured in the melancholy of Wah's mourning with no end, the questions that cannot be answered, function as a form of resistance. The refusal to be cured of sadness is an affect working against the lures of assimilation. As David Eng and Shinee Han recognize in their argument for depathologizing melancholia, the racialized subject engages with both forms of grief. Eng and Han argue that 'the process of assimilation is a negotiation between mourning *and* melancholia. The ethnic subject does not inhabit one or the other – mourning *or* melancholia – but mourning *and* melancholia coexist at once in the process of assimilation. This continuum between mourning and melancholia allows us to understand the negotiation of racial melancholia as *conflict* rather than *damage*' (363). Indeed, the importance of relinquishing the idea of damage in relation to racial grief becomes all the more urgent when it is understood within the context of the insistence upon 'health' in the dominant culture. In *The Melancholy of Race* Anne Cheng suggests that the cultural assumptions around health that preoccupy dominant American culture are questionable at best and the presumption of a 'cure' 'remains dubious so long as health and pathology remain tethered to race and so long as assimilation reinforces the logic of incorporation that in turn repeats and prolongs the susceptibility of the already susceptible racialized body' (94). Moreover, the idea of a cure can function as a form of coercion: 'The question of how to "get over" the racial issue has profound implications for the future of social relations in America. American idealization of health, cure, and mourning (i.e., "getting over" something, or "moving on") is itself symptomatic of the culture's attachment to coercive normality' (95). In its preoccupation with the question of grief, the desire to speak to the dead, and the awareness of the ways in which death bequeaths death, Wah's poetry rejects the curative norms of mourning, refusing to fully let go of the father who fell too young, whose heart was broken too soon.

In the refusal to 'get over it' there is a stubborn attachment to the rawness of the displacement, of, in the case of Chinese Canadian migrant history, a history of labour exploitation, indirect indenture, and head-tax racism. In this sense, the refusal to be cured functions as a persistent reminder of the hostility of the present location. The nostalgic diasporic subject is not just someone who wallows in the familiar comfort of Chinatown enclaves or fantasies about an idealized homeland to which she can never return, but an agential reminder of the unhomeliness of a place where she will be continually cast as migrant, from away. Nostalgia may be hostile to history, in the sense of a history of teleological progression, but it is not necessarily hostile to memory. Instead, it suggests that there might be another register of remembering that is not embedded in history, but in the body.

In 'Between Memory and History: Les Lieux de Mémoire,' Pierre Nora traces memory's affiliation with the corporeal. Marking a difference between history and memory, Nora notes that seemingly abstract and objective remembering in the form of history has superceded a more concrete and subjective form of remembering that he has termed 'true memory.' Recalling the ties that bind, Nora differentiates between the history that binds a community and the memory that a community shares in its collectivity:

> Memory is blind to all but the group it binds – which is to say, as Maurice
> Halbwachs has said, that there are as many memories as there are groups,
> that memory is by nature multiple and yet specific; collective, plural, and
> yet individual. History, on the other hand, belongs to everyone and to no
> one, whence its claim to universal authority. Memory takes root in the con-
> crete, in spaces, gestures, images, and objects; history binds itself strictly
> to temporal continuities, to progressions and to relations between things.
> Memory is absolute, while history can only conceive the relative. (9)

The collectivity of memory lies in a materiality that history can only claim
in the abstract, in representation. Nora's differentiation between history
and memory marks a crucial possibility because it contests the notion
that the only way to remember the past is to historicize it. He proposes
the possibility of an alternative remembering that resides outside of history and yet still within the realm of shared communal knowledge. Within the concrete, Nora identifies a particular kind of memory that has
escaped the eradicating abstractions of historicism. 'True memory,' Nora
argues is a form of remembering, 'which has taken refuge in gestures and
habits, in skills passed down by unspoken traditions, in the body's inherent self-knowledge, in unstudied reflexes and ingrained memories' (13).
That is, the memory of the body, and not just individual memory within
the individual body, but cultural memory within collective bodies.

Wah' s poetry can be read as a repository of true memory. Loss, pain,
and anger move inward not only through the body, but also between
generations and across communities. An earlier poem, 'my father hurt-/
ing,' articulates loss as a process that flows 'very very far / inside' both
as a form of alienation between generations, but also as that which
connects:

    my father hurt-
    ing at the table
    sitting hurting
    at suppertime
    deep inside very
    far down inside
    because I can't stand the ginger
    in the beef and greens
    he cooked for us tonight
    and years later tonight
    that look on his face

appears now on mine
my children
my food
their food
my father
their father
me mine
*the* father
very far
very very far
inside (*Waiting* 7)

The poem reels, a tunnel inward down the page, down the lines of descent and the explosive resentment of taste. The hurting that emerges in the enjambment of the first four lines speaks to a legacy of pain that carries down through the lines of the remainder of the poem. In a later prose-poem about ginger, Wah speaks of ginger as a 'site of an implicit racial qualification,' where a taste for ginger stands in for a Chineseness that is accepted, swallowed, in all of its 'delicate pungency' (*Diamond* 11). Around ginger, 'this knurled suffix of gradated foreignicity,' the secret gestures of hurt and anger will superimpose themselves upon one generation and then the next and the next after that. And in the superimposition of gesture along the lines of the page, of descent, Wah collapses the expanse of time in the repetition of his temporal reference: 'he cooked for us tonight / and years later tonight.' Tonight and tonight again, the presence of the past emerges repeatedly in unexpected spaces of true memory, the passing on of gesture, of grimace, of taste: 'that look on his face / appears now on mine.' In the lines 'my food / their food / my father / their father / me mine' – in the single melodic line of, in Giorgio Agamben's words, 'this schism between sound and sense'[9] – homophony produces homophyly. The body recurs in the reiteration of 'food' and 'father,' and it is at the level of taste, a transgenerational recurrence of gesture, of the body writing itself through a very old code, that we can capture the glimpse of the painful transpiring of memory's transmission.

The transmission of memory occurs not only in the immediacy of familial bodies at suppertime but also in strange intimacies of a transpacific smell-taste experience. Writing about *juk*, a savoury rice soup that his family makes with leftovers, Wah suggests a way in which taste, as it surges along the tongue and through the neural networks of the body, functions as one of the refuges of the body.

Juk is even better than bird's-nest soup, though both soups share an intrinsic proprioceptive synapse: memory. While slurping a bowl of juk with the
January snow still swirling outside, the memory of the bird itself, only a few
weeks old, triangulates with a smoky star-filled night in China. Likewise,
with the gelatinous bird's-nest soup, the taste carries images of men climb-
ing the walls of dark caves in Yunan collecting the spaghetti-like translucent
strands of bird's nests, the frightened cries of the swallows themselves as
piercing as a foreign language. (*Diamond* 167–8)

The proprioceptor is a sensory nerve ending in muscles, tendons, and
joints that provides a sense of the body's position by responding to stimu-
li from within the body. In suggesting that *juk* and bird's nest soup share
a proprioceptive synapse, memory, Wah situates the body as a crucial
site of memory. The body, in this poem, does not simply exist abstractly
in space but is aware, through a series of synaptic jolts, of its location in
particular geographies, of its displacement and emplacement.

Wah's suggestion signals the work accomplished in neuropsychology,
in experimental psychology, and on cognition in the sciences, and pushes against the limits of this knowledge at the same time. While there had
been some debate about the precise pathways of the connections, scien-
tists have known for a long time that there is a connection between the
physiological response of memory and that of smell or, in the rational
language of science, 'that olfactory inputs reach hippocampus through
connections with entorhinal cortex and that the hippocampus has out-
puts that influence primary olfactory cortex' (Mair, Harris and Flint 50).
The hippocampus, the part of our brain that is widely understood as, in
laymen's terms, 'the seat of memory,' is connected to the ways in which
we recognize and process the smells we encounter. Wah takes this scientific body of knowledge even further though when he suggests that
taste can evoke a memory that is not specific to an individual body but
a memory that taps into a transpacific archive of experience. Taste can
carry within it the sense of a particular location. Wah's identification of
taste as a proprioceptive synapse suggests a way in which taste and smell
situate the body not only in space but also within a larger geography. In
this sense, Wah's writing pushes the scientific rationale of memory and
poses a challenge to it, asserting another order of experience wherein
the synapse produces a syndetic experience across physical space, gesturing towards a collectivity of experience. In 'these straits and islands /
of the blood … biology recapitulates geography; place becomes an island
in the / blood' (*Diamond* 22–3). *Juk* is more than just a highly personal-

ized synapse, and the body maps onto the transpacific in the way that the geography of transpacific migration has mapped itself onto a collective body.

Not only does Wah write of the way the body positions itself in geographical space and place through a complex chain of synaptic responses through the proprioceptive workings of memory, he also positions his reader within this process as well. Wah's use of the imperative in several of the *Diamond Grill* poems conducts the reader through a series of motions, leading us both inward and outward at the same time. In a poem about Chinese turnip, *lo bok*, Wah guides his reader into the geography of longing. He writes of

a craving for some Chinese
food taste that I haven't been able to pin down. An absence that
gnaws at sensation and memory. An undefined taste, not in the
mouth but down some blind alley of the mind. (*Diamond* 67)

He describes stumbling across this un-named but not forgotten taste in a Chinese food market. Seeing a pile of Chinese turnips being rapidly picked over by numerous shoppers, he asks a woman in the market how to use the vegetable. Thus, he finds this lost taste and invites his reader into the space of the fulfilment of craving. He tells us that we must

Buy a good sized Chinese white turnip, or lo bok. Even Safeway
will sometimes carry them. Start the dish by washing and setting
aside to soak about a tablespoon of small, dried shrimp. Peel the
turnip and cut it up into french-fry sized strips. Blanch by bringing
to a boil and then take out and pour cold water over. Slice and stir-
fry some beef with garlic and soy sauce. You can use a little onion if
you want to (my mother doesn't). Strain the cooled turnips and add
them to the stir-fry along with the shrimp and the water it's been
soaking in. Simmer in the liquid until the turnip just starts to soften.
Add a little more water if necessary and serve thin that way or
thicken with a little corn starch. During cooking the lo bok turns
from white to a light taupe. The taste roots itself as a miscegenated
bitterness of soil and ocean transfused by the dark brown soya into
guttural pungency. (67)

He repeats these instructions as the woman at the market would have given them to him. Wah takes our hand and asks us to follow him through that blind alley of the mind where there might be an absence gnawing at sensation and memory. This is not food as a sentimental return to a utopic past. This is not about comfort food only as comfort food. This is about the process of memory – of the body moving through space, preparing food, and retracing with another body the route towards a memory where the materiality of food has left its trace, viscerally forcing the past into the present. Wah's instructions for cooking *lo bok* are not a recipe, but a repetition of the way the diasporic body transforms the rawness of absence into the presence of cooked turnip rooting itself in the memory of the body. Finding the lost taste of *lo bok* is not so much a cause of celebration in Wah's text as it is a sad remembering of 'the bitterness of soil and ocean,' of the 'guttural pungency' of memory.

It is important that Wah locates this lost taste from a stranger. The route he poses for a diasporic memory of the body occurs in the community of dislocation, of one stranger bringing another stranger into a memory. The nostalgia for *lo bok* is one that emerges in dislocation and can only be re-experienced in dislocation. He posits unabashedly the possibility of collectivity in dislocation. Diasporic nostalgia is not for a particular homeland necessarily, or even for *lo bok* specifically, but for a sense of the communal bound by the alienations of dislocation. For Anne Cheng, racialized communities in the United States (the site of her investigation) are bound not by ethnicity but by grief. Cheng suggests that private grief teaches 'us about the advantages and disadvantages of forming a collective communal identity united not by ethnic homogeneity but by racial grievance' (91). In losing something private, the taste of a vegetable that had been part of a private, familial memory, and then finding it through the tastes of a stranger, Wah suggests that it is not only grief and loss that bind racialized diasporic subjects, but also hunger and the ways in which being lost can also lead to the profound joys of being found.

There is a collectivity to the processes of Wah's remembering. He has extended a hand towards others who have lost the taste of *lo bok* and asked them to move through the kitchen with him, simmering the liquid, soaking the shrimp. The imperative of Wah's language draws us into the internal space of personal craving and towards the public one of its fulfilment in a Chinatown market and the recipe that is not so much a recipe as a record of the process of retracing the body's movement in space. The collectivity of *lo bok* roots itself in the possibility of future repetitions by different bodies in differently dislocated situations. In this sense, the path of nostalgia is not only a reaching back into memory, into the past, but also a process of reaching forward and outward, away from individual longing and into process of shared memory in the preparation of *lo bok*.

In her essay 'The Memory of the Senses,' Nadia Seremetakis situates taste as a route to collective cultural memory. She argues that nostalgia has been fundamentally misread in contemporary culture.

> In Greek the *nostalghó* is a composite of *nostó* and *alghó*. *Nostó* means I return, I travel (back to homeland); the noun *nóstos* means the return, the journey ... *Alghó* means I feel pain, I ache for, and the noun *alghós* characterizes one's pain in soul and body, burning pain (*kaimós*). Thus *nostalghía* is the desire or longing with burning pain to journey. It also evokes the sensory dimension of memory in exile and estrangement ... In this sense, *nostalghía* is linked to the personal consequences of historicizing sensory experience which is conceived as a painful bodily and emotional journey. (4)

For Seremetakis, 'the senses are also implicated in historical interpretation as witnesses or record-keepers of material experience' (6). In this understanding, nostalgia is a means through which the body bears the record of experiences rooted in the materiality of the day-to-day.

Although Seremetakis suggests that nostalgia has been undervalued and misread in contemporary Western thought, I want to take her project one step further and propose that the relegation of nostalgia to the realm of the sentimental and inconsequential needs to be read within a specific history of European Enlightenment's denial of sensual memory as a form of history. In *Scent*, Annick Le Guérer traces the philosophical suppression of taste and smell as legitimate routes to knowledge. From Hegel to Freud, Le Guérer locates a general anathema in Enlightenment thought to the odiferous and therefore uncivilized space of the 'lesser' senses.[10] Similarly, Classen, Howes, and Synnott, in *Aroma*, uncover the deliberate suppression of smell because of its intensely corporeal and personal nature. Unlike sight, where one's relationship to the object does not affect the object itself, smell shifts according to the subject of its encounter. Smell refuses abstraction. Despite the advances of the chemical reproduction of certain scents, smell is irreproducible; it frustrates a modernity concerned with mechanical reproduction. Classen, Howes, and Synnott argue that 'smell has been marginalized because it is felt to threaten the abstract and impersonal regime of modernity by virtue of its radical interiority, its boundary-transgressing propensities and its emotional potency' (5). In this sense, the denial of taste and smell to function as repositories of alternative histories and true memories is an integral part of the project of European Enlightenment to maintain a particular social order. Returning to Nora, in conjunction with Seremetakis, it becomes clear that the suppression of smell and taste in Enlightenment thinking is closely related to the project of the obliteration of memory through history.

As I have been suggesting throughout this discussion, against the obliteration of memory *Diamond Grill* powerfully asserts a poetics of memory that is deeply embedded in the corporeality of the racialized diasporic body. For Wah, in the 'still-dark in the half-dream breathing silence,' we can find the 'silent rehearsal of / the memory of taste,' where 'the first language / behind his closed eyes is a dreamy play-by-play about making beef / and lotus root soup' (*Diamond* 174). In the declaration that memory and taste can be a 'first language' wherein the tongue waters 'at the palpable flavour of words' Wah traces another text of memory.

This is a collectivity born out of and borne in shared longing, a craving that cannot be suppressed in the abstractions of identity politics. The 'common possession,' to return to David Scott's phrase (124),[11] of Chinese diaspora culture lies not in animating figures such as Indenture and Asia – not only because it is mistaken to suggest that the experience of indenture and the idea of Asia are parallel to Slavery and Africa – but in the idiosyncratic inheritance of, in Wah's evocation, 'real Chinese food ... ox tail / soup, deep fried cod, chicken with pineapple and lichee – things we / don't always taste willingly but forever after crave' (*Diamond* 46). It is not that the sadness of indenture and dislocation is not relevant to this common possession. Rather, it is constitutive of it. However, the problem that this chapter wants to attend to is the way in which this sadness has been transmitted. It is within this question of transmission that I propose 'real Chinese food' as the mode by which the inheritance of unresolved racial grief surges to the surface of the everyday. Echoing Wah, I use this phrase, 'real Chinese food,' in order to emphasize the discourse of dissensus and consensus that the idea of 'real Chinese food' evokes. This is contested terrain. It is this contestedness, Scott argues, that we should treasure. As my discussion of Wah's poetry has emphasized, I am not interested in 'real Chinese food' as an identifiable object of debate, but rather in the subjective and material experience of it, of taste, craving, longing. In addition to oxtail soup and chicken with pineapple and lichee, we might also add sweet and sour pork, beef and greens with slivered ginger, lotus root soup, juk. As the debate on Chineseness reveals, the point of 'real Chinese' is not an authorized cultural authenticity, about getting the 'right' Chinese food, but is about authenticating the experience of craving, longing for something that defies the binds of historicism – a collective gustatory desire.

To authenticate an experience or a desire is not to authorize it. To authenticate the possibility of a collective gustatory desire as a route to an alternative history, as I have been arguing, is simply to give credence to a mode of knowing that has been suppressed and misnamed as sentimental. As Keya Ganguly presciently argues, 'The question of authenticity has more to do with the phenomenal click of the presence of the past, of some ideal of truth occluded ... than it does with the retroactive click of a deferred action in which experience becomes the remembrance of something that was never true in the first place' (134). 'Real Chinese food' then is the mode by which 'the phenomenal click of the presence of the past' surges through the neural networks of the body to produce a proprioceptive synapse: memory. It is a synapse that situates the body in space, that mediates the gap between the past and the present, between China and Chineseness, in order to make sense of a longing for plain white rice, or lo bok cooked simmered in soy with shrimp. In an interview with Jonathan Goddard, Wah articulates the relationship between food and racialized memory with a characteristic simplicity that confounds transparency: 'Race is not something you can feel or recognize, and that's one of the things I'm investigating in [*Waiting for Saskatchewan*]. It turns out race is food. I feel Chinese because of the food I enjoy, and that's because my father cooked Chinese food. But I don't know what it feels like to feel Chinese' (41). Wah's deceptively simple answer – 'I feel Chinese because I like the food my father cooked,' immediately turns in on itself when he declares, 'But I don't know what it feels like to feel Chinese.' I read in Wah's answer not a contradiction but a contralateral positioning of Chineseness. To know what it feels like to feel Chinese works in conjunction with its opposite, with not knowing what it feels like to feel Chinese. Knowing Chineseness can only emerge in dialectical tension with not knowing. Within this uncertainty, the ebb and flow of memory emerges.

Emerging out of, and coalescing within, true memory, recuperated from history, diasporic communities pose a challenge to dominant cultural power. One of the ways in which we can read for diasporic resistance lies in their stubborn attention to memory. Diasporic communities can be understood as constituted by the imminence of memory rather than by the backward browsings of historicism. Diasporic criticism risks reinscribing the suppression of alternative histories in relegating nostalgia solely to the realm of the inconsequentially sentimental. Underneath the pathologizing of nostalgia lies the anxieties of colonialism's own unresolved sickness for a home that never existed. The nostalgia of diasporic subjects is not necessarily one that yearns for an impossible authenticity in fictive narratives of homeland. One part of theorizing and thinking through the possibilities of diasporic resistance lies in recuperating the histories that might otherwise remain buried in the rubbish of sentiment. In recuperating nostalgia from sentiment and memory from history I hope to have moved towards an awareness of an unofficial history embedded in the gestures and longings of the racialized body. Against the Kantian notion of taste as deeply subjective, as individually idiosyncratic,[12] I have been gambling on the possibility of community constituted in that which has precisely been rejected as too subjective, too individual, and too nostalgic for the formation of community. Wah's poetry suggests that there are communities formed out of a 'taste burnt right through to the spine' (*Diamond* 74). While I am committed to the question of what it is that makes the diasporic subject diasporic, my exploration of an answer has been speculative, a wager on the possibility that we might have tastes that might not be entirely our own.

# Conclusion

HIS HALF-DREAM IN THE STILL-
   DARK BREATHING SILENCE IS

the translation from the bitter-green cloudiness of the winter melon
soup in his dream to the sweet-brown lotus root soup he knows
Shu will prepare later this morning for the Chinese staff in the
cafe. He moves the taste of the delicate nut-like lotus seeds through
minor degrees of pungency and smokiness to the crunchy slices of
lotus root suspended in the salty-sweet beef broth. This silent
rehearsal of the memory of taste moves into his mind so that the
first language behind his closed eyes is a dreamy play-by-play
about making beef and lotus root soup. Simple: a pound of short
ribs and a pound of lotus root in a small pot of water with some
soy sauce and salt, a little sliced ginger, maybe a few red Chinese
dates. Shu will surely touch it with a piece of dried orange peel
because it's close to Christmas. He feels his tongue start to move
as his mouth waters at the palpable flavour of words.

(Wah, *Diamond* 174)

Before the modern restaurant became a restaurant, it was an object rather than a place. It was a bowl of soup, a restorative broth, *un restaurant*.
In eighteenth- and nineteenth-century France, it was a highly condensed
bouillon served in small cups to those who deemed themselves too delicate to digest meats and vegetables, preferring instead these 'essences'
of chicken, beef, and so on. While the story of the European restaurant's
transformation from 'miniature soup-cup to Rabelaisian excess, from

sensibility to politics' is a story told elsewhere (Spang 3),[1] in a book about small town Chinese restaurants it seems fitting then that we circle back to soup, the first course. We will close where the restaurant begins.

I used to find Chinese soups suspicious. They were too much like Chinese medicine. Too many ingredients I couldn't name. And nobody ate any of these things on TV. Give me something from that ubiquitous red and white can, warmed up in the old steel pot, any day. At the Diamond Grill, you could order Chicken Rice, Chicken Noodle, Cream Mushroom, Consomme Clear, Vegetable, Cream Tomato, Clam Chowder, Cream Celery, Dinner Soup. No lotus root in beef broth. No winter melon. Shu makes the lotus root soup for the Chinese staff at the café. Why isn't it on the menu? Are there communities of taste? Wah's poem seems to suggest that there might be something we might call a 'Chinese taste.' The woeful inadequacy of this phrase already points to part of the problem of how we can talk about something that might just be outside the bounds of that which can be articulated. When your tongue waters at the palpable flavour of words, at the memory of pungent and smoky lotus seeds and the sweet-saltiness of beef broth, does it water in the same way as mine? Against the Kantian notion of taste as deeply subjective, as individually idiosyncratic, I have been gambling on the possibility of community constituted in that which has precisely been rejected as too subjective, too individual, and too nostalgic for the formation of community. While I am committed to the question of what it is that makes the diasporic subject diasporic, my exploration of an answer has been speculative, a wager on the possibility that we might have tastes that might not be entirely our own.

In the chapter 5, I have been trying to think through what David Scott termed the 'demand' of diaspora criticism as a problem of memory (127). Terdiman suggests that memory has a materiality. But does this materiality have a collectivity? Can we think of memory as not only transgenerational, but also as something that traverses individual subjectivities. It seems to me that it does, even though we may not be able to articulate how exactly this might work. In their 'Dialogue on Racial Melancholia,' David Eng and Shinhee Han write about Rea Tajiri's video *History and Memory*. The video is about a Japanese American girl whose parents survive the internment. Her mother has suppressed all memories of the event. The daughter has nightmares she cannot explain of a young woman at a watering well and enters a state of depression. 'Eventually, the daughter discovers that these nightmares are reenactments of the mother's histories in the camp. Ironically, the mother has history but no memory, while the daughter has memory but no history' (Eng and Han 354). Tajiri's work posits a 'theory of melancholia that is not individually experienced but intergenerationally shared' (ibid.). Both Anne Cheng's work and that of Eng and Han suggests the possibility of inter-subjective melancholia, wherein the 'historical traumas of loss are passed down from one generation to another unconsciously' (ibid.).

While Tajiri's work is a specific, and very compelling, example of the possibility of the psychic manifestations of the residual of loss, of that which remains and gets passed on across generations and individuals, this book has not been about a singular historical trauma or event. Part of the challenge of writing about the Chinese diaspora without giving in to historical triumphalism lies in resisting the urge to spectacularize the large, nameable events of historical trauma. That is not to say that sweeping, horrifying events that have displaced so many people – the indenturing of Chinese labourers, the Nanking Massacre, the Boxer Rebellion, the rise of the gulag labour system, to name just a few – are not significant. But this by no means inclusive list of some of the traumas that might be associated with Chinese diaspora history in itself suggests and masks the multiplicity of losses and displacements. Further, we cannot overlook the smaller, pedestrian events that accrue day after day. In the previous chapter, I resisted naming indenture as being akin to slavery in David Scott's reformulation of Kamau Braithwaite's 'profoundly oppositional Afro-Caribbean tradition,' wherein 'slavery is the name of a trial and a tribulation, and Africa the name of an identity\difference' (127). Whereas slavery names a trial and tribulation shared by most of the black diaspora, indenture does not name a singular, shared event in Asian-Pacific migration. That does not dispel its importance as one of the primary sources of nineteenth- and twentieth-century mass trans-Pacific migration, but suggests the need to resist the urge to name singular traumas for the Chinese diaspora.

While I have insisted from the beginning of this book that diaspora must retain a sense of its relationship to the historical oppressions and dislocations of colonialism and imperialism in its many forms, and thus that there is an integral relationship between old and new diasporas, I have also resisted naming indenture as the only defining experience of the Chinese diaspora. To be sure, I have insisted on the contemporaneity of indenture, on the need to consider it as a feature of the present rather than relegating it to a forgettable past in the desire to move on, to progress into a future of global cosmopolitanism. This insistence connects to my sense that diaspora studies need to retain their relationship with postcolonial studies. However, I do not want to name an originary role for indenture in the Chinese diaspora. Rather, my hope is that diaspora allows for a way to embrace the multiple forms of sadnessess and loss that emerge from displacement, one form of which is the legacy of indenture. It is not that the restaurant is directly related to indenture, or that Chinese labourers were technically indentured (although they were called coolies for a reason and the conditions of their work pose a challenge to the idea of free labour), or that those who worked on the railway then went on to work in restaurants (although this did happen); rather, the small town Chinese restaurant illuminates the gap between indenture as an event firmly embedded in the past and the way in which the residuum of indenture continues to emerge in the present. This book is about the small acts of resistance and recalcitrance, the overlooked forms of agency embedded within everyday exchanges and interactions. It is devoted to the slow accrual of meaning that occurs in the act of passing a menu back and forth across the counter over the years, the conversations that unfold while people sit in booths and order their food, the hunger for that preternaturally red sauce on sweet and sour pork.

Within this commitment to the everyday, we can locate the collective forms of loss and trauma that form the sometimes irrational ties that bind – irrational because they cannot always be explained within the forms of knowledge we have at hand. How do you explain a daughter who dreams a mother's history? How do you rationalize the longing for the taste of *juk*, which is 'even better than bird's-nest soup, though both soups share an intrinsic proprioceptive synapse: memory' (Wah, *Diamond* 167). Memory is not always rational. As Dipesh Chakrabarty notes about the difference between memory and history with regard to Partition in India, 'History seeks to explain the event; the memory of pain refuses the historical explanation and sees the event as a monstrously irrational aberration' (*Habitations* 119). This book is committed to memory's refusal of history, to the possibilities of that which is not always rational but which is nonetheless a part of our world.

When you eat lotus root, it tears into multiple threads as it separates on the edge of your teeth. They become cobwebs in your mouth. Perhaps we can read in that moment before swallowing not a silence but what Homi Bhabha calls a 'caesura,' a break in the rhythm of history that allows for a different story (246). In the half-dream that translates bitter-melon into the silken webs of lotus root, we can read for the history's otherness, for memory that traverses collectivities and constitutes communities.

This book began with the problem of opposing the premature requiem for the small town Chinese restaurant which has not died, for those diasporic populations outside of the metropole who have not disappeared. It emerges out of a concern for the way in which discussions of transnationalism, the global movement of migrants, and the rise of the visibly diasporic in the First World collapse the nonmodern with the backward. That is, diasporas are a problem for the First World. I have argued that small town Chinese restaurants in Canada function as a locus for examining diasporic culture. They lie at the juncture between old and new diasporas and illuminate how one is constitutive of the other. They illuminate not just cultural survival, but also the negotiations and transformations that are the stuff of survival.

Overall, this book has tried to recuperate the reputedly nonmodern from the dustbins of backwardness and to see in that which has been declared backward the possibilities of alternative histories, and submerged or suppressed agency. Against a history that seems to suggest a population that was largely passive, that took their beatings without major protest, that was outraged and yet acquiescent, this project has tried to look for something else. In Chinese Canadian history, there are no major rebellions or revolutions on the order of the rebellion of the Santals in 1855 India, or that of the Haitian revolution, or the Philippino sugar strikes in early-twentieth-century Hawaii, and yet this does not mean that there was no protest. Chapter 1 argued for a conception of agency in diaspora that shares much with the work of Subaltern Studies, but also differs from it. In diaspora, you are not the (colonized) majority. In diaspora, you are not 'native.' But you work; you cook; you serve food; you change the names of dishes, tell jokes, and share memories; you eat food that you crave and you long for things you cannot always name. As this book has shown, agency, resistance, and recalcitrance can take less noisy, less visible forms in diaspora. We have to read differently.

Reading differently, I want to conclude by casting a backward glance at the book through the lens of one last photograph (see figure 8). It was taken in 1905 at the MacInnes lumber camp in Elkmouth, British Columbia. A loose assembly of burly lumber workers stands rough and tall, shoulder to flannel shoulder, in the centre. Some smile. Most don't. It is hard work. They are in the middle of nowhere, logging, living months on end at a camp that is known only by the name of their employer. Hugh MacInnes, the owner of the camp, stands in the front, arms folded across his chest. The only one wearing a sports jacket, he stares sternly into the camera. At the end of the front row, on the right-hand side, there is a

8  MacInnes Lumber Camp, Elkmouth, British Columbia, 1905. Courtesy of Glenbow Archives.

Chinese man, the only one in the group. He is a little shorter than every-one else. He wears a cap, a shapeless, dark, button-front coat over many other layers, and tough workpants like everyone else. Thumbs in his pockets, arms out, he stands broadly, looking straight into the camera.

The photograph is archived at the Glenbow Museum in Calgary, Al-berta. On the back of the photograph is a note: 'Chinese man, front right, was a woman in disguise.' The note comes from Richard MacInnes, grandson of the Hugh, who donated the materials to the Glenbow a few years ago. The story that has been passed around in the MacInnes family is that she was the best camp cook Hugh MacInnes ever had. After that things get fuzzy. How did he know? Did everyone else in the camp know? As a cook, she kept different hours than everyone else. She slept behind the cooking shed, at a distance from the rest of the camp. Maybe they didn't know. Maybe they did. Why was she disguised? Nobody seems to remember her name. She worked, disguised as a man, for the MacIn-neses for a few years and then left. Where and why, again, nobody seems to know. The records are incomplete and full of questions for which nobody seems to have any answers. Tucked away amidst archival files on lumber camps and logging, she interrupts presumptions of bachelor societies, of how women came and what they did. She suggests another, hidden history of Chinese women in Canada that scholarship on Chi-nese immigration and Chinese diaspora studies has yet to grasp.

Throughout the time that I have worked on this book, I have often asked myself about the place of women in this project. I have taken this question to be about two broadly related concerns. I understand the first to be a more straightforward concern with presence: Where are the women? The second I take to be about the problem of methodology and praxis: What is the place of feminist critique for a project that seems to be almost entirely about men? From Ah Lum in Hong Kong to Hoy Fat Leong and Charlie Chew Long in New Dayton, to Fred Wah mourning the death of a father, Chinese women seem to be far from the centre of this project. Feminist work is not only about engaging with women as objects of inquiry, but also, among other things, is a methodological engagement and a commitment to subjective experience and subjectiv-ity. As the woman cook cross-dressed at the MacInnes lumber camp sug-gests, the purported absence of women can be more richly understood as an indication of the creativity of women who assert their presences in ways that are not always obvious and not always visible. I hope that the commitment to exploring an alternative, interruptive temporality, to the multiple planes of history as Reinhart Koselleck puts it, has demonstrated one way of doing feminist work even when there *seem* to be no women in the picture.

With the problem of presence, my response has been two-fold. First, according to all the documents, the census data, the immigration records, and the official histories, there were very simply few Chinese women in Canada before 1947. Feminist historians such as the Women's Book Committee of the Chinese Canadian National Council tried to address this problem of presence with the publication of *Jin Guo: Voices of Chinese Canadian Women* in 1992. The book records the histories of several Chinese Canadian women and fills an important gap in our historical record. However, addressing the problem of presence does not modify the dominance of the bachelor society in this history, nor does it dislodge what the immigration records and the *Chinese Immigration Act* flatly declare: that, before the end of Exclusion, Chinese women entered Canada through two categorical ports of entry, wife or prostitute. My second response to the problem of presence lies, as my meditation on the photo of the MacInnes lumber camp indicates, in recognizing that there were women that we do not yet know about.

One cross-dressed Chinese woman does not necessarily mean that there are many more, nor does she invalidate the hardships and history of a bachelor society that survived against the edicts of immigration laws that intended otherwise. However, her particularity should not be ignored or treated as unique. She is neither the exception nor the rule, but a figure of possibility. There are other histories yet to be unfolded. As cultural critics, we do not explode the particular into the general, but examine the way in which it complicates the general narrative, the way in which it presents an interruption to what we think we know.

If the demand of diaspora criticism has been that of negotiating between cultural nationalism and deconstruction, perhaps the obligation of diaspora criticism is to the otherness of history, to memory and the spaces where modernity sometimes stammers. Memory has a collectivity, cutting across generations and individuals, but where is the place of the disguised lumber-camp cook in our remembering? In this backward glance, this project looks forward as well towards the work that has yet to be done. While Gayatri Spivak has insisted that the experience of being in diaspora is a fundamentally uneven one for Third World women,[2] diaspora studies have yet to work out the contours of that unevenness.

The photograph of the lumber camp illuminates the overdetermined sense of gender that attends to considerations of early Chinese migrant labour and the Chinese diaspora. It raises questions about the seemingly unknown and barely visible history of women labourers, cross-dressing, and gender performance. It complicates the questions about the effeminization of Asian male labourers. The photograph points directly to an over-written history of male migration and the tendency towards discursive generalization of Chinese migrants – the way the definite article hovers over the entire history of Chineseness in Canada, implying a specificity and knowability to a constantly shifting subjectivity. The Chinese Restaurant. The Chinese Labourer. The 'Coolie.' Against the attempts to pin down Chineseness through a project of persistent universalization, this project has been committed to the specificities of diasporic arrival. As my backward glance through the doors of the restaurant and into a long disbanded lumber camp makes clear, this is an unfinished commitment.

# Notes

## Introduction

1 My deepest thanks to this listener, and to all the others, who wrote and called with their enthusiasm for the project and their memories. My thanks also to Judy Hamill at CBC Radio One, Edmonton, for insisting that I do the interview even though I thought I didn't have anything to say.

2 This information would have been impossible to find without the help of the archivists at the Galt Museum in Lethbridge, Alberta, and the New Dayton Historical Society. My sincere thanks to them for their help.

3 In a preface written in memoriam to Claire Johnston, Morris shares Paul Willemen's interpretation of the film *Trop Tôt Trop Tard* (Too Soon Too Late), by Jean-Marie Straub and Danielle Huillet, noting that 'there is a need "for things being *both* too soon and too late" if "even a moment" of eventfulness is to be possible ... This, more than anything to do with a "postmodern" pragmatism, describes the activating principle of Claire Johnston's feminist film theory' (xxiii).

4 See Jean Anthelme Brillat-Savarin, *The Physiology of Taste* and Barthes, *Mythologies*.

5 See Douglas, 'Deciphering a Meal' and Visser, *The Rituals of Dinner*.

6 See Spang, *The Invention of the Restaurant*.

7 See Rushdie, *Imaginary Homelands*.

8 See Chow, 'The Secrets of Ethnic Abjection' in *The Protestant Ethnic and the Spirit of Capitalism*, and 'Introduction: On Chineseness as a Theoretical Problem.'

9 See Brah, *Cartographies of Diaspora*, esp. 181–95, Dufoix's *Diasporas*, and Tololyan, 'Rethinking Diaspora(s).'

## 1. Sweet and Sour

1   This a brief summary of the poisoning. Accounts of the event appear in a
    number of histories of Hong Kong, including Nigel Cameron's *Hong Kong:
    The Cultured Pearl* and G.B. Endacott's *A History of Hong Kong* (44–60, 93–4).
    In popular history, the story has been retold by Jan Morris in *Hong Kong*
    (42–3). Each of these accounts names Cheong Ah Lum as the principal per-
    petrator. The most thorough account of the specifics of Ah Lum's trial can
    be found in James William Norton-Kyshe's 1898 *The History of the Laws and
    Courts of Hong Kong* (414–18).

2   In *The Potlatch Papers* Christopher Bracken makes a similar point regarding
    the multiple spellings of the 'potlatch' in the settler colonial archive.

3   The main currency at this time was the silver dollar. The problem of cur-
    rency has been a constant factor of doing business in Hong Kong, where
    transactions were often transnational. Endacott notes that a May 1845
    proclamation set a number of coins as legal tender in addition to sterling
    and British coins: 'the East India Company's gold mohur at 29s. and 2d.;
    the rupee at 1s. 10d. and the half, quarter, and one-eighth rupees, pro rata;
    the dollar of Spain, Mexico and any South American state at 4s. 2d. and the
    Chinese copper cash at 288 for one shilling' (76–7). These equivalents re-
    mained in force until the growth of trade and forgery prompted then gover-
    nor Sir Hercules Robinson to insist on a series of new coins for Hong Kong
    and the declaration of silver Spanish, Mexican and South American dollars
    to be legal tender in the colony (Endacott 117). The use of these particular
    currencies makes an interesting comment on early Pacific Rim trade and
    the intersection between British and Spanish imperial interests.

4   From the beginning, the Hong Kong legal system differentiated its subjects
    on the basis of race. The problem of finding an appropriate legal system
    of governance for the colony haunted the Hong Kong administrators for
    decades. As the proclamation declaring Chinese inhabitants to be subjects
    of the Queen of England makes clear, Hong Kong began with a dual system
    – British settlers would be governed by English law and Chinese inhabitants
    would be governed by Chinese law. However, despite a series of subsequent
    ordinances, there were still a number of problems with this system. As Enda-
    cott notes, 'The official attitude towards the Chinese was liberal enough in
    theory, but much of the legislation providing for law and order discrimi-
    nated against them' (70). Endacott's discussion of early Hong Kong gover-
    nance, particularly under Sir John Davies, highlights many of the problems
    that the colonial administration encountered in their attempts to apply
    English law in the colony. Peter Wesley-Smith's chapter 'Statutory Provisions

Importing English Law' in *The Sources of Hong Kong Law* discusses these issues in some depth.

5  See Guha, 'The Prose of Counter-Insurgency,' esp. 78–84, and *Elementary Aspects of Peasant Insurgency*, esp. 251–77; and Chakrabarty, 'Conditions for Knowledge of Working-Class Conditions,' esp. 225–30.

6  A.A. Brill's 1918 translation of *Totem and Taboo* highlights the text's preoccupation with race more explicitly than does James Strachey's subsequent translation in the Standard Edition. Brill's translation of the same line from the preface suggests that the essays in the book 'represent [Freud's] first efforts to apply view-points and results of psychoanalysis to unexplained problems of *racial psychology*' (ix , my emphasis). Strachey's translation of the term *Völkerpsychologie* suppresses the racial undertones of the text. However, neither the Strachey nor the Brill translation is satisfying. Both seem anachronistic in their readings of the compound adjective *Völkerpsychologie*. This instability around the translating of *Völkerpsychologie* itself points to a larger issue in the text around the situating of cultural others.

7  In her essay 'Anthropology and Race in Brazilian Modernism' Zita Nunes also writes of the relationship between race, cannibalism, and the problem of the residual or what is leftover.While my argument has taken a detour through the issue of identification and Freud's totem meal, Nunes's analysis focuses more specifically on the problem of race in Brazil and a reading of Brazilian modernism. Nunes focuses on the Brazilian modernist movement's emphasis on cultural cannibalism articulated in texts such as Oswald be Andrade's *O manifesto pau Brazil* (The brazilwood manifesto) and *O manifesto antropofago* (The cannibalist manifesto). Writing of the Brazilian modernist movement's approach to cultural mixing and miscegenation through the cannibalist method, Nunes notes that the desire to consume and absorb what is useful in a culture and excrete the rest fails to recognize the exclusions inherent in excretion: 'The law of assimilation is that there must always be a remainder, a residue – something (someone) that has resisted or escaped incorporation, even when the nation produces narratives of racial democracy to mask this tradition of resistance' (125). For Nunes, the remainder constitutes a problem for the state.

In her essay 'The Melting Pot of Assimilation: Cannibalizing the Multicultural Body' Sneja Gunew also discusses the idea of cannibalism in relation to multiculturalism, specifically that of multicultural food festivals. Through the work of Julia Kristeva, Gunew argues that 'while food signifies actual bodies it also stands in for … language itself. Thus, the dominant culture engages with multicultural cuisine as a way of not acknowledging multicultural words' (147). Gunew explores mother–daughter relationships in a number of Australian minority writers and charts some of the ways in which food replaces language and, in the sense of Deleuze and Guattari's work on Kafka, 'deterritorializes the language from within' (155).

8  In 'Rereading Chinese Head Tax Racism' I explore the discursive production of Chinese as a legal category in the 1885 *Report of the Royal Commission on Chinese Immigration.*

9  For an account of 'everyday resistance' as it has been theorized in postcolonial studies see David Jefferess, *Postcolonial Resistance.* Of particular relevance to the present discussion is Jefferess's account of 'resistance as subversion,' which, in his analysis, 'constitutes the disruption or modification of colonial modes of knowledge and authority' (20).

10  These criticisms are most cogently argued in texts such as Aijaz Ahmad's *In Theory* and Arif Dirlik's '*The Postcolonial Aura: Third World Criticism in the Age of Global Capital.*'

11  In *Postcolonialism* Robert Young traces the history of the deployment of the idea of imperialism and differentiates imperialism in its direct form (conquest) from indirect forms such as political or economic influence, which functions as an effective domination (27). Also, see pp. 15–43 for an excellent discussion of the historical emergences of colonialism and imperialism and the distinction between the two.

12  There have been a series of race riots targeting Chinese immigrants in Canadian history, including the 1907 Vancouver riot that caused enough concern at both a local and a national level that then–prime minister Wilfrid Laurier stepped in to police the situation. For detailed discussions of anti-Chinese riots and anti-Chinese legislation (the two often went hand in hand) see Peter Li's *The Chinese in Canada*, Patricia Roy's *A White Man's Province*, Peter Ward's *White Canada Forever*, and Edgar Wickberg's *From China to Canada.*

13  See Li, *The Chinese in Canada* and Wickberg, *From China to Canada* for excellent historical surveys of some of the 'push' and 'pull' factors that mark early-nineteenth- and late-twentieth-century Chinese emigration to Canada.

14  For detailed discussions of the trajectories and histories of Chinese indentured labour, see Walter Look Lai, *Indentured Labour, Carribean Sugar*; Brij Lal, Doug Munro, and Edward Beechart, eds., *Plantation Workers: Resistance and Accommodation*; Moon-Ho Jung, *Coolies and Cane*; and Kay Saunders, *Indentured Labour in the British Empire.*

## 2. On the Menu

1  Although Patricia Roy has argued that Chinese railway workers were not technically coolies because they came to work voluntarily, most historians

agree that the conditions of their labour were almost identical to that of indenture. Roy writes that 'the Chinese … were not technically [coolies] having come to Canada as free laborers or under voluntary term contracts: the true coolie was usually a captive who had no choice about where he went or what he did' (18). However, Chinese railway workers had very little choice about where they went and the conditions of their arrival produced an informal indenture system. Chinese laborers usually had their head tax and transportation fees paid for first by a contractor or subcontractor and they would be expected to eventually work off those debts, producing a system of indentured labour that was never formally named as such in Canada. The elaborate system of subcontracting made it particularly easy for the Canadian government to declare that it was not employing indentured labour. See Lee 47, Li 20–3, and Wickberg 20–4.

2  See also Spivak's 'Diasporas Old and New' and Mishra's 'The Diasporic Imaginary.'

3  Ian Baucom notes that Gilroy's notion of a ruptured, nonsynchronous temporality is by no means exclusive to *The Black Atlantic*, but has been previously explored by Althusser, Bloch, Braudel, and Derrida. See Baucom, 'Introduction: Atlantic Genealogies' 8–12.

4  While Laura Chrisman's 'Journeying to Death: Gilroy's *Black Atlantic*' and Neil Lazarus's 'Is a Counterculture of Modernity a Theory of Modernity?' argue that Gilroy's analysis fails to address the conditions of the reproduction of blackness, Chris Bongie's 'A Street Named Bissette: Nostalgia, Memory, and the Cent-Cinquantenaire of the Abolition of Slavery in Martinique (1848–1998),' David Scott's chapter 'An Obscure Miracle of Connection' in *Refashioning Futures*, and Charles Piot's 'Atlantic Aporias: Africa and Gilroy's *Black Atlantic*' seek in various ways to think through the problem of memory and 'tradition' that Gilroy poses, particularly in the latter half of the book.

5  Williams connects the rural-to-urban migration flows with those of the flows from the colonies or ex-colonies to the metropolis, noting that 'ironically, unemployment in the colonies prompted a reverse migration, and following an ancient pattern the displaced from the "country" areas came, following the wealth and stories of wealth, to the "metropolitan" centre, where they were at once pushed in, overcrowded, among the indigenous poor, as had happened throughout in the development of the cities' (283).

6  While I am clearly indebted to Williams's argument, I also depart from him in terms of his sense of the progression of history. In chapter 24, 'The New Metropolis,' which connects imperialism with the metropolitan, Williams suggests a sense where the postcolony occupies the space once held by the English countryside: 'We can remember our own early literature of

mobility and the corrupting process of cities, and see many of its themes reappearing in African, Asian and West Indian literature, itself written, characteristically, in the metropolitan languages which are themselves among the consequences of mobility. We can read of the restless villages of so many far countries: in Nkem Nwankwo's *Danda*, in George Lammings's *In the Castle of My Skin* ... And Chinua Achebe, who in *Things Fall Apart* and *Arrow of God* showed the arrival of the alien system in the villages, shows us the complicated process of education mobility and new kinds of work in the city in *No Longer at Ease* and *Man of the People*' (Williams 288). In making these important connections between the postcolony and the English countryside, Williams betrays a subscription to a notion of progress where the postcolony replicates and re-enacts the effects of capitalism within England itself and is thus somewhere further behind on the timeline of development. Despite the importance of recognizing the possibilities of 'a common history' (ibid.), the early literature of English rural mobility is not quite the literature of decolonization.

7 There is a significant body of scholarship on Chinatowns and the following is a sample of some of the work that has been most useful for my understanding of Chinatown as both a physical and social formation. For historical, geographical, and sociological work, see Kay Anderson's *Vancouver's Chinatown*, Hsiang-Shui Chen's *Chinatown No More*, chapter 5 ('Building Permanent Chinese American Communities ... 1920–27') of Shehong Chen's *Being Chinese, Becoming Chinese American*, David Lai's *Chinatowns: Towns within Cities in Canada*, Peter Kwong's *The New Chinatown*, Jan Lin's *Reconstructing Chinatown*, Wing Chung Ng's *The Chinese in Vancouver 1945–80*, and chapter 15 ('Chinatowns') of Lynn Pan's *Sons of the Yellow Emperor*. In literary work, A. Robert Lee's essay 'Imagined Cities of China: Timothy Mo's London, Sky Lee's Vancouver, Fae Myenne Ng's San Francisco' argues that each of these texts reproduces a cultural China, an imaginary and transplanted Chinese world, within each of the cities in which the novels are set. Also, within literary criticism, Maria Ng's 'Representing Chinatown: Dr. Fu Manchu at the Disappearing Moon Café' argues that Chinatown functions as an overly stereotyped site of racial identifications in the literature of Sky Lee, Irene Lin-Chandler, and Sax Rohmer. While I agree with Ng that we must always be vigilant against the perpetuation of stereotype, we must also be attentive to overly easy parallels that occlude critique. There are, for example, crucial differences between London's Limehouse district of Sax Rohmer's work – which departs significantly from North American Chinatowns – and the Chinatown of Sky Lee's novel.

8 Although they reinforce the idea of Chinatown as an ethnic enclave or, to

borrow David Lai's phrase, towns within cities, most of the literature argues against viewing Chinatowns as racially or socially homogeneous enclaves. Hsiang-Shui Chen, Shehong Chen, and Peter Kwong in particular argue for an understanding of the heterogeneity of the Chinatowns of their respective studies. Extending this vision of heterogeneity, the work of both Michel LaGuerre and Jan Lin insist on the need to understand Chinatowns as locally grounded sites with deeply global connections. In this sense, their work focuses on Chinatown as a site that mediates the flows of culture and capital transnationally and yet still remains within a clearly bounded ethnic enclave. Departing somewhat from this work, Kay Anderson's book on Vancouver's Chinatown argues that Chinatowns are bounded from without. Anderson traces the racist urban planning policies that have created a racially ghettoized community. Recently, her thesis has been taken up by Ng Wing Chung, who contests Anderson's reading and argues for something like a subaltern history of the emergence of Vancouver's Chinatown.

9 Michel Laguerre notes that the grammatical rules behind the naming of enclaves reveals a hierarchical spatial ordering system: 'In contrast to the ways in which minoritized quarters are stigmatized as "little" places, the mainstream refers to its space in terms of a new reality, as in "New" England, "New" Britain, "New" London, and "New" York' (6).

10 Chinese workers were often abandoned wherever the contracts for work on the railway line ended and unemployment in these areas produced drifting communities. In some of the worst cases, starving workers resorted to petty theft and eating garbage from the streets. See Morton 106–107.

11 In many ways, this chapter has taken Gilroy's work as its departure point. I acknowledge this debt in the spirit of Khachig Tölölyan's argument that the black diasporic communities are exceptional in their experiences of racism both historically and in contemporary realities. Recognizing this exceptionality means that we need to think through the ways in which black diaspora criticism offers a space of engagement for Chinese diaspora criticism. There has been relatively little engagement with black diaspora criticism in work on Chinese diasporas. Neither the essays in Wei-Ming Tu's *The Living Tree* nor Ling-Chi Wang and Gungwu Wang's two-volume anthology *The Chinese Diaspora* raise possible connections with black diaspora criticism. Although Rey Chow's work does not directly refer to diasporic experiences outside of Chinese diasporic ones, her work can be seen as overlapping with Gilroy's in terms of her concern for deconstructing 'Chinese' as a centre of ethnic identification. See, in particular, 'Can One Say No to China?' and the introduction to *Writing Diaspora*. Ien Ang's writing on the Chinese diaspora in *On Not Speaking Chinese* does refer at several moments to Gilroy's work. Ang

focuses largely on ideas of hybridity developed by Gilroy, Homi Bhabha, and Garcia Canclini as an alternative to what she has marked as the ethnic conservatism that pervades the Chinese diaspora. See, for example, her final chapter of the book, 'Togetherness-in-difference (the uses and abuses of hybridity).'

12 In first chapter of *The Last Days of Haute Cuisine*, Patric Kuh traces the arrival of the concept of haute cuisine in North America to a reclaimed landfill site in the borough of Queens, New York, 1939. Very briefly, the story goes like this: This was the site of the French Pavilion of the 1939 World's Fair. Where the English brought the Magna Carta (which, needless to say, was largely ignored), the French brought a four-hundred-seat restaurant, Le Pavillon de France. The restaurant was run by a hand-picked, government-supported team of restaurant staff culled from some of the most famous restaurants in France. The pavilion opened with a gala dinner for dignitaries. The menu that night began with *Double Consommé de Viveur served with Paillette Dorés* – a dish that would be translated in the *Times* the next day as 'Chicken consomme with twisted cheese sticks' (Kuh 10). Although the restaurant began with the markings of exclusivity, it served 18,401 meals to the average fairgoer; in the second month, 26,510 people had a meal at Le Pavillon de France (Kuh 11). In 1940 the maître d'hôtel, Henri Soulé, ended up back in New York by order of the French prime minister and finally opened up Le Pavillon, his own restaurant, in 1941. These were the first days of haute cuisine in North America. For a more detailed account, please see Kuh 1–35.

13 Peter Li situates the exclusion of Chinese immigrants from Canada's vision of itself within economic terms where state-sanctioned ideological racism supports and complements economic desires: 'Thus an ideology defining a racial group as unassimilable and inferior becomes useful, and indeed necessary, to rationalize racial exploitation. This explanation suggests that institutional racism against the Chinese was a structural imperative at a time when pioneer industries depended on cheap casual labour' (Li 38). In the US context, Lisa Lowe takes up this point, arguing that 'in the last century and a half, the Amercian *citizen* has been defined over against the Asian *immigrant*, legally, economically, and culturally' (4). In the first chapter of *Asian/American*, David Palumbo Liu extends Lowe's argument to a discussion of the way in which the exclusion of Asian Americans haunts conceptions of US citizenship. See also Yen Le Espiritu's *Asian American Women and Men* 9.

14 In her work on the idea of racial grief, *The Melancholy of Race*, Anne Anlin Cheng begins by giving a brief history of the damage hypothesis and tracing several decades of social pyschological work that focuses particularly on

racial damage experienced by children of colour. Cheng begins with the 1930s experiments of Kenneth and Mamie Clark which found that the vast majority of black children, given the choice, preferred to play with white dolls, identifying them as 'good,' rather than black dolls, which the children often referred to as 'bad.' The Clark dolls tests came to be important evidence in the 1954 *Brown v. Board of Education* case that ended the segregated school system in the United States. The Clark doll tests have been contested in subsequent years but, as Cheng notes, the pain that the tests highlighted has not gone away: 'Racial ideals continue to drive those most oppressed by it. Even market researchers have become invested in this question of racial preference ... The toy giant Mattel, who spent millions of dollars in market research and new product development only to find ... what Kenneth Clark could have told them nearly fifty years ago: that African American (and other ethnic) children given the chance, would rather play with a blond, blue-eyed Barbie than dolls that "look more like themselves"' (Cheng 6). Arguing that 'the connection between subjectivity and social damage needs to be formulated in terms more complicated than either resigning colored people to the irrevocability of "self-hatred" or denying racism's profound, lasting effects,' Cheng turns to exploring the idea of racial grief (7).

15 What has been known as the Chinese Exclusion Act, formally the 1923 Chinese Immigration Act, was repealed in 1947. Chinese immigrants were the only immigrant group to be targeted with legal exclusion. For an extended discussion of the Exclusion Act, see the chapter on exclusion in Wickberg.

16 Although I am making a claim about the overlap between the menu, the map and the nation, I am not suggesting that this is the making of a national cuisine in the sense that Arjun Appadurai has established in his work on Indian cookbooks. Also, depending on a textualized reading of food through the menu, my discussion departs from work of social anthropologists who have written extensively about the relationship between food and ethnic or national identity. In this work, much of which focuses on the ideas of foodways, the analyses emerge from interviews and participant observational work rather than reading the representation of food through a text such as a menu. Writers draw out the ways in which communities, usually racially or ethnically defined communities, mark out their differences through food, retain a sense of an ethnic identity (constructed or otherwise), and perform ethnic identity. I am thinking in particular of Susan Kalcik's 'Ethnic Foodways in America' and Richard Raspa's 'Exotic Foods among Italian-Americans in Mormon Utah.' Raspa, for example, argues that 'preparing and eating exotic food [i.e., goat's head] allow[s] the performers to recreate their ethnic identity, maintain traditional boundaries with

the dominant culture, and nurture familial closeness' (193). The work on foodways constitutes a significant body of knowledge in social anthropological work and largely focuses on food prepared for consumption within the private sphere of the home and community. In contrast, this project dwells on food served in public space, prepared by Chinese cooks for non-Chinese consumers.

17 See Ashcroft, Griffith, and Tiffin's *The Empire Writes Back*, and Ania Loomba's chapter 'Colonialism and Literature' in *Colonialism/Postcolonialism*.

18 Although the Provincial Archives of Alberta does not have a date for the New Dayton menu, I have dated the menu to the 1920s. In conversation with archivists at the Galt Museum in Lethbridge, Alberta, we have agreed that this is a reasonable approximation of the period of this menu. According to a publication of the New Dayton Historical Society, Hoy Fat Leong came to New Dayton in 1917 with his son Charlie Chew Leong. They bought land from Jim Reid and then operated the first café in New Dayton. In 1923 the café was destroyed by fire. Charlie Chew rebuilt the café with four tables, stools, a glass counter, and modern gas lamps (a big improvement on the old kerosene ones). The menu we now have, which includes items such as pastries that could be displayed at a glass counter and ice cream sodas, would have been part of the menu of the rebuilt New Dayton Café. Also, the menu names 'C.L. Chew' as the proprietor and not Charlie's father, Hoy Fat Leong.

19 In *On Not Speaking Chinese*, Ien Ang sets the up the problem 'real' and 'fake' Chineseness by relating it to an anecdote about Chinese food. Ang opens with a description of a one-day trip to China and the pain of her experience of wanting to identify and not identify with the kinds of Chineseness that she confronts. This experience of simultaneous alientation from and interpellation into Chineseness culminates in a scene at a restaurant. Let me take a minute to revisit it. She writes:

We were served a lunch in a huge, rather expensive-looking restaurant complete with fake Chinese temple and a pond with lotus flowers in the garden, undoubtedly designed with pleasing international visitors in mind, but paradoxically only preposterous in its stereotypicality. All twelve of us, members of the tourist group, were seated around a typically Chinese roundtable. Lan-lan [the tourist guide] did not join us, and I think I know why. The food we were served was obviously the kind of Chinese food that was adapted to European taste: familiar, rather bland dishes ... not the 'authentic' Cantonese delicacies I was subconsciously looking forward to now that I was in China. (Wrong assumption, of course: you have to be in rich, decadent, colonial capitalist Hong Kong for that, so I found out.) And we did not get bowl and chopsticks, but a plate with spoon and fork. I was shocked, even though my chopstick competence is not very great. An instant sense of alienation took hold of me. Part of me wanted to leave immediately, wanted to scream out loud that I didn't belong to the group I was with, but another part of me felt compelled to take Lan-lan's place as tourist guide while she was not with us, to explain, as best I could, to my fellow tourists what the food was all about. I realized how mistaken I was to assume, since there seems to be a Chinese restaurant in virtually every corner of the world, that 'everybody knows Chinese food.' For my table companions the unfamiliarity of the experience prevailed, the anxious excitement of trying something new (although they predictably found the duck skin "too greasy," of course, the kind of complaint about Chinese food that I have heard so often from Europeans). (22–3)

I have quoted Ang at length because she nicely sets a series of binaries that attend to the problem of Chineseness – fake vs authentic, outside vs inside, tourist vs native, fork and spoon vs chopsticks and a bowl. These are binaries that persist throughout discussions of Chineseness. The problem of assimilation versus non-assimilation emerges for Ang in the scene of the restaurant and the serving of a Chineseness back to her in the form of fake Chinese food on a plate accompanied by a fork and a spoon.

20 See Lisa Lowe's chapter 'Immigration, Citizenship, Racialization' in *Immigrant Acts*. See also Yen Le Espiritu's *Asian American Women and Men* 9.

21 This is far and away not an exhaustive list and I recognize that I have simplified the many complex interventions that have been made in these texts regarding the work of Asian American literature for the sake of drawing out the larger contours of the discussion. I am thinking for example of: Elaine Kim's *Asian American Literature*, chapter 5 of Yen Le Espiritu's *Asian American Women and Men*, 'Ideological Racism and Cultural Resistance: Constructing our own images'; Sau-Ling Wong's *Reading Asian American Literature*, and chapter 5 of Lisa Lowe's *Immigrant Acts* 'Decolonization, Displacement, Disidentification: Writing and the Question of History.' In terms of anthologies, I have in mind work such as Shirley Lim , Mayumi Tsutakawa and Margarita Donnelly's *The Forbidden Stitch* and Amy Ling's *Yellow Light*.

22 Although Butler does not make this specific reading regarding temporal succession in Althusser, we can already see in his text the attempt to justify the dependence on temporal progress which he then, only a few lines later, tries to suppress. Describing the scene of the hailing, Althusser writes, 'Nat-

urally for the convenience and clarity of my little theoretical theatre I have
had to present things in the form of a sequence, with a before and an after,
and thus in the form of a temporal succession' (174). He then illustrates the
now famous scene of the individual who 'turns round, believing/suspect-
ing/knowing that it is for him, i.e. recognizing that "it really is he" who is
meant by the hailing. *But in reality these things happen without any succession.*
The existence of ideology and the hailing or interpellation of individuals as
subjects are one and the same thing' (175, my emphasis). Althusser's initial
rationalizing belies the paradox of the argument. Ostensibly, he describes
the scene in terms of temporal succession only for the sake of clarity. However, this one and the same of the existence of ideology and the interpellation of the subject into ideology then belies the necessity of the subject
already anticipating the interpellation prior to the act. There is, despite Althusser's attempt to 'suppress the temporal form in which' he has presented
the scene to us, always, as Butler notes, a moment prior to the hailing in
which the subject is formed.

23 See my 'Rereading Chinese Head Tax Racism.'
24 Chow's analysis is focused on the problem of the desire for the authentic
   racial other in the Western academy and she refers to a range of texts, including her experience on a hiring committee for a Chinese language and
   literature specialist at the University of Minnesota, Julia Kristeva's *About Chinese Women*, and Malek Alloula's *The Colonial Harem.*
24 Although Bhabha's thinking on the concept of the time lag unfolds
   throughout *The Location of Culture*, and is, perhaps, one of the central, unifying concepts of the book, it is best captured in the closing pages of the conclusion, 'Fanon, Race and the Time of Modernity' 246–56. Bhabha argues
   that the 'progressive myth of modernity ... is an attempt ... to universalize
   the spatial fantasy of modern cultural communities as living their history
   "contemporaneously," in a "homogenous empty time" of the People-as-
   One that finally deprives minorities of those marginal, liminal spaces from
   which they can intervene in the unifying and totalizing *myths* of the national
   culture' (249). For Bhabha, then, the time lag is a space from which to
   enunciate the disjunctive that, as he argues in 'The Postcolonial and Postmodern,' is the space of agency: 'This emphasis on the disjunctive present
   of utterance enables the historian to get away from defining subaltern consciousness as binary, as having positive or negative dimensions. It allows the
   articulation of subaltern agency to emerge as relocation and reinscription.
   In the seizure of the sign ... there is neither dialectical sublation nor the
   empty signifier: there is a contestation of the given symbols of authority that
   shift the terrains of antagonism' (193).

25  There is substantial overlap between Gilroy's thinking on race and the time of modernity and Bhabha's thinking on the same subject. While they both emphasize the disruptive possibilities of the disjunctive temporality of diasporic time, the difference between their two considerations lies in their conceptions of agency. For Bhabha, the time lag is the space from which agency is articulated. For Gilroy, the disjunctive time of black counterculture is itself constitutive of modernity and black identity. Citing Ralph Ellison on the experience of temporal disjunction, Gilroy notes: 'Instead of the swift and imperceptible flowing of time, you are aware of its nodes, those points where time stands still or from which it leaps ahead. And you slip into the breaks and look around." A precious sense of black particularity gets constructed from several interlocking themes that culminate in this unexpected time signature. They supply the accents, rests, breaks *and* tones that make black identity possible' (202).

26  In 'Migrant Identities: Personal Memory and the Construction of Selfhood,' Keya Ganguly traces a similar trajectory in the experience of middle-class Indian men emigrating to the United States, where 'the representation of identity involves a complex distancing from the past. The attempt to consolidate respectability in the bourgeois, diasporic context requires constructing the past as the undesirable other. However, the devaluation of the past indicates and itself produces the present, hybrid identity of immigrant men' (38). Much of this essay reappears as the third chapter of *States of Exception*, 'Personal Memory and the Contradictions of Selfhood.' As the difference in the title suggests, Ganguly's latter version of the essay highlights the ways in which this desire to keep the past separate from the present is more about the contradictions of this hybrid state than the construction of selfhood.

## 3. Disappearing Chinese Café

1  In this chapter I will refer to the music of Joni Mitchell and Sylvia Tyson under the generalized category of 'folk' and 'folk music.' I understand that Tyson's later music can be considered to be more closely associated with the category of 'country music' rather than 'folk.' I also appreciate that there are significant differences between the music of Mitchell and Tyson and what might be considered 'authentic' folk music, and that Mitchell and Tyson might more accurately fall under the headings of 'folk revivalist' or 'folk rock.' However, I use the term 'folk' and 'folk music' in deference to Robert Cantwell, whose history of the music of the 1960s has influenced much of the work in music history, criticism, and ethnomusicology that followed. Although the subtitle of Cantwell's book *When We Were Good* is 'The

Folk Revival,' Cantwell generally refers to the music of the 1960s as 'folk music' throughout the book and argues for an understanding of this music as connected to what might be considered the more authentic folk music tradition. While there are parts of Cantwell's analysis, particularly in terms of the universality of 1960s folk music, with which I do not entirely concur, I find his handling of this issue of definitions to be very useful.

2  I acknowledge Marc Redfield's point regarding the curiously phantom-like quality of the *Bildungsroman* genre, that it is at once terribly general and so specific as to have no exemplar: 'On the one hand it is certainly true that under the lens of scholarship this genre rapidly shrinks until, like a figure in Wonderland, it threatens to disappear altogether. Even *Wilhelm Meister* has proved resistant to being subsumed under the definition it supposedly inspired ... But on the other hand, Germanists seem all the more ideologically committed to the truth of this "critical fiction" for having examined it and found it ontologically wanting.' (Redfield 41). However, Redfield himself concedes, one of the reasons why the *Bildungsroman* has persisted lies precisely in this peculiar and contradictory generality and particularity.

3  When it came time to consider emancipation in Jamaica, the British discovered that the slaves already earned enough to live on doing one day's worth of free labour: 'The key question, therefore, was "What, except compulsion, shall make them work for six?"' (Holt, *Problem* 43). This is the problem of freedom.

4  'Unchained Melody' was originally written by Hy Zaret (lyrics) and Alex North (music) for a 1955 prison-farm film, *Unchained*, starring Elroy 'Crazy Legs' Hirsch. It reached the number one spot on the Billboard charts with a version by Les Baxter. Versions by Al Hibbler, Roy Hamilton, and June Valli kept the song on the charts throughout the rest of the 1950s. In 1965 (a year that has now become significant in folk revivalism's history because of the events at the Newport Folk Festival) the song was a number four hit for the Righteous Brothers.

5  'Canadian Sunset,' written by Norman Gimbel and Eddie Heywood, peaked on the Billboard charts at number seven with a version by Andy Williams.

6  The songs also speak to a particular understanding of a historical moment in North America when folk festivals, coffee-houses, and tiny, smoke-filled living rooms in the East Village constituted a bourgeois public sphere in precisely the sense of the Habermasian ideal. While this is not the purpose of my chapter, let me briefly point out that both the space of the Chinese restaurant and the 1960s folk-music revival can be understood as public spheres. In the case of the former, as historians of Canadian small towns have noted, Chinese restaurants were often the only communal gathering

place. Similarly, there are many affinities between the production and circulation of folk music in the 1960s and the structure of the Habermasian
bourgeois public sphere. Not only did much of the music emerge out of
New York coffee-houses, not only did the musical discourse permeating
these coffee-houses also disseminate through print media dedicated to this
coffee-house discourse (*Broadside* and *Sing Out!*), but the music was also
understood as a discursive institution that was outside of the state and yet
was deeply engaged in the project of political commentary. In his history
of 1960s folk music and culture, David Pichaske suggests the way in which
folk music of the 1960s could be seen as a sphere of its own: 'And the songs
were printed in *Broadside* and *Sing Out!* and they were sung in the streets
and coffeehouses of New York and Boston and Philadelphia and across the
South and finally on records and on FM stations, and they have thus found
their way into American consciousness, a permanent record of early sixties
protest' (58). For more detailed histories of this music and its political implications, please see also Robert Cantwell's *When We Were Good* and Richie
Unterberger's *Turn!Turn!Turn!*

7  Linking the culture of the 1960s folk-music scene and the civil rights movement of the time, David Pichaske argues that 'the music of the sixties saves
us. It offers the most accurate record of persons and places and spirits.
More important, it provides a common history. We may not have been in
Montgomery, Alabama, but we have all sung or heard sung "We Shall Overcome"' (xx).

8  Geoff Eley's 'Nations, Publics, and Political Cultures' summarizes much of
this critique, noting that Habermas idealizes the normative category of the
bourgeois subject at the expense of attention to other popular social movements: 'On the one hand, the actual pursuit of communicative rationality
via the modalities of the public sphere at the end of the eighteenth century
reveals a far richer social history than Habermas' conception of a specifically bourgeois emancipation allows; on the other hand, Habermas' concen-
tration on *Öffentlichkeit* as a specifically *bourgeois* category subsumes forms
of popular democratic mobilization that were always already present as
contending and subversive alternatives to the classical liberal organization
of civil society in which Habermas' ideal of the public sphere is confined'
(330–1). Oscar Negt and Alexander Kluge's *Public Sphere and Experience*
explores the possibilities of a proletarian public sphere that Habermas
more or less ignores throughout his analysis. Eley also raises the problem
of Habermas's idealizing of the public sphere as a particularly male space.
Feminists such as Joan Landes, Nancy Fraser, Carole Pateman, and Marie
Fleming in particular have taken up some of the issues involved in this ide-

alization and argued for the constitutive role of gender in the conception of the public sphere.

9  Keya Ganguly notes that Stewart's narrativization risks occluding the materiality of her subject matter. Citing a passage in which Stewart collapses the actual process of being born into a discussion of the emergence of subjectivity, Ganguly argues that 'this kind of narratological explication depends upon dissimulating a materialist interest in the world of objects and of reality (however qualified). In actuality, the argument is entirely analogical, even more than it is metaphorical. It is predicated on a presumed though not necessarily established resemblance among elements of the series posited (cell, body, enclosure, birth, separation, loss, signifier, meaning, and so on) ... In the process, [Stewart] blurs the very line between truths and their representation' (*States* 131).

10  Although I do not think Habermas aimed to provide a comprehensive historical survey of the seventeenth- and eighteenth-century French, German, and English public spheres, I also do not want to diminish the important historical work that has resulted from the critiques that followed. Harry C. Boyte argues that Habermas's 'account is meant in a sense to prompt historical investigation. This it has certainly achieved' (343). Also, Joan Landes notes, Habermas's project inspired both a series of historical critiques, but also a renewed interest in histories of public spheres: 'The path taken by the independent European reception of the book leads towards feminist and critical theorists who are reconstructing the original model of the public sphere, and to those scholars who are charting the possibilities for what is variously called the "new historicism" or the "new cultural and intellectual history"' ('The Public and the Private' 92). Landes's own book reconstructed the eighteenth-century French public sphere and emphasized in particular the crucial role of women in this sphere. Similarly, both David Zaret's call for further attention to the role of religion and science as well as Mary Ryan's conception of early US feminist uses of the public sphere provide further historical facets to the Habermasian public sphere.

11  Cantwell's account has been considered as definitive and has influenced many ethnomusicologists who came after him. What interests me in particular is Cantwell's insistence on the 'goodness' of sixties folk-music culture. Noting the political influences on the folk revival, Cantwell argues that left politics had less influence than some might argue, but that a general desire to 'be good' permeated the revival: 'For we were good, and wanted to be' (22). In Cantwell's view, a general desire for transcendent goodness superseded overt political concerns: 'Nothing was more tiresome, once the revival was in full swing, than to endure the contributions of some antediluvian

communist songster with a bag of "banker and bosses" songs, stirring as they must have been in their time, who imagined that the labor movement of the thirties had come back to life … What had been their movement became our revival – and we insisted on assigning our own meanings to it' (22).

12  Theodor Adorno and Max Horkheimer were perhaps the first to declare *The Structural Transformation of the Public Sphere* as too tied to the Enlighten-ment concepts of reason and rational discourse. Craig Calhoun notes that the book 'originated as Habermas' *Habilitationschrift* (thesis for postdoctoral qualification required of German professors) and was intended for submis-sion to Max Horkheimer (and Theodor Adorno) at Frankfurt. Horkheimer and Adorno, however, apparently thought it at once insufficiently critical of the illusions and dangerous tendencies of an Enlightenment conception of democratic public life, especially in mass society, and too radical in its politi-cally focused call for an attempt to go beyond liberal constitutional protec-tions in pursuit of truer democracy. Habermas successfully submitted it to Wolfgang Abendroth at Marburg' (4).

13  Please see Negt and Kluge's *Public Sphere and Experience.*

14  Although Habermas does not cite this particular passage, he draws most of his reading of Marx from the early writings and, in particular, 'On the Jewish Question,' wherein Marx writes: 'The state in its own way abolishes distinctions based on *birth, rank, education* and *occupation* when it declares birth, rank, education and occupation to be *non-political* distinctions, when it proclaims that every member of the people is an equal participant in popular sovereignty regardless of these distinctions, when it treats all those elements which go to make up the actual life of the people from the stand-point of the state. Nevertheless the state allows private property, education, and occupation to *act* and assert their *particular* nature in *their* own way, i.e. as private property, as education and as occupation. Far from abolishing these *factual* distinctions, the state presupposes them in order to exist, it only experiences itself as *political state* and asserts its *universality* in opposi-tion to these elements' (219).

15  Habermas writes: 'According to this new model, autonomy was no longer based on private property; it could in principle no longer be grounded in the private sphere but had to have its foundation in the public sphere itself. Private autonomy was a derivative of the original autonomy which alone constituted the public of a society's citizens in the exercise of the functions of the socialistically expanded public sphere' (128).

16  In *The Sexual Contract* Carole Pateman argues that the bourgeois social con-tract secured civil rights for men at the expense of those for women.

17  While the critique of Enlightenment reason can be seen as implicit in a

wide range of postcolonial critical theory, Gayatri Spivak offers a particularly pointed critique in her deconstruction of Kant in *A Critique of Postcolonial Reason*, where she examines what she calls the 'double bind of practical reason' (25). Noting that Kant's notion of reason is both free and bounded by an understanding of what it means to be human, Spivak pushes Kant at the limits of his universalism by tracking the figure of what she calls the 'native informant' in his text. Please see in particular pp. 17–37. In addition, the final chapter of Srinivas Aravamudan's *Tropicopolitans* contains a reading of the Enlightenment from the postcolonial perspective, not as a critique, but as a project of locating the places where postcolonial subjects appropriated the logic of the Enlightenment. In particular, Aravamudan explores the way in which Toussaint L'Ouverture 'tropicalized' the Enlightenment and, more generally, the way in which the revolutionaries in Haiti reworked French Enlightenment thought in order to support their anticolonial work.

18 Drawing from the work of L. Stephen and H. Reinhold, Habermas counts the existence of more than three thousand coffee-houses in London by the first decade of the eighteenth century (32).

19 In the course of my research, I have been surprised by the lack of material on the predication of the Habermasian public sphere on colonialism and imperialism. As I note throughout this chapter, there is no shortage of material engaging with Habermas critically on all kinds of fronts, including a sustained feminist critique and an extension of his thinking in the field of media and communications studies (the set of essays in Craig Calhoun's *Habermas and the Public Sphere* provides an excellent overview of many of the critiques). However, I have not yet come across a sustained and detailed critique of the Habermasian public sphere from the perspective of postcolonial and colonial studies.

## 4.  Diasporic Counterpublics

1 *The Beanery* was a recreation of a popular bar on Route 66, Barney's Beanery, in West Hollywood. Kienholz chemically impregnated the installation with the smell of beer and filled it with a soundtrack of people chattering in the bar. The faces of the mannequins in the installation were replaced with clocks set to 10:10. Outside the installation, he placed a newspaper vending machine with the headline 'Children Kill Children in Vietnam' splashed across the paper.

2 Please see Mishra, 'The Diasporic Imaginary' 427, 435, and 442 and *The Literatures of the Indian Diaspora* 3; Spivak, 'Diasporas Old and New' 245; and Ong, *Flexible Citizenship* esp. 16–21.

3 In a more recent essay, 'Transnationalizing the Public Sphere,' Fraser acknowledges that her earlier critique of the concept of the public sphere 'did not go far enough' (3). In this essay, she takes up the problem of the reliance of the public sphere on a Westphalian concept of the nation-state. This critique is much more sceptical of the possibilities of the public sphere and Fraser still writes with a view to repoliticizing, and thus recuperating, the theory of the public sphere (2).

4 Although there is no definitive collection or collective under the banner 'The Feminist Public Sphere,' the feminist critique and recuperation of the public sphere has also been crucial and in many ways the most theoretically nuanced and diverse response to the Habermasian concept. I will take this critique up in more detail later in this chapter.

## 5. 'How taste remembers life'

1 Regarding the politics of the black diaspora specifically, Scott takes 'a demand of black diaspora criticism in the present that it neither wants the cultural nationalist dream of a full and homogeneous blackness nor the postmodern hope of an arbitrary, empty and "unscripted" one' (127).

2 I am thinking of modern US poetry's romance with things Chinese. This is the legacy of diffusion from Fenellosa to Pound and from Pound to a whole range of modern US poets. In *Orientalism, Modernism, and the American Poem* Robert Kern argues that 'the issue here is not the direct or indirect influence of Chinese on American writing but a romantic or mythologized – and Western – conception of language that is imposed upon Chinese and then appropriated as a model – one that embodies values, authorizes procedures, and represents possibilities seemingly unavailable in Western languages' (6). As his reference to Said's *Orientalism* suggests, Kern proposes that the Chinese language and poetic tradition which reinvigorated modern US poetry in the twentieth century became an orientalist object of fascination rather than a cross-cultural engagement. In *ABC of Influence*, Chris Beach convincingly traces Pound's influence on Olson, Duncan, Levertov, and Snyder. The relationship between things Chinese and modern poetry is necessarily an uneasy one. For a further discussion of this relationship in terms of Asian American poets such as John Yau, please see Wang's 'Undercover Asian.'

3 I am gesturing to the title of her introduction to *boundary 2* 25, 'Introduction: On Chineseness as a Theoretical Problem,' which I will take up in the next section.

4 Most of the response to the living-tree argument can be found in the pages

of *boundary 2*. In 1998 Rey Chow edited a special issue of *boundary 2*, which was then republished, with additional essays, as *Modern Chinese Literary and Cultural Studies in the Age of Theory: Reimagining a Field* in 2000. Ien Ang's contribution to the collection, 'Can One Say No to Chineseness?' takes up Tu's living-tree metaphor specifically and questions the organicist premises of his metaphor.

5 Melancholy does not have a good reputation. As Walter Benjamin traces so thoroughly in *The Origin of German Tragic Drama*, the 'codification' of melancholy as a syndrome 'dates from the high middle ages, and the form given to the theory of the temperaments by the leader of the medical school of Salerno, Constantinus Africanus, remained in force until the Renaissance. According to this theory the melancholic is "envious, mournful, greedy, avaricious, disloyal, timorous, and sallow," and the *humor melancholicus* is the "least noble complexion"' (*Origin* 145). Reading the emblem of the stone in Albrecht Dürer's engraving *Melencolia*, Benjamin notes that the stone retains a 'genuinely theological conception of the melancholic, which is to be found in one of the seven deadly sins. This is *acedia*, dullness of the heart, or sloth' (155). Not only was it associated with one of the deadly sins, melancholia also becomes pathologized as being akin to rabies, such that Aegidius Albertinus described both states in very similar terms (152).

6 I am deliberately echoing Homi Bhabha's use of the idea of unhomeliness. In his introduction to *The Location of Culture*, Bhabha suggests that the unhomeliness of subjects displaced by colonialism challenges the distinctions between public and private spheres that have been forgotten or suppressed: 'Such a forgetting – or disavowal – creates an uncertainty at the heart of the generalizing subject of civil society, compromising the "individual" that is the support for its universalist aspiration' (10). Drawing together Freud's notion of the *unheimlich* and Hannah Arendt's work in *The Human Condition* on the separation between public and private spheres, Bhabha argues that 'the unhomely moment relates the traumatic ambivalences of a personal, psychic history to the wider disjunctions of political existence' (11).

7 Aihwa Ong's *Flexible Citizenship* opens with this image (1).

8 Although the existence of line breaks in a prose-poem is ambiguous and there is no clear general protocol for citation, I have chosen to retain the original line breaks in my citations of Wah's prose-poems.

9 Citing the medieval Italian poet Nicolò Tobino's definition of enjambment, in *The End of the Poem* Agamben notes that 'it often happens that the rhyme ends, without the meaning of the sentence having been complete' (*Multiocens enim accidit quod, finita consonantia, adhuc sensus orationis non est finitus*). All poetic institutions participate in this noncoincidence, this schism of

sound and sense – rhyme no less than caesura. For what is rhyme if not
a disjunction between a semiotic event (the repetition of a sound) and a
semantic event, a disjunction that brings the mind to expect a meaningful
analogy where it can find only homophony?' (110).

10  *Scent* devotes approximately one essay to each of the major Enlightenment
thinkers. I will very briefly summarize Le Guérer's discussion. Eighteenth-
and nineteenth-century European thought elevated sight as the primary
sense of civilized man. Darwin's theory of evolution argued that bipedalism
lifted homo sapiens from dependence on the odours of the ground and
upwards towards development relying mainly on sight. Following Darwin,
Freud suggested that infants revelling in the world of odours would grow
into an increasing appreciation of visual pleasures. Adults who clung to
smell in their pleasures were thus arrested in their development. Hegel
linked the separation between the forehead and the nose and lips as a clear
sign of the superiority of the mind and the eyes over smell and taste. Smell,
and in relation to it taste, were repeatedly devalued as senses in a European
intellectual project that sought again and again to differentiate the civilized
from the primitive. For a fascinating and thorough discussion of smell and
the French body politic, please see Alain Corbin's *The Foul and the Fragrant:
Odor and the French Social Imagination.*

11  Scott suggests that the black diaspora constitutes a 'community and tradition ... [that] are discursively constituted principally (though not exhaus-
tively) in and through the mobilization of a common possession, namely,
the historically constituted figures of "Africa" and "Slavery," and their
deployment in the ideological production of effects of identity\difference,
of community ... The minimal condition of participation in the moral
community of a black diaspora discourse or tradition is the mobilization of
the common possession of the figures of Africa and slavery as markers of
identity\difference. In this way, insofar as these figures are in play, there is
the potential for recognition and solidarity on the part of a black diasporic
subject' (124–6).

12  For example, in the *Critique of Judgement*, Kant argues that, regarding 'the
*agreeable* every one concedes that his judgement, which he bases on private
feeling, and in which he declares that an object pleases him, is restricted
merely to himself personally. Thus he does not take it amiss if, when he says
that Canary-wine is agreeable, another corrects the expression and reminds
him that he ought to say: It is agreeable *to me*. This applies not only to the
taste of the tongue, the palate, and the throat, but to what may with any
one be agreeable to the eye or the ear ... With the agreeable, therefore, the
axiom holds good: *Everyone has his own taste* (that of sense)' (51–2).

## Conclusion

1  Please see Spang's introduction, 'To Make a Restaurant.'
2  Please see 'Diasporas Old and New.'

# Works Cited

Agamben, Giorgio. *The End of the Poem: Studies in Poetics.* Trans. Daniel Heller-Roazen. Stanford: Stanford UP, 1999.

Althusser, Louis. 'Ideology and Ideological State Apparatuses (Notes towards an Investigation).' In *Lenin and Philosophy and Other Essays*, trans. Ben Brewster. New York: Monthly Review Press, 1971. 127–85.

Anderson, Kay. *Vancouver's Chinatown: Racial Discourse in Canada, 1875–1980.* Montreal and Kingston: McGill-Queen's UP, 1990.

Ahmed, Aijaz. *In Theory: Classes, Nations, Literatures.* London and New York: Verso, 2008.

Ang, Ien. 'Can One Say No to Chineseness? Pushing the Limits of the Diasporic Paradigm.' *boundary 2* 25.3 (1998): 223–42.

– *On Not Speaking Chinese: Living between Asia and the West.* London and New York: Routledge, 2001.

Aravamudan, Srinivas. *Tropicopolitans: Colonialism and Agency, 1688–1804.* Durham: Duke UP, 1999.

Backhouse, Constance. *Colour-Coded: A Legal History of Racism in Canada, 1900–1950.* Toronto: U of Toronto P, 1999.

Baker, Jr, Houston A. 'Critical Memory and the Black Public Sphere.' In *The Black Public Sphere*, ed. The Black Public Sphere Collective. Chicago and London: U of Chicago P, 1995. 5–38.

Bakhtin, M.M. *The Dialogic Imagination.* Trans. Caryl Emerson and Michael Holquist. Austin: U of Texas P, 1996.

Banting, Pamela. *Body, Inc.: A Theory of Translation Poetics.* Calgary: Turnstone P, 1995.

Barker, Francis, Peter Hulme, and Margaret Iverson, eds. 'Introduction.' In *Colonial Discourse / Postcolonial Theory.* Manchester: Manchester UP, 1994. 1–23.

Barthes, Rolande. *Mythologies.* Trans. Annette Lavers. New York: Hill and Wang, 1972.

– 'Toward a Psychosociology of Contemporary Food Consumption.' In *Food and Culture: A Reader*, ed. Carole Counihan and Penny Van Esterick. New York: Routledge, 1997. 20–7.

Baucom, Ian. 'Introduction: Atlantic Genealogies.' *South Atlantic Quarterly* 100.1 (2001): 1–14.

Beach, Chris. *ABC of Influence: Ezra Pound and the Remaking of American Poetic Tradition*. Berkeley: U of California P, 1992.

Bell, David, and Gill Valentine. *Consuming Geographies: We Are Where We Eat*. London and New York: Routledge, 1997.

Bell, Derrick A., Jr. 'Brown v. Board of Education and the Interest-Convergence Dilemma.' *Harvard Law Review* 93 (1980): 518–33.

Belu, Françoise. 'The Empire and the Middle Kingdom, or the Dream Exchange.' In *Gold Mountain Restaurant Montagne d'Or*. Montreal: MAI (Montréal, arts interculturels), 2006. 8–20.

Benhabib, Seyla. 'Models of Public Space: Hannah Arendt, the Liberal Tradition and Jurgen Habermas.' In *Habermas and the Public Sphere*, ed. Craig Calhoun. Cambridge, MA, and London: MIT Press, 1992. 73–98.

Benjamin, Walter. *Illuminations*. Trans. Harry Zohn. New York: Schocken Books, 1969.

– *The Origin of German Tragic Drama*. 1977. Trans. John Osborne. London and New York: Verso, 1985.

Berlant, Lauren. *The Queen of America Goes to Washington City: Sex and Citizenship*. Durham and London: Duke UP, 1997.

Bhabha, Homi. *The Location of Culture*. London and New York: Routledge, 1994.

Black Public Sphere Collective. *The Black Public Sphere*. Chicago and London: U of Chicago P, 1995.

Bloch, Ernst. *A Philosophy of the Future*. Trans. John Cumming. New York: Herder and Herder, 1970.

Bongie, Chris. 'A Street Named Bissette: Nostalgia, Memory, and the Cent-Cinquantenaire of the Abolition of Slavery in Martinique (1848–1998).' *South Atlantic Quarterly* 100.1 (2001): 215–58.

Bove, Paul. Afterword. *Modern Chinese Literary and Cultural Studies in the Age of Theory: Reimagining a Field*. Durham and London: Duke UP, 2000.

Boyte, Harry C. 'The Pragmatic Ends of Popular Politics.' In *Habermas and the Public Sphere*, ed. Craig Calhoun. Cambridge, MA, and London: MIT Press, 1992. 340–58.

Bracken, Christopher. *The Potlach Papers: A Colonial Case History*. Chicago: U of Chicago P, 1997.

Brah, Avtar. *Cartographies of Diaspora: Contesting Identities*. London and New York: Routledge, 1996.

Brennan, Timothy. *At Home in the World: Cosmopolitanism Now.* Cambridge and London: Harvard UP, 1997.

Bürger, Peter. *Theory of the Avant-Garde.* Trans. Michael Shaw. Minneapolis: U of Minnesota P, 1985.

Butler, Judith. *The Psychic Life of Power: Theories in Subjection.* Stanford: Stanford UP, 1997.

Cadava, Eduardo. *Words of Light: Theses on the Photography of History.* Princeton: Princeton UP, 1997.

Calhoun, Craig. 'Introduction: Habermas and the Public Sphere.' In *Habermas and the Public Sphere*, ed. Calhoun. Cambridge, MA, and London: MIT Press, 1992. 1–50.

Cameron, Nigel. *Hong Kong: The Cultured Pearl.* Hong Kong: Oxford UP, 1978.

Cantwell, Robert. *When We Were Good: The Folk Revival.* Cambrige and London: Harvard UP, 1996.

Chakrabarty, Dipesh. 'Conditions for Knowledge of Working-Class Conditions.' In *Selected Subaltern Studies*, ed. Ranajit Guha and Gayatri Chakravorty Spivak. London and New York: Oxford UP, 1988. 179–232.

– *Habitations of Modernity: Essays in the Wake of Subaltern Studies.* Chicago: U of Chicago P, 2002.

– *Provincializing Europe: Postcolonial Thought and Historical Difference.* Princeton and Oxford: Princeton UP, 2000.

Chao, Lien. 'Anthologizing the Collective: The Epic Struggles to Establish Chinese Canadian Literature in English.' *Essays on Canadian Writing* 57 (1995): 145–71.

Chen, Hsiang-shui. *Chinatown No More: Taiwan Immigrants in Contemporary New York.* Ithaca and London: Cornell UP, 1992.

Chen, Shehong. *Being Chinese, Becoming Chinese American.* Urbana and Chicago: U of Illinois P, 2002.

Cheng, Anne Anlin. *The Melancholy of Race: Pyschoanalysis, Assimilation and Hidden Grief.* Oxford: Oxford UP, 2001.

Cho, Lily. 'Rereading Chinese Head Tax Racism: Redress, Stereotype and Antiracist Critical Practice.' *Essays on Canadian Writing* 75 (2002): 62–84.

– 'The Turn to Diaspora.' *Topia* 17 (2007): 11–30.

Chow, Lily. *Chasing Their Dreams: Chinese Settlement in the Northwest Region of British Columbia.* Prince George, BC: Caitlin Press, 2000.

Chow, Rey. *Ethics after Idealism: Theory, Culture, Ethnicity, Reading.* Bloomington: Indiana UP, 1998.

– 'The Fascist Longings in our Midst.' In *Linked Histories: Postcolonial Studies in a Globalized World*, ed. Pamela McCallum and Wendy Faith. Calgary: U of Calgary P, 2005. 21–43.

– 'Introduction: On Chineseness as a Theoretical Problem.' *boundary 2* 25.3 (1998): 1–24.

– *The Protestant Ethnic and the Spirit of Capitalism.* New York: Columbia UP, 2002.

– *Writing Diaspora: Tactics of Intervention in Contemporary Cultural Studies.* Bloomington: Indiana UP, 1993.

Chow, Rey, ed. *Modern Chinese Literary and Cultural Studies in the Age of Theory: Reimagining a Field.* Durham and London: Duke UP, 2000.

Chrisman, Laura. 'Journeying to Death: Gilroy's Black Atlantic.' *Race and Class* 39.2 (1997): 51–64.

Chun, Allen. 'Fuck Chineseness: On the Ambiguities of Ethnicity as Culture as Identity.' *boundary 2* 23.2 (1996): 111–37.

Classen, Constance, David Howes, and Anthony Synnot. *Aroma: The Cultural History of Smell.* London and New York: Routledge, 1994.

Clifford, James. *Routes: Travel and Translation in the Late Twentieth Century.* Cambridge and London: Harvard UP, 1997.

Cohen, Robin. *Global Diasporas: An Introduction.* Seattle: U of Washington P, 1997.

Corbin, Alain. *The Foul and the Fragrant: Odor and the French Social Imagination.* Cambridge, MA: Harvard UP, 1986.

Davey, Frank. Introduction. In *Tish No. 1–19.* Vancouver: Talonbooks, 1975. 7–12.

Davey, Frank, ed. *Tish No. 1–19.* Vancouver: Talonbooks, 1975.

Day, Iyko. 'Interventing Innocence: Race, "Resistance," and the Asian North American Avant-Garde.' In *Literary Gestures: The Aesthetic in Asian American Writing,* ed. Rocio Davis and Sue-Im Lee. Philadelphia: Temple UP, 2005. 35–54.

Deer, Glenn. 'Asian North Americans in Transit.' *Canadian Literature* 161.2 (1999): 5–15.

Derksen, Jeffrey. 'Making Race Opaque.' *West Coast Line* 29.3 (1996): 63–76.

Derrida, Jacques. *Dissemination.* Trans. Barbara Johnson. Chicago: U of Chicago P, 1981.

Dirlik, Arif. *The Postcolonial Aura: Third World Criticism in the Age of Global Capital.* Boulder, CO: Westview P, 1998.

Douglas, May. 'Deciphering a Meal.' In *Food and Culture: A Reader,* ed. Carole Counihan and Penny van Esterick. New York and London: Routledge, 1997. 36–55.

Dufoix, Stéphane. *Diasporas.* Berkeley: U of California P, 2008.

Eagleton, Terry. *The Function of Criticism: From the Spectator to Post-Structuralism.* London and New York: Verso, 1984.

– *Ideology of the Aesthetic.* London: Blackwell, 1990.

Eley, Geoff. 'Nations, Publics, and Political Cultures: Placing Habermas in the Nineteenth Century.' In *Habermas and the Public Sphere*, ed. Craig Calhoun. Cambridge, MA, and London: MIT Press, 1992. 289–339.

Endacott, G.B. *A History of Hong Kong*. 2nd ed. Hong Kong: Oxford UP, 1973.

Eng, David, and Shinhee Han. 'A Dialogue on Racial Melancholia.' In *Loss: The Politics of Mourning*, ed. David Eng and David Kazanjian. Berkeley: U of California P, 2003. 343–71.

Espiritu, Yen Le. *Asian American Women and Men*. Thousand Oaks, CA: Sage, 1997.

Fisher, Susan. 'Japanese Elements in the Poetry of Fred Wah and Roy Kiyooka.' *Canadian Literature* 163 (1999): 93–110.

Fleming, Marie. 'Women and the "Public Use of Reason."' In *Feminists Read Haberams*, ed. Johanna Meehan. New York and London: Routledge, 1995. 117–38.

Fraser, Nancy. 'Rethinking the Public Sphere: A Contribution to the Critique of Actually Existing Democracy.' In *Habermas and the Public Sphere*, ed. Craig Calhoun. Cambridge, MA, and London: MIT Press, 1992. 109–42.

– 'Transnationalizing the Public Sphere.' In *Globalizing Critical Theory*, ed. Max Pensky. New York: Rowman and Littlefield, 2005. 37–47.

Freud, Sigmund. 'Beyond the Pleasure Principle.' In *Standard Edition of the Works of Sigmund Freud*, vol. 4. Trans. James Strachey. London: Hogarth Press, 1958.

– 'Instincts and Their Vissicitudes.' In *Standard Edition*, vol. 14. Trans. James Strachey. London: Hogarth Press, 1955. 109–40.

– 'Mourning and Melancholia.' In *Standard Edition*, vol. 14: 243–58.

– 'Screen Memories.' In *Standard Edition*, vol. 3: 299–322.

– 'Totem and Taboo.' In *Standard Edition*, vol. 13. Trans. James Strachey. London: Hogarth Press, 1950. vii–162.

– *Totem and Taboo*. Trans. A.A. Brill. New York: Vintage Books, 1946.

Frow, John. *Time and Commodity Culture: Essays in Cultural Theory and Postmodernity*. Oxford: Clarendon P, 1997.

Fuss, Diana. *Identification Papers*. London and New York: Routledge, 1995.

Gandhi, Leela. *Postcolonial Theory: A Critical Introduction*. New York: Columbia UP, 1998.

Ganguly, Keya 'Migrant Identities: Personal Memory and the Construction of Selfhood.' *Cultural Studies* 6.1 (1992): 27–50.

– *States of Exception: Everyday Life and Postcoloniality*. Minneapolis and London: U of Minnesota P, 2001.

Gilroy, Paul. *Against Race: Imagining Political Culture beyond the Color Line*. Cambridge, MA: Harvard UP, 2000.

– *The Black Atlantic: Modernity and Double Consciousness*. Cambridge and London: Harvard UP, 1993.

Goddard, John. Interview with Fred Wah. *Books in Canada*, October 1986: 40–1.

Goddard, Peter. 'Sweet-sour Memories at Shangri-la Café.' *Toronto Star*, 22 July 2006: H7.

Goellnicht, Donald C. 'Tang Ao in America: Male Subject Positions in China Men.' In *Reading the Literatures of Asian America*, ed. Amy Ling. Philadelphia: Temple UP, 1992. 191–212.

Gotanda, Neil. 'A Critique of "Our Constitution Is Colour-Blind."' *Stanford Law Review* 44 (1991): 1–68.

Guha, Ranajit. *Elementary Aspects of Peasant Insurgency in Colonial India*. Delhi: Oxford UP, 1983.

– 'The Prose of Counter-Insurgency.' In *Selected Subaltern Studies*, ed. Ranajit Guha and Gayatri Spivak. New York and Oxford: Oxford UP, 1988. 45–88.

Gunew, Sneja. 'The Melting Pot of Assimilation: Cannibalizing the Multicultural Body.' In *Transnational Asia Pacific: Gender, Culture, and the Public Sphere*, ed. Shirley Geok-Lin Lim, Larry E. Smith, and Wimal Dissanayake. Urbana: U of Illinois P, 1999. 145–58.

Gupta, Akhil, and James Ferguson. 'Beyond "Culture": Space, Identity, and the Politics of Difference.' In *Culture, Power, Place: Explorations in Critical Anthropology*, ed. Akhil Gupta and James Ferguson. Durham and London: Duke UP, 1997. 33–51.

– 'Culture, Power, Place: Ethnography at the End of an Era.' In *Culture, Power, Place*, 1–32.

Habermas, Jürgen. *The Structural Transformation of the Public Sphere: An Inquiry into a Category of Bourgeois Society*. Trans. Thomas Burger. Cambridge, MA: MIT Press, 1989.

Habib, Jasmin. *Israel, Diaspora, and the Routes of National Belonging*. Toronto: U of Toronto P, 2004.

Hall, Stuart. 'When Was "The Post-Colonial"? Thinking at the Limit.' In *The Post-Colonial Question: Common Skies, Divided Horizons*. London and New York: Routledge, 1996. 242–60.

Harris, Cheryl. 'Whiteness as Property.' *Harvard Law Review* 106 (1991): 1709–91.

Hennessy, Rosemary. *Materialist Feminism and the Politics of Discourse*. London and New York: Routledge, 1993.

Holt, Thomas. Afterword. 'Mapping the Black Public Sphere.' In *The Black Public Sphere*, ed. The Black Public Sphere Collective. Chicago and London: Chicago UP, 1995. 325–9.

– *The Problem of Freedom*. Baltimore and London: Johns Hopkins UP, 1992.

Hongo, Garrett. Introduction. In *The Open Boat: Poems from Asian America.* New York: Doubleday, 1993. xvii–xlii.

JanMohammed, Abdul, and David Lloyd. Introduction. In *The Nature and Context of Minority Discourse.* Oxford and New York: Oxford UP, 1990. 1–16.

Jefferess, David. *Postcolonial Resistance: Culture, Liberation, and Transformation.* Toronto: University of Toronto Press, 2008.

Jung, Moon-ho. *Coolies and Cane: Race, Labor and Sugar in the Age of Emancipation.* Baltimore: Johns Hopkins UP, 2006.

Kalcik, Susan. 'Ethnic Foodways in America: Symbol and Performance of Identity.' In *Ethnic and Regional Foodways in the United States,* ed. Linda Keller Brown and Kay Mussell. Knoxville: U of Tennessee P, 1984. 37–65.

Kamboureli, Smaro. 'Faking It: Fred Wah and the Postcolonial Imaginary.' In *Études Canadiennes / Canadian Studies: Revue interdisciplinaire des études Canadiennes en France* (Assn Française d'études Canadiennes, Talence) 54 (2003). 115–32.

Kant, Immanuel. *The Critique of Judgement.* Trans. James Creed Meredith. Oxford: Oxford UP, 2007.

Kelley, Robin. *Race Rebels: Culture, Politics, and the Black Working Class.* New York: Free Press, 1994.

Kern, Robert. *Orientalism, Modernism, and the American Poem.* Oxford: Oxford UP, 1996.

Kim, Elaine H. *Asian American Writing: An Introduction to the Writings and Their Social Context.* Philadelphia: Temple UP, 1984.

Koselleck, Reinhart. 'Modernity and the Planes of History.' In *Futures Past: On the Semantics of Historical Time,* trans. Keith Tribe. London and Cambridge, MA: MIT Press, 1985. 3–20.

Kuh, Patric. *The Last Days of Haute Cuisine: America's Culinary Revolution.* New York: Viking, 2001.

Kwan, Cheuk. *Chinese Restaurants.* Toronto: Tissa Films, 2005.

Kwong, Peter. *The New Chinatown.* New York: Hill and Wang, 1987.

Lachance, Sylvie. 'Foreword.' In *Gold Mountain Restaurant Montagne d'Or.* Montreal: MAI (Montréal, arts interculturels), 2006. 4–8.

Lai, David. *Chinatowns: Towns within Cities* in Canada. Vancouver: UBC P, 1988.

Lai, Walter Look. *Indentured Labor, Caribbean Sugar: Chinese and Indian Migrants to the British West Indies, 1838–1918.* Baltimore: Johns Hopkins UP, 1993.

Laguerre, Michel S. *The Global Ethnopolis: Chinatown, Japantown and Manilatown in American Society.* New York: St Martin's Press, 2000.

Lal, Brij, Doug Munro, and Edward Beechart, eds. *Plantation Workers: Resistance and Accommodation.* Honolulu: U of Hawaii P, 1993.

Landes, Joan B. 'The Public and the Private Sphere: A Feminist Reconsideration.' In *Feminists Read Haberams*, ed. Johanna Meehan. New York and London: Routledge, 1995. 91–116.

– *Women and the Public Sphere in the Age of the French Revolution*. Ithaca and London: Cornell UP, 1988.

Laplanche, Jean, and J.-B. Pontalis. *The Language of Psychoanalysis*. Trans. Donald Nicholson-Smith. New York: W.W. Norton, 1973.

Lazarus, Neil. 'Is a Counterculture of Modernity a Theory of Modernity?' *Diaspora* 4.3 (1995): 323–39.

Lee, A. Robert. 'Imagined Cities of China: Timothy Mo's London, Sky Lee's Vancouver, Fae Myenne Ng's San Francisco.' *Wasafiri* 22 (1995): 25–30.

Lee, Days. 'Memories of a Chinese-Canadian Restaurant.' In *Gold Mountain Restaurant Montagne d'Or*. Montreal: MAI (Montréal, arts interculturels), 2006. 37–49.

Lee, Jennifer 8. *The Fortune Cookie Chronicles: Adventures in the World of Chinese Food*. New York: Twelve, 2008.

Lee, Leo Ou-fan. 'On the Margins of the Chinese Discourse: Some Personal Thoughts on the Cultural Meaning of the Periphery.' In *The Living Tree*, ed. Tu Wei-ming, 221–44.

Lefebvre, Henri. *The Production of Space*. Trans. Donald Nicholson-Smith. London: Blackwell, 1991

Le Guérer, Annick. *Scent: The Mysterious and Essential Powers of Smell*. Trans. Richard Miller. London: Chatto and Windus, 1993.

Lever-Tracy, Constance, and David Ip. 'Diaspora Capitalism and the Homeland: Australian Chinese Networks into China.' *Diaspora* 5.2 (1996): 239–73.

Li, Peter. *The Chinese in Canada*. 2nd ed. Toronto and Oxford: Oxford UP, 1998.

Lim, Shirley Geok-Lin, and Wimal Dissanayake. Introduction. In *Transnational Asia Pacific: Gender, Culture and the Public Sphere*, ed. Shirley Geok-Lin Lim, Larry E. Smith, and Wimal Dissanayake. Urbana and Chicago: U of Illinois P, 1999. 1–10.

Lin, Jan. *Reconstructing Chinatown: Ethnic Enclave, Global Change*. Minneapolis and London: U of Minnesota P, 1998.

Look Lai, Walter. *Indentured Labor, Carribean Sugar: Chinese and Indian Migrants to the British West Indies, 1838–1918*. Baltimore: Johns Hopkins UP, 1993.

Loomba, Ania. *Colonialism/Postcolonialism*. London and New York: Routledge, 1998.

Lowe, Lisa. *Immigrant Acts: On Asian American Cultural Politics*. Durham and London: Duke UP, 1996.

Lukács, Georg. 'Walter Scott and the Historical Novel.' In Lukács, *Marxism and Human Liberation*, ed. E. San Juan Jr. New York: Delta, 1973. 132–78.

Mair, Robert G., Loredana M. Harris, and David L. Flint. 'The Neuropsychology of Odor Memory.' In *Memory for Odors*, ed. Frank R. Schab and Robert G. Crowder. Mahwah, NJ: Lawrence Erlbaum, 1995. 71–92.

Marshall, P.J., and Glyndwr Williams. *The Great Map of Mankind: Perceptions of New Worlds in the Age of Enlightenment*. Cambridge, MA: Harvard UP, 1982.

Marx, Karl. 'On the Jewish Question.' In *Early Writings*, trans. Rodney Livingstone and Gregor Benton. New York: Vintage, 1975. 211–42.

Massey, Doreen. *Space, Place and Gender*. Minneapolis: U of Minnesota P, 1994.

Matthews, Robin. Preface. In *Poetry and the Colonized Mind*. Oakville, ON: Mosaic Press, 1976. 7–12.

McGonegal, Julie. 'Hyphenating the Hybrid "I": (Re)Visions of Racial Mixedness in Fred Wah's *Diamond Grill*.' *Essays on Canadian Writing* 75 (2002): 177–95.

Meehan, Johanna, ed. *Feminists Read Habermas: Gendering the Subject of Discourse*. New York and London: Routledge, 1995.

– Introduction. In *Feminists Read Habermas*, 1–20.

Memmi, Albert. *The Colonizer and the Colonized*. Boston: Beacon Press, 1967.

Mill, John Stuart. *On Liberty*. 1859. New York: Penguin, 1985.

Mishra, Vijay. '(B)ordering Naipaul: Indenture History and Diasporic Poetics.' *Diaspora* 5.2 (1996): 189–237.

– 'The Diasporic Imaginary: Theorizing the Indian Diaspora.' *Textual Practice* 10.3 (1996): 421–47.

– *The Literature of the Indian Diaspora*. London: Routledge, 2007.

Mo, Timothy. *Sour Sweet*. New York: Aventura, 1985.

Moretti, Franco. *The Way of the World: The Bildungsroman in European Culture*. London: Verso, 1987.

Morris, Jan. *Hong Kong: Epilogue to an Empire*. London: Penguin Books, 1997.

Morris, Meagan. 'Things to Do with Shopping Centres.' In *The Cultural Studies Reader*, ed. Simon During. London and New York: Routledge, 1993. 391–409.

– *Too Soon Too Late: History in Popular Culture*. Bloomington and Indianapolis: Indiana UP, 1998.

Morton, James. *In the Sea of Sterile Mountains: The Chinese in British Columbia*. Vancouver: J.J. Douglas Ltd, 1974.

Mufti, Aamir, and Ella Shohat. Introduction. In *Dangerous Liaisons: Gender, Nation and Postcolonial Perspectives*. Minneapolis and London: U of Minnesota P, 1997. 1–14.

Nancy, Jean-Luc. 'Finite History.' In *The States of 'Theory': History, Art, and Critical Discourse*, ed. David Carroll. New York: Columbia UP, 1990. 149–74.

Nandy, Ashis. *The Intimate Enemy: Loss and Recovery of the Self under Colonialism*. Oxford: Oxford UP, 1983.

Negt, Oskar, and Alexander Kluge. *Public Sphere and Experience: Toward an Analy-*

*sis of the Bourgeois and Proletarian Public Sphere.* Trans. Peter Labanyi, Jamie Owen Daniel, and Assenka Oksiloff. Minneapolis: U of Minnesota P, 1993.

New Dayton Historical Society. *Memories: New Dayton and District 1900–1978.* Lethbridge, AB: Robins Southern Printing Ltd, 1978.

Nielsen, Aldon Lynn. *Black Chant: Languages of African-American Postmodernism.* Cambridge: Cambridge UP, 1997.

Ng, Maria. 'Chop Suey Writing: Sui Sin Far, Wayson Choy, and Judy Fong Bates.' *Essays on Canadian Writing* 65 (1998): 174, 185.

– 'Representing Chinatown: Dr. Fu-Manchu at the Disappearing Moon Café.' *Canadian Literature* 163 (1999): 157–75.

Ng, Wing Chung. *The Chinese in Vancouver 1945–80.* Vancouver: UBC P, 2002.

Nora, Pierre. 'Between Memory and History: Les Lieux de Mémoire.' Trans. Marc Roudebush. *Representations* 26 (1989): 7–25.

Norton-Kyshe, James William. *The History of the Laws and Courts of Hong Kong.* 1898. 2 vols. Hong Kong: Vetch and Lee, 1970.

Nunes, Zita. 'Anthropology and Race in Brazilian Modernism.' In *Colonial Discourse / Postcolonial Theory,* ed. F. Barker, P. Hulme, and M. Iverson. Manchester: Manchester UP, 1994. 115–25.

Ong, Aihwa, and Donald Nonini. *Buddha Is Hiding: Refugees, Citizenship, the New America.* Berkeley: U of California P, 2003.

– 'Experiments with Freedom: Milieus of the Human.' *American Literary History* 18 (2006): 229–44.

– *Flexible Citizenship: The Cultural Logics of Transnationality.* Durham: Duke UP, 1999.

– *Ungrounded Empires: The Cultural Politics of Modern Chinese Transnationalism.* New York: Routledge, 1996.

Ortiz, Fernando. *Cuban Counterpoint: Tobacco and Sugar.* Trans. Harriet de Onís. 1947. Durham and London: Duke UP, 1995.

Palumbo-Liu, David. *Asian/American: Historical Crossings of a Racial Frontier.* Stanford: Stanford UP, 1999.

Pan, Lynn. *Sons of the Yellow Emperor: A History of the Chinese Diaspora.* Boston: Little, Brown, 1990.

Parry, Benita. 'Resistance Theory / Theorizing Resistance or Two Cheers for Nativism.' In *Colonial Discourse / Postcolonial Theory,* ed. F. Barker, P. Hulme, and M. Iverson. Manchester: Manchester UP, 1994. 172–96.

Pateman, Carole. *The Sexual Contract.* Stanford: Stanford UP, 1988.

Pichaske, David. *A Generation in Motion: Popular Music and Culture in the Sixties.* Granite Falls, MN: Ellis Press, 1989.

Piot, Charles. 'Atlantic Aporias: Africa and Gilroy's Black Atlantic.' *South Atlantic Quarterly* 100.1 (2001): 155–70.

Prakash, Gyan. 'Postcolonial Criticism and Indian Historiography.' In *Dangerous Liaisons: Gender, Nation and Postcolonial Perspectives*, ed. Aamir Mufti and Ella Shohat. Minneapolis and London: U of Minnesota P, 1997. 491–500.

Raspa, Thomas. 'Exotic Foods among Italian-Americans in Mormon Utah: Food as Nostalgic Enactment of Identity.' In *Ethnic and Regional Foodways in the United States*, ed. Linda Keller Brown and Kay Mussell. Knoxville: U of Tennessee P, 1984.185–94.

Redfield, Marc. *Phantom Formations: Aesthetic Ideology and the Bildungsroman.* Ithaca and London: Cornell UP, 1996.

Reiter, Ester. *Making Fast Food: From the Frying Pan into the Fryer.* 2nd ed. Montreal and Kingston: McGill-Queen's UP, 1996.

Richards, Keith. *Poetry and the Colonized Mind: Tish.* Oakville, ON: Mosaic Press, 1976.

Roy, Patricia E. *A White Man's Province: British Columbia Politicians and Chinese and Japanese Immigrants 1858–1914.* Vancouver: UBC P, 1989.

Rudy Dorscht, Susan. 'mother/ father things I am also': Fred(,) Wah, Breathin' His Name with a Sigh.' In *Inside the Poem: Essays and Poems in Honour of Donald Stephens*, ed. W.H. New. Oxford: Oxford UP, 1992. 216–24.

Rushdie, Salman. *Imaginary Homelands: Essays and Criticism 1981–1991.* New York: Penguin, 1992.

Ryan, Mary P. 'Gender and Public Access: Women's Politics in Nineteenth-Century America.' In *Habermas and the Public Sphere*, ed. Craig Calhoun. Cambridge, MA, and London: MIT Press, 1992. 259–88.

Said, Edward. *Culture and Imperialism.* New York: Vintage, 1993.

Saul, Joanne. 'Displacement and Self-Representation: Theorizing Canadian Biotexts.' *Biography* 24.1 (2001): 259–72.

Saunders, Kay. *Indentured Labor in the British Empire, 1834–1920.* London: Croom Helm, 1984.

Schwarcz, Vera. 'No Solace from Lethe: History, Memory, and Cultural Identity in Twentieth-Century China.' In *The Living Tree*, ed. Tu Wei-ming, 64–87.

Scott, David. *Refashioning Futures: Criticism after Postcoloniality.* Princeton: Princeton UP, 1999.

Seremetàkis, C. Nadia. 'Benjamin, Bloch, Braudel and Beyond.' In *The Senses Still: Perception and Memory as Material Culture in Modernity*, ed. C. Nadia Seremetakis. 1994. Chicago and London: U of Chicago P, 1996. 19–22.

– 'The Memory of the Senses, Part I: Marks of the Transitory.' In *The Senses Still*, 1–18.

– 'The Memory of the Senses, Part II: Still Acts.' In *The Senses Still*, 23–44.

Sharpe, Jenny. 'Is the United States Postcolonial?' *Diaspora* 4.2 (1995): 181–99.

Shih, Shu-Mei. 'Toward an Ethics of Transnational Encounters, or, "When"

Does a "Chinese" Woman Become a "Feminist."' In *Minor Transnationalism*, ed. Françoise Lionnet and Shu-Mei Shih. Durham: Duke UP, 2005. 73–108.

Smith, A.J.M., ed. *The Book of Canadian Poetry*. Chicago and Illinois: U of Chicago P, 1943.

Spang, Rebecca. *The Invention of the Restaurant: Paris and Modern Gastronomic Culture*. Cambridge and London: Harvard UP, 2000.

Spivak, Gayatri Chakravorty. *A Critique of Postcolonial Reason: Toward a History of the Vanishing Present*. Cambridge, MA: Harvard UP, 1999.

– 'Diasporas Old and New: Women in the Transnational World.' *Textual Practice* 10.2 (1996): 245–69.

– 'Introduction. Subaltern Studies: Deconstructing Historiography.' In *Selected Subaltern Studies*, ed. Ranajit Guha and Gayatri Chakravorty Spivak. London and New York: Oxford UP, 1988. 3–34.

Stanley, Timothy J. '"Chinamen, Wherever We Go": Chinese Nationalism and Guangdong Merchants in British Columbia 1871–1911.' *Canadian Historical Review* 77.4 (1996): 475–503.

Stewart, Kathleen. *Ordinary Affects*. Durham and London: Duke UP, 2007.

Stewart, Susan. *On Longing: Narratives of the Miniature, the Gigantic, the Souvenir, the Collection*. Durham and London: Duke UP, 1993.

Stoddart, D. Michael. *The Scented Ape: The Biology and Culture of Human Odour*. Cambridge and New York: Cambridge UP, 1990.

Sugars, Cynthia. 'The Negative Capability of Camouflage.' *Studies in Canadian Literature* 26.1 (2001): 27–45.

Terdiman, Richard. *Present Past: Modernity and the Memory Crisis*. Ithaca and London: Cornell UP, 1993.

Tölölyan, Khachig. 'Rethinking Diaspora(s): Stateless Power in the Transnational Moment.' *Diaspora* 5.1 (1996): 3–36.

Tu, Wei-Ming. 'Cultural China: The Periphery as Center.' In *The Living Tree*, 1–34.

Tu, Wei-Ming, ed. *The Living Tree: The Changing Meaning of Being Chinese Today*. Stanford: Stanford UP, 1994.

Ty, Eleanor. *The Politics of the Visible in Asian North American Narratives*. Toronto: University of Toronto Press, 2004.

Unterberger, Richie. *Turn! Turn! Turn!: The 60s Folk-rock Revolution*. San Francisco: Backbeat Books, 2002.

Visser, Margaret. *The Rituals of Dinner: The Origins, Evolution, Eccentricities and Meaning of Table Manners*. New York: Grove Weidenfeld, 1991.

Wah, Fred. *Diamond Grill*. Edmonton: NeWest P, 1996.

– *Pictograms from Interior B.C.* Vancouver: Talonbooks, 1975.

– *Waiting for Saskatchewan*. Winnipeg: Turnstone Press, 1985.

Wang, Dorothy. 'Undercover Asian: John Yau and the Politics of Ethnic Self-Identification.' In *Asian American Literature in the International Context: Readings of Fiction, Poetry, and Performance*, ed. Sami Ludwig and Rocio Davis. Hamburg and London: Lit Verlag, 2002. 135–56.

Wang, Ling-chi, and Wang Gungwu. *The Chinese Diaspora: Selected Essays.* 2 vols. Singapore: Times Academic Press, 1998.

Ward, W. Peter. *White Canada Forever: Popular Attitudes and Public Policy toward Orientals in British Columbia.* Montreal: McGill-Queen's UP, 1978.

Warner, Michael. *Publics and Counterpublics.* New York: Zone Books, 2002.

Wesley-Smith, Peter. *The Sources of Hong Kong Law.* Hong Kong: Hong Kong UP, 1994.

Wetherell, Donald, and Irene Kmet. *Town Life: Main Street and the Evolution of Small Town Alberta, 1880–1947.* Edmonton, U of Alberta P, 1995.

Wickberg, Edgar. *From China to Canada: A History of the Chinese Communities in Canada.* Toronto: McClelland and Stewart, 1983.

Williams, Raymond. *The Country and the City.* Oxford and New York: Oxford UP, 1973.

– *Marxism and Literature.* London: Oxford UP, 1977.

Wong, Sau-ling Cynthia. *Reading Asian American Literature: From Necessity to Extravagance.* Princeton: Princeton UP, 1993.

Wong, Shelley. 'Sizing Up Asian American Poetry.' In *A Resource Guide to Asian American Literature*, ed. Sau-ling Cynthia Wong and Stephen H. Sumida. New York: Modern Language Association of America, 2001. 285–308.

Wu, David Yen-ho. 'The Construction of Chinese and Non-Chinese Identities.' In *The Living Tree*, ed. Tu Wei-ming, 148–67.

Young, Robert. *Postcolonialsim: An Historical Introduction.* London: Blackwell, 2001.

Zaret, David. 'Religion, Science, and Printing in the Public Spheres in Seventeenth-Century England.' In *Habermas and the Public Sphere*, ed. Craig Calhoun. Cambridge, MA, and London: MIT Press, 1992. 212–35.

# Index

## CULTURAL SPACES

*Cultural Spaces* explores the rapidly changing temporal, spatial, and theoretical boundaries of contemporary cultural studies. Culture has long been understood as the force that defines and delimits societies in fixed spaces. The recent intensification of globalizing processes, however, has meant that it is no longer possible – if it ever was – to imagine the world as a collection of autonomous, monadic spaces, whether these are imagined as localities, nations, regions within nations, or cultures demarcated by region or nation. One of the major challenges of studying contemporary culture is to understand the new relationships of culture to space that are produced today. The aim of this series is to publish bold new analyses and theories of the spaces of culture, as well as investigations of the historical construction of those cultural spaces that have influenced the shape of the contemporary world.

*Books in the Series:*
Peter Ives, *Gramsci's Politics of Language: Engaging the Bakhtin Circle and the Frankfurt School*
Sarah Brophy, *Witnessing AIDS: Writing, Testimony, and the Work of Mourning*
Shane Gunster, *Capitalizing on Culture: Critical Theory for Cultural Studies*
Jasmin Habib, *Israel, Diaspora, and the Routes of National Belonging*
Serra Tinic, *On Location: Canada's Television Industry in a Global Market*
Evelyn Ruppert, *The Moral Economy of Cities: Shaping Good Citizens*